THE FASTEST THIRTY BALLGAMES

A Ballpark Chasers World Record Story

*Douglas 'Chuck' Booth Craig B.
Landgren & Kenneth A. Lee*

authorHOUSE

AuthorHouse™
1663 Liberty Drive
Bloomington, IN 47403
www.authorhouse.com
Phone: 1-800-839-8640

First published by AuthorHouse   6/6/2011

ISBN: 978-1-4520-8679-8 (sc)
ISBN: 978-1-4520-8680-4 (e)

Library of Congress Control Number: 2011908015

Printed in the United States of America

Any people depicted in stock imagery provided by Thinkstock are models,
and such images are being used for illustrative purposes only.
Certain stock imagery © Thinkstock.

This book is printed on acid-free paper.

TO BRYAN MCCRON,
1961-2010

You were a dedicated friend who always put others ahead of yourself and your own personal need. If it wasn't for your due diligence in helping me with a new job—and helping me out as I journeyed onto these quests, there is a great chance I would not achieved this feat. You will be forever remembered as a kind soul who would always be there listening and sharing words of wisdom while gracing us with your infectious smile. I wished you could have celebrated this record with me when I am verified—like you celebrated with me when I broke the record in 2009—but I know you are looking down from somewhere. We all could learn a lesson from how you treated people. I miss you friend!!

TO JIM MACLAREN,
<u>1963-2010</u>

It was with great sadness that I learned you had passed away this past summer of 2010-without ever getting a chance to meet you in person. Your inner strength and ability to overcome adversity while making the best of life— served as a defining moment that changed me forever. Furthermore, I really appreciated you sending me your positive energy with personal messages—in order to pursue this record and campaign for the charity you were so personally involved with. I always remembered your perseverance towards whatever quest you were undertaking and how it motivated me for my own physical and mental ability. It took everything I had to chase down this world record.

I will continue your motto of "Choosing Life." You will be missed my friend. Please check out Jim's story at <u>www.jimmaclaren.com</u>

INTRODUCTION

"I sat in the Houston International Airport awaiting the flight that would take me to the last baseball double header in Arlington Texas. I had felt a huge sense of accomplishment in arriving on time for this 5:15 PM departure. Still I had thought this would be a tight squeeze from the moment I booked and purchased the flight.

I was lucky the Houston Astros game had wound up in the two hour and forty-five minute window I needed—with them beating the New York Mets.

During a hot and humid day indoors, I watched with curious energy as the last out was recorded, I then raced to the corner of Crawford and Congress—where my sedan driver was in his car, gas running and ready to head out to the airport.

I had beaten the general attendance out of the game because I had positioned myself near the exit while watching the final inning. The game was close enough to be in question so people were not leaving early.

My driver had been the same driver I called on the previous month when I made my first visit to Houston. Ironically, it was the also the third day of the month, and was also a day game, except for this game was on a weekend, and that game was on a Thursday.

Traffic was light on that Sunday, and I took a look at my boarding pass that I had printed out in the airport earlier that morning when I had arrived from Minnesota. I then looked at my remnants of a black travel bag that had already travelled Forty-Thousand Miles through the journey.

The bag used to be heavier, but I started throwing things out towards the end of my trip to make it lighter. I also had a black briefcase which had been the best ally to travel with since it could double as a place for extra clothing—along with carrying schedules, game tickets, hotel reservations, car reservations, maps and electronics for my equipment to document the evidence of this streak.

I was dressed in shorts that had the colors of the British Flag, red white and blue. I was also wearing my black number 23-'Don Mattingly New York Yankee t-shirt Jersey, I also had sandals on, and a black baseball cap that was severely weathered from being to Twenty-Eight different ballparks in the last Twenty Six days.

My stomach was full of pizza I had eaten at the baseball game. At this point of the trip I knew I had gained about thirty five pounds in the 5 weeks since I left home. I shot from One Hundred and Eighty-Five pounds to Two-hundred and Twenty. I was going to work that off when I returned home to Canada. Another thing to be gone was the beard dangling from my face that had never been so long in my life.

Heading up Highway Fifty-Nine up North, I started to see clouds in the distance, as we approached the airport more, it was apparent we were going to the eye of a rainstorm. I felt a little uneasy as I paid the driver and cleared through security, all the while I was looking through the glass of the airport to monitor the weather towards my pending gate.

It was 4:15 PM in the afternoon. My driver had made good time in reaching the airport from 'Minute Maid Park' in twenty-five minutes, and I made it through security in only a few minutes as well.

Everything felt ominous from the time I reached the area of the boarding jet way for this scheduled flight. Most notably, there was no sign of a plane. As rain continued gaining momentum outside the gate, I talked with an airline agent and she told me a plane was supposed to be coming in—and was only late by ten minutes. According to her, we would be able to make the set departure time.

I took a seat after buying a Coke, (another habit I was going to stop after the trip was finished), and began watching 'CNN'. There was yet another debate going on with Barack Obama and Hillary Clinton for the Democratic race.

Having been on forty plus flights in a month, I was well versed in every avenue of this given political race. All the airport TV monitors carried 'CNN' as the only channel.

Another gust of wind, followed by a heavy thunderclap, and the rain came feverishly to the ground outside the airport. The lights momentarily flickered throughout the entire inside of the airport. I became worried. No sooner then two minutes later the clock for the impending flight to Dallas Fort Worth changed by thirty minutes ahead.

This caused me to bury my head into my hands. Already if the flight was on time I needed a perfect flight, timely sedan pick up in Dallas, and to have traffic not be so bad in Dallas, so I could run go through the turnstiles at 'The Ball Park In Arlington', for the first pitch. First pitch was five minutes after seven. My map told me it was about eleven miles of distance to cover, and could take thirty-five minutes in traffic to get there.

I called my buddy Justin in Canada, I asked for the weather report in Dallas for the game. My thought was that, "If it is raining here it may be raining there, and that could cause a rain-delay, then I might be able to make the first pitch still." He confirmed it was raining in Dallas and that it loomed in the forecast pretty heavy for the next few hours but was supposed to clear up after that.

At this point I had a little bit of optimism, the very same thing had happened to me in Cincinnati the previous month. There was a big traffic accident on the Seventy-One Highway South on the 'Fourth of July' heading from Indianapolis Airport to 'The Great American Ball Park'. The start of the game was delayed, and I made it there on time to qualify for the game.

I drank my beverage and was ready to call my sedan driver in Dallas to go over the game plan after the flight time change. I then noticed that not only was there not a plane in my gate yet, but that I had not even seen a plane in any of the other dozen gates from the time I had arrived there.

From that instant, my flight to Dallas, (that had already been delayed by thirty minutes)—jumped from one gate—all the way to other side of the airport gate and the time changed to 7:00 PM. I swore out loud.

I swore so loud that about fifty people looked in my direction with angst. It was a natural reaction without any time to even think about it. It was not the first time in the trip I had been caught swearing either, and it would not be the last. The next few times I swore I managed to do it under my breath. I ran to the bathroom. It was an excruciating few minutes.

After all the chasing I had done, radio interviews, newspaper articles that had been written about the streak in pursuit for charity, months of planning, years of saving up money, dedication to learning the craft of the stadium chase, having been on the road for Thirty-Five days straight, traveling on planes, trains, automobiles, public transit, losing sleep entirely throughout the process, all culminating in the chance to break the record—which was now officially over and it was not my fault. A spill over, rogue Gail storm, left over from some of the worst Hurricane season in the lower 'Southern Belt Area" of the summer had wreaked enough havoc to ground and/or re-route planes to nearby airports in Mobil and Gulfport.

All I could do was tie the record that was stated by the fine people at "The Guinness Book of World Records." The given streak chase was: "The Fastest to See All 30 Major League Baseball Parks." The record stood at Thirty-games in Twenty-nine days, although I had seen articles and websites of a couple of Canadians who had accomplished the feat in 'Twenty-Eight' days.

My official best I could do was-Thirty-Games in Twenty-Nine days now. During those brief moments I knew that I might not even be able to tie the 'World Record' should "GWR" have given the 'Canadians' the new record. I was mad.

I temporarily wished that I had never tried for the record knowing that I had my scheduled holiday always with the three days off for the All-star break.

I had initially not planned to shoot for the record when I booked my vacation. My original version of the six week trip was to see all the parks over the course of six weeks. The break was in week number three. During a day of planning online, I decided to see what the world record was for seeing all the parks. That is when I saw the thirty games in twenty-eight days record website. It took me two weeks of looking at Baseball's schedule to see if I could try for the record even with the three day penalty. There were going to be some costs incurred for altering some of my already purchased schedule. I was willing to live with that. Besides, I could re-sell some of my baseball tickets. It was only April still, two months before the whole chase started.

The skinny of it all-was that any record I submitted would have the three days of July 14-16/2008 as a blank. To make up the necessary games I was going to need six successful double headers—to bring in a thirty games in twenty-seven days streak. I had a Thirty-games-in Twenty-Six games bid scheduled. With some more diligent planning, I even was able to have a re-set attempt on July.9th, some ten days into the first bid attempt, should the streak go awry to begin with. I had exercised that chance, hit on five out of six double headers with this second streak attempt, with the seventh chance being foiled due to this rain.

There was another game I missed when a Toronto bound flight was delayed from O'Hare International Airport for a day game.

Normally I would have rented a car from Chicago to drive to Cleveland to make up the only doubleheader game that I missed—except I was to meet my mom in Toronto for that game—and she was already there having flown in from Montreal. I flew to Canada instead and took a zero for the day. This all led up to streak now sitting at Twenty-Seven games in Twenty-Six days. The last three-games would be in Texas, Toronto and Chicago.

After calling my step-mom Nancy in Canada, I waited for my delayed flight to Texas, and thought about Jim McLaren's dedication to his life, and how I should not ever 'give up' even when you are truly feeling like crap.

Besides, the way it worked out, I was going to visit the last baseball park in my stadiums list! I had been to several of the other parks multiple times each already but never to Arlington. It was kind of nice the way it was going to work out. It was my salvation in an otherwise horrendous day of emotions.-(Little did I know at that point, I was going to have another shot at the record in the summer of 2009!) To show you where I went from this time, I must show you were this all originated from back on another rainy day in 2005.

<u>2005</u>

"Back in 2005 I was listening to the **Jim Rome** Show in my hometown of White Rock B.C., when he had a special motivational guest speaker come on named **Jim Maclaren (1963-2010)** - <u>www.jimmaclaren.com</u>.

I often thought I had a difficult life at that point until I heard his story. Jim was an all-American guy in the mid-80s, who had played football in college and aspired to make it in Hollywood. He stood 6-foot-5 and weighed almost 300 lbs. He had life by the tail, until he was riding his bike in New York City and a bus hit his bicycle head on and knocked him off into the air.

Jim was pronounced dead on arrival at hospital and doctors were shocked when a while later he came back to life. His accident did not come without any permanent damage as one of his legs was amputated. He now had some serious obstacles to overcome. Since Jim was a great athlete, he started riding a bike and spending time in the pool.

His new will was to test his physical limits, despite his leg. For eight years he routinely beat able-bodied competitors in triathlons and other tests of physical endurance. In an Ironman contest in California in 1993 he was riding his bike in a competition when he heard screams in the distance. A van had been swerving and headed for him without any warning. Jim was flung from the van and smashed into a street sign far from the point of impact. This time he also lived but he had to face another fact, he was left a quadriplegic. Jim struggled with this news and sunk into a depression that caused him to have several inner battles to which he fought drugs, thoughts of suicide and most of all loneliness.

At a turning point in his life he decided to live his life to the fullest despite all the things physically that were working against him. Jim changed his entire outlook on life and found a deep inner peace with himself and knew he was ready to live his life.

He would spend hours rehabilitating his injuries and willed his own self to walk in a pool and regained some use in his arms. Doctors marveled at Jim's unwillingness to give up. Soon Jim realized that he had lots of advice to give to others because he had been at the bottom of everything life has to offer in the negative fashion and risen to live a normal life. Normal for Jim is doing thing that others routinely take for granted like tying up shoe laces, moving across a room, doing the dishes after a meal. Jim has touched so many people with his tale of courage to live. If you ask him, he will tell you that, "he has been given a gift with the life he has led, for he has seen the light in what makes him happy." He would not change any of it for anything. Hearing this story I pulled over to the side of the road and took some personal inventory of my own life. I was nearly in tears hearing his story and inspired to achieve things in my life from that point forward. I wrote down all the goals I wanted to achieve that day to make me happy. One of them was to write the two novels I had always procrastinated about as an adult. I did that and had them both published in 2008 and the third one is in circulation now with this book. The other goals were to set foot in all 50 States, (I completed this in 2010) and the last goal was see all the Major League Baseball stadiums in my life which I accomplished by August of '08. At the original point of the change though, it took some re-tooling my schedule. I was going to have to work harder, smarter and focus to realize this dream.

It had not been my fault I was in such bad financial shape. My wife Stella had Tourette's Syndrome—and was on government assistance that had been cut off the moment we were married in 2002. It was a most devastating bad turn of events. My jobs were delivering newspaper and pizza for about sixty hours a week. I should have had enough money to pay the bills with what I made, but a bad run of car repairs for years upon years had sunk us to the level we were at. The worst part was that we could not live in an apartment, because of her involuntary ticks had caused a disturbance in every building we lived in—enough to force five moves in five years.

Finally I had us situated in a secluded house that was costly in rent, but I could afford it if I could just clear the credit card debt.

After promising myself changes to come after the Jim McLaren interview, I also added an additional thirty hours of work at a week at a gas station. This brought my weekly work total up to ninety hours. The extra money was actually helping me to balance my expenses and even save a few dollars. Changes were still coming, and I could not pay off my credit balance but it was satisfying to be making more money then spending now.

In June of Two-Thousand and Five I was burnt out from working ninety hours a week for six months straight. However I arrived to my first vacation in six years. The trip was easy, my wife and I would drive my repaired Nineteen Eighty One Mustang to Seattle, Oakland, San Francisco, Los Angeles and San Diego, before returning home up Las Vegas to Nevada before California again.

We sat on the third base side at 'Safeco Field.' I felt an adrenaline rush hit my body as I stood up for the National Anthem. The Mariners were playing the New York Mets. It was my first Major League baseball game since 1996 when I saw the Montreal Expos play at 'Olympic Stadium.' I was really happy to watch the Mariners starting pitcher Jamie Moyer pitch to one of my favorite catchers of all time in Pat Borders. They were both Forty-Two years old. I was watching history as their cumulative age marked the oldest pitcher-catcher tandem ever in MLB.

Somehow throughout the whole game, I knew my life was about to change for the better. I had been brought back to the game I loved.

It was my first road trip of baseball games. Two days after the Seattle game, I watched the Oakland A's play on Father's day at 'McAfee Coliseum', the very next night I watched the San Francisco Giants play at then 'Pacific Bell Park/now AT&T Park.' During batting practice that day, Shawn Green of the Diamondbacks launched a baseball off the red brick past the right center field bleachers———and it promptly ricocheted right to my feet. That was it, I was hooked. No matter what it took I was going to come to baseball games every year if it killed me. What an awesome few days. I saw two of the best stadiums in baseball with Seattle and San Francisco's parks.

I closed off the trip by seeing the Los Angeles Angels play at Angels Stadium, that game was followed up by a trip to 'Petco Park' to see the Padres play.

I returned from that trip having now seen six out of the thirty active ball parks.

I did declare bankruptcy in early 2006, but managed to sneak away to see two games at 'Dodgers Stadium' and 'Yankee Stadium,' (to bring the stadium count up to 8) along with a handful of games at 'Safeco Field.'

I was still sitting at 8 Stadiums in early 2007-and wanted to see a few stadiums that year but it was all depending on how well the cars could perform.

My three cars had been good to me on repairs for years of 2005 and 2006.

With my debt being cleared off with bankruptcy in early 2006—I would be able to pay my bills with the extra money and have left over cash for traveling—provided I did not get blistered on car repairs like how it had happened to create such a financial mess before.

I had a momentary scare when the gas station closed in late 2006 and I was out of that job's money, but I quickly replaced the earnings with a community based newspaper that I could pick my own hours. While my pizza delivery job and major newspaper routes had been set on deadlines—and specific hours to work, the community based newspapers I could do whenever I had the time.

It was going to take a physical torque on my body to keep up with the ninety hour work week, but it was necessary to keep the savings up in order to take off a couple of weeks a year to baseball stadium chase.

March of Two Thousand and Seven provided more drama in a week then I wanted to deal with. I had to sell the Eighty One Mustang because gasoline prices were at a record high. I then used that money to sink into the Nineteen Eighty-Four Toyota Celica I owned, only to have the master chain break on the engine and render the car un-drive-able a few days after picking it up from the service garage.

This left me with one car that had already been through the gauntlet of hard city driving for all the seven years I had been a courier. That car was a Nineteen Ninety-One Chevy Cavalier.

I was worried about the car expenses killing any dream of baseball watching in the future should they start piling up again.

In an act of desperation, I resorted to bidding (via E-Bay) on another Ninety-One Chevrolet Cavalier in a town that was two hours south of Toronto. I won the bid for a bargain. The only problem was that I had to fly out East 3000 miles and drive it back across the country. I knew this when bidding, so I planned on seeing some baseball games coming back on the trip.

My thought process at this time was: "At least if the thing breaks down en route back home I can have a baseball vacation out of it."

I flew to Toronto first and drove a rental car down 2 hours to the remote town of Strathroy, Ontario where I took my used Cavalier car into a repair garage—to have the guy's price out a repair job for servicing the car.

I planned this all along. I figured it would take two to three days to fix whatever problems that car had with it, so in the meantime I would drive down to Cincinnati and Cleveland to knock them off the schedule of baseball stadiums left to see. It was opening week of the 2007 Major League Season.

When the Cavalier was finished being repaired, I was going to also see 'Wrigley Field' and the 'Metrodome' on the way back to Vancouver, BC Canada. This 4 game tour would bring me up to 12 parks.

It was only April though, and it was snowing all over the Eastern Seaboard jeopardizing the games I was going to watch. I was cancelled out of the opening game in Cleveland before I took in a last minute hockey game in Columbus en route to Cincinnati.

I was able to see Ken Griffey Jr. play right field for the Cincinnati Reds at 'The Great American Ballpark' in near freezing weather despite a small snowfall. It was so cold outside that day that when the game was over I went into the 'Cincinnati Baseball Hall Of Fame' just to warm up for a few hours.

The next day I drove back to Cleveland to watch a newly announced doubleheader between the Mariners and Indians. When I showed up, the games were both cancelled because the stadium had a foot of snow surrounding it——I got the consolation prize of viewing the 'Rock and Roll Hall Of Fame'. So then I drove the rental car back to Toronto—and met up with my brother for a Blue Jays game in Toronto.

Memories came back to me of my first pro game ever returned as I entered 'Skydome'. It was my thirteenth birthday in Nineteen Eighty-Nine, the very first year of the existence of the retractable skyline roof in Toronto.

I talked with my oldest brother Trent about the rental car I had. We were eating hot dogs and sitting in the bleachers level in the Five Hundred Deck on $2 opening Tuesday night. It was the day after the opener.

"You drove the car rental Fifteen Hundred Miles in Four Days and had full insurance for the average of Fifty dollars a day?" Trent asked as the sound system echoed from the latest theme song being played for Canadian Matt Stairs of the Toronto Blue Jays. It was a wrestling song from the 'WWE.'

"Yeah, that it is a pretty good price for a nice car like a Pontiac G6, that is almost as much as I pay per day to drive the crappy cars I have been driving," I answered as I thought about my 3 cars some more.

"Doug, I have been renting cars for years now and have never heard of those rates in Canada."

"I am going to investigate that when I get home, maybe I can work it out for the courier jobs. I sure hope this car makes it all the way home without conking out."

"You have guts brother."

"The car should be fine, but this snow is something else." I was excited yet nervous about driving to Wrigley the next day.

"Did you hear about the Indians-Angels series being moved to Miller Park?"

"No, starting tomorrow?"

"All series," Trent explained.

"I am going to buy a ticket for that game too. Milwaukee is only a hundred miles away from Miller and the game is during the day in Chicago."

"Dude, I don't know if you are going to pull that off in this weather, the Ninety Four Highway gets pretty jammed in cold weather."

"I got to try. I am not going to see Miller Park this year if I don't."

Trent finished his food, "I am just saying you won't see every pitch."

"I don't like that aspect but I will stay for the whole game in Chicago first."

▲▲▲

The game in Chicago was cancelled a few days later. I sat across the street from Wrigley Field flabbergasted. I had come all this way and for the game to be called was crazy. The car had made it thus far with all the new parts and accessories. I was now well versed in the disappointment one faces in a stadium visit that is all dependent on the weather.

I wish all of the stadiums had roofs that day. During the first few minutes after the notification, a local news camera interviewed some people outside the ballpark. I made my way to the camera and explained how far I was from home to come to this historic park. It was there where I would not give up on this dream. During the interview I snapped. "I was going to ask for a refund for the ticket, but I just decided to risk my job and make my wife upset by changing the ticket to two days from now to see the 'Reds' play." Snow was pelting off my spring beige jacket as I said this. It was a true statement. I was supposed to have gone to Minnesota after the Milwaukee game that night. A few days later I was to be home and back at work. It was a calculated risk too, it may have kept snowing the whole time till that game and then I would have nothing to show for the trip to Chicago.

It was the first sign of things to go my way. My brother was right about the traffic to Milwaukee too. I was thinking about how I was going to find out an excuse to justify my prolonging of the trip to include Wrigley Field. I went to the game at Miller Park, when I returned to my car the front left wheel was deflated—un-drive able—and was just losing air slowly to suggest it was a small leak. There was my out.

I took the car in the next day to a Tire place in Milwaukee, and attended the Angels and Indians game for a second straight day, (Field View Tickets for ten dollars).

I was able to attend Wrigley Field the next day, in cold but sunny weather I saw the Cubs jump out to a five run lead before in classic style, they surrendered the lead and lost to the Cincinnati Reds 6-5.

I got to live another disappointment loss with the 'Wrigley fans.' It was a great moment, seeing baseball without all the modern day amenities, seeing the ivory in the outfield, man-operated scoreboard that only has seven spots for the A.L teams and six for the N.L teams so there is always one score that does not get posted.

The next day I drove to Minnesota-and watched a game from the "Metrodome." It felt like being at home because we have a similar stadium back in British Colombia Canada in "BC PLACE." It is also one of two stadiums in the Majors that have Canadian flags prominently displayed.

Since I delayed my return home by a few days, I wanted to gun it as fast as humanly possible from Minnesota to Seattle. It was a test of endurance and pride that I reached Seattle a mere Twenty Six Hours after leaving Minnesota, thus covering almost Seventeen Hundred Miles.

The whole trip left me wanting more after building my parks list up to 13 parks. The Chevrolet car was successful enough to make it through the next few months without repairs so I was able to plan out another trip back East.

I had searched the internet for rates on car rentals when I returned home with my Cavalier in the spring of 2007. I found no such deals that would compare to what I found during my trip in April, besides I just sank a thousand dollars into the Chevy Cavalier, and it was working.

My first trial into hardcore ballpark chasing started that summer. I had ten days of vacation and planned to see ten baseball games in eight days.

Since I did not have a passport at this time, and the United States required foreign travelers to fly domestic flights within the States with one—I had to fly to Montreal first in order to rent a car—and drive down to the States instead.

Day one was a game in Toronto, then it was onto, Baltimore, New York to see the Mets and Philadelphia as part of a day-night double header in two different cities, this was to be followed up by Detroit, the Chicago White Sox, the Cleveland Indians, and a doubleheader in Pittsburgh, Boston and to be concluded in New York to see a Yankees game at Yankee Stadium.

The trip was Four Thousand Miles of all driving. I brought my wife Stella along with me. She was going to visit the 'Rock N Roll Hall Of Fame', Times Square in New York, and was going to meet 'Dog The Bounty Hunter' in a bookstore in Taylor, Michigan.

I loved my wife Stella at this point, and I did not think it was fair to have a ten day vacation without her so she came along. Many different events happened though out chasing these stadiums that threw a wrench into our marriage. I would not see them for months afterwards, but it was a problem with us, I never attributed them to the baseball directly although it was the catalyst.

Doing a schedule like this made me realize how hard traveling can be. I missed the second game of the trip in Baltimore outright because the drive from Toronto to Philadelphia, then onto Baltimore took way longer then I thought it would. Some of these directions you receive online are just mileage charts—they don't take construction, weather, and traffic into consideration. Deciding not to drive to Baltimore was a wake-up call that I needed to fine-tune the preparations I took from that point forward.

After completing the Shea Stadium, Citizen's Bank doubleheader, I was schooled again on the drive from Philadelphia to Detroit. I never made it to Comerica Park until the second inning.

The next day we were late arriving to 'US Cellular Field' because 'Dog The Bounty Hunter' arrived late to his book store signing in Taylor, Michigan. I hate missing any pitch for baseball games, and vowed right there never to miss any starts or ends of the game from that point forward! I have since made the opening pitch for 110 straight games.

I will also get to ranking and talking about all the stadiums during the streak chasers later in future chapters. I ended the trip seeing nine different home games in nine days. The biggest shock of the trip was returning the rental car in Montreal—only to find that when we parked out car in a New York Valet Parking near Times Square, someone had dinged it against the wall.

I guess because I was tired from the trip, I forgot when booking the car contract online, that we had taken full insurance for the car and were covered entirely for the damages. My fears of paying for the car and cutting into my pocketbook were subsided instantly.

My wife and I fought the whole time we drove from New York City to Montreal, at it was apparent she did not have the physical fortitude to come on big road trips that test your endurance. I, on the other hand, was invigorated by the process and was contemplating a huge summer long vacation the following year that included going to all the ballparks.

I spent four hours on the computer verifying that the latest car offer was real. I found out that the website that I reserved my rental contract for that ten day summer trip also offered a deal for fully insured rental cars for just over a Thousand Dollars a month.

The reason I thought my first rate on my spring trip was such a deal was because it was low season for traveling. Car rentals are spiked from June to September.

Whether it was fate or not, a couple of weeks into being home that August, the Chevy Cavalier started to show signs it was headed for major car repairs. Again I was prompted to the computer.

This time I searched every car rental place in the book. I remembered what got me to this point in my life success the last few years—it was tireless work towards my time management schedule. I finally came to a conclusion that would be questioned for years in logic, for me it was a revelation.

The best thing I ever did as a courier was chart down every expense for gas, repairs, purchase prices, insurance, car washes and oil changes. I doubled that with charting all the mileage for the pizzeria and papers—along with daily money earned for the driver job and for the paper routes. I roughly knew what I was paying per mile to operate a car. It was six years of research that told me a tale. I sat with a calculator for a full day straight crunching numbers.

It was a decision that I needed help with. My dad is a car salesman, and he knows the car business like no tomorrow. I ran the idea by him—he counter-offered a loan for a reliable used Toyota Yaris. I was touched by the prospect, but I have a knack for mathematics and knew that buying a car would be the worst thing I could do. I left the conversation telling him that I would try the car rental for three months and see how it turned out. At worst, I could always take him up on his offer after. My mind was working overtime. I broke it down like this.

3000 miles per month is what I averaged in driving.

Rental Car-Estimated Charges

Heavy price tag-at $925 per month (plus $75 a month to have one of the Cavalier's on the road so I qualified for Plus Insurance-meaning a rental cars collision would cover the loss of a rental car. It is a loophole in the province's insurance package that I found)-so $1000 a month.

Gas on a new car for the 3000 miles driven for Rental Car of a 2007 Toyota Corolla was-$400 (My rental car at Thrifty)

Total Operation money for the car was:-$1400/month or 46.7 Cents per mile.

Chevy Cavalier-Estimated Charges

Car Insurance (For Delivery Insurance—(which Rental Cars do not need to have because they have Fleet Insurance) $150, plus $75 for the second old Cavalier for emergency use incase the first one breaks down for a total of $225 a month rare for insurance. This did not include if I caused the accident, my own vehicle would have to be replaced at my own expense and the subsequent premiums would rise even higher.

Gas on 3000 miles was $575 per month average on the 91' Cavalier.

Average depreciation per mile was 4 cents so-$125 per month.

Future purchase price towards a—New Car-$125 per month.

Average Repairs on 3000 miles on 15 year old car (moderate) is 15 cents a mile

So total average per month of $450.

Car washes and Oil Changes on 3000 miles per month is $50.

Total operation Money was $1550 or 51.7 cents per Mile, plus no coverage if the car was wrecked. Meaning I would have to pay for a new car without having collision.

At minimum I figured I would spend $150 dollars less a month. With the rental car I would also have the knowledge I was not going to spend one-to five days a month in the car repair shop waiting for a car to be repaired. Oh, and lest we forget that this was a month to month comparison analysis.

What if the Cavalier's engine seized, or a transmission was blown? This would wipe out my personal savings. With the set dollar total for the rental car I would be able to set a budget for the first time ever as a carrier.

Another thing I always had to worry about was crossing the border to Washington State from the province of British Colombia. I live three miles from the first gas station in Blaine, WA. The price difference per gallon translates to about a dollar a gallon savings going to Blaine Washington. If my cars had any slight problems in the past I would not even risk the car breaking down in the States, thus I paid the crazy fuel charges Canadians pay. That worry went away with the rental cars.

Immediately my life improved ten-fold. No longer was I worried about mileage on cars. At work I was offered some of the higher paying routes that no one wanted to do because of a mileage on a car—well now with unlimited miles I could take country routes that required more driving then physical walking and for half of the time elapsed. This opened up my income to take on more community newspapers, having that extra energy in reserve.

The first month I switched to the rental cars, I made a $1000 more dollars then the previous month. I actually tallied about 3500 miles on the car too.

Another thing I learned was that every 16 days that I rented a car—I received a free day car rental to use anywhere in North America(from Thrifty Car Rental)——including my summer baseball trips where I could save 60-70 dollars per day for those mid-week rentals in cities like St. Louis, Chicago, New York and Philly. This meant an additional $125 on the good side of the ledger.

I have long known for years that the United States also has a cheaper cost of living. Many times on prolonged road-trips I would bring back the $700 worth of goods exemptions from the USA-back into Canada. Compared to what we pay in Canada that could be a savings of nearly half off.

The town of Bellingham, Washington is Twenty-Five Miles from my house. I started travelling there three times a week to pick up $15-20 worth of food, clothing and whatever else was cheaper there. Usually the border guards would not impose duty when I returned to Canada on the way back. Since mileage was not an issue for me, I reveled in the amount of miles I tacked on the cars. I was driving new Toyota cars that all had Ten-Thousand Miles on them or under. After a month, I would take the car back to the rental place, and trade for a fully detailed similar car. It was an awesome feeling. I even was able to drive a few of the cars under a thousand miles. Sometimes I would keep these cars for longer then a month.

At the pizzeria, I used to be moan and groan when there were far off single deliveries, this unlimited mileage deal eliminated all of that. I was driving almost three times more then the average driver. People started questioning the logistics of it all. They would ask questions about leasing or buying being better? I had to reply them these answers: "I can not lease a car because I put on 36 to 40000 miles a year. Second is the delivery insurance, thirdly, I could not buy a car from any bank because I just declared bankruptcy. I was lucky enough that there are 'secured credit card's' out there that grant you all the benefits of a regular Visa—but you must deposit whatever you want you credit limit to be though.

Having more money on a monthly basis also freed up the ability to buy other food items, and other household items that had reward air miles from specific grocery stores like 'Safeway.' Air miles that could get you hotel gift certificates and airline vouchers. I had always done this but was afraid of carrying to much inventory of one or two items in my house for fear of running out of money. I could now carry inventory of items for up to six months at a time if the deal was right.

Every week I sat in my house with my calculator and crunched the value of the air miles in connection to the products listed. In some instances the value of the air miles was worth more money then the product itself.

I will give you an example:

There is a deal for 32 oz Coke bottles (3 for $3 at Safeway.) For every 6 bottles you buy, you receive 40 Air Miles. An Air Mile is worth 16 cents each when you redeem them for Best Western Hotel Gift Cards. So you buy (6) 32-oz cokes for $6, in exchange you receive 40 Air Miles at .16 worth for $6.40 in return. I would buy hundreds of dollars worth of the deal—and then sell them to my manager at the pizzeria. She just wanted the best deal in town equivalent and she would give the money for that price point.

I would line up the Air Miles dollar for Dollar-with the money spent on the Coke—and then resell them to manager at like 50% percent of the money spent   the rest of that money was pure profit. I will get into how I made $2000 for my first streak chase when it comes to that chapter from another Air Miles deal. This was money made from the road while I was going to baseball games for 6 weeks.

My community newspaper I was delivering for, also was thrilled I wanted to work extra, so they gave me more work. There was a problem with the amount of people who did not want this given newspaper on the house lists though. About 15 percent of the houses for every route on average did not want the paper.

The problem was that I was getting shipped a hundred extra papers (including the subsequent huge volume of flyers to be inserted in the papers) of the stopped houses. They were piling up in my shed at my house. That is when I remembered a guy at the 'big newspaper job' used to talk about receiving a few dollars a day for recycling about five big bundles of newspapers near his house. I asked him for the address and how this all worked.

It was yet another victory for me after finding out the specifics. They paid about Thirty-Five Dollars a Metric Ton—or about fifteen dollars a full car load from one of the Toyota's I was renting. I had a new business.

On the way back from the States border—there was a community recycling plant in which several bad carriers dumped their entire paper routes every two or three days. Every two days I went for gas I came back with a full car of newspapers—and headed right over to the recycling plant. This profited me fifteen dollars for about forty-five minutes of work. I just had to protect the rental cars from the newspaper ink—wouldn't you know I used free blanket giveaways from baseball stadiums to do this. This business netted me an extra Two-Hundred Dollars of money per month.

I was now in a situation where I could make as much money as the amount of hours I was willing to work. Between the newspapers and delivering pizza seven days a week I was making money from every direction—also at this time the Canadian dollar was worth $1.10 for every American dollar. I started buying all the U.S money I could get my hands on for the future trip.

Also because of the vast amount of money I was making, (delivering to nearly 600 hundred houses)—as opposed to 250 the year before—for that Christmas I made nearly $2000 in Christmas tips, more then the $700 then the year before. I saved $14000 dollars from September 2007 to March of 2008.

The best part about my new schedule was I actually decreased the amount of time involving work because my days of being in a repair shop were over. From September to December I wrote a full science fiction novel—and re-edited my first novel ever written about a teenage gambling ringmaster. I wrote for fifteen to twenty hours a week without fail.

In January of 2008, I purchased the ability to self publish both books for Thirteen Hundred Dollars Total. Now it was a matter of one more final edit. Out of the goals I set forth for myself, they were all a realistic achievement now—with enough money to see the remainder stadiums, (with the bonus of seeing all the other nineteen stadiums again also) and the books being published. The other goal I had was to visit all the Fifty States in America.

At this point in time I was sitting at Twenty-Five States out of the Fifty. However I was going to do the baseball trip it would include every other State I had not yet seen except for Alaska.

By March I was ready for the tickets to go on sale for every ball club—and for them to post the remaining time of game starts on the schedule. Unlike the previous summer, my wife would not be going with me for the road trip. I had initial talks with all other family members, with most of them agreeing to meet me at various times to watch some baseball. I printed up two months worth of the schedule and studied up at the course I wanted to take. I made some early purchases of tickets for this schedule.

A few weeks later, I was online and searched for the 'World Record' holder of the "The Fastest to see all 30 Ballparks in MLB." I knew the record was 28 days—and now I had to re-think this whole trip if I wanted to attempt history. It took me about a week to iron the changes necessary to go for the record streak chase. The total cost to alter the plane trips and buy additional tickets was about a Thousand Dollars when all was said and done. I was ready for the tickets portion. Before I even bought the tickets I strategically mapped out how the plane fares would work, and the mapping of each park, from one to another, after each game.

For years it had been my dream to visit all Fifty-States through visiting baseball games—both minors and majors league games alike. For this very reason, I was good at United States geography.

Being a Canadian doing this trip I had to study the geography even harder. I also had to contend with a slipping dollar now too-as it had slipped to $0.92. From the actual trip expenses I was lucky enough to have purchased all of my plane tickets when the dollar was at par. In all, Forty Flights were arranged.

Out of the plane fares, some of the tickets were of the multi-city variety. I was traveling to a lot of cities one-way. The main site I used was "Kayak." The plane fares had to be searched in relevance to price right after I picked the main schedule I went ahead with. After months of this practice I practically memorized the entire three letter airport codes of all the airports in North America.

The main thing about the streak was that I had to leave myself outs in the double headers should I miss the second game for that day. For this concept, it is somewhat parallel to establishing a flush in poker. Your back end of the schedule kind of looked like your front schedule. This was new territory to me. I was confident of my travel ability because I had already been to nineteen of the ballparks. This element both helped me and hindered me in this quest.

Before the streak started I would see three games. I started my journey by catching a 'Quick Shuttle Bus" From White Rock to Seattle-where I was flying to Oakland. My friend Bryan Mccron sat with me and waited until I boarded the bus—and wished me luck-boy was I going to need it.

2008
STREAKS
1&2

		G		30 GAMES
		A		26 DAYS
		M		
HOME TEAM	**DATE**	E		OPPONENT TIME
	JULY	#		GAME TIME
OAKLAND	SAT-28	0	MCAFEE COLISEUM	GIANTS 6:05 PM
NY METS	SUN-29	0	SHEA STADIUM	YANKEES 1:05 PM
NY YANKEES	M-30	0	YANKEE STADIUM	RANGERS
CW-SOX	JULY	0	US CELLULAR	ATHLETICS 7:11 PM
	1ST			
STREAK STARTED ON THE 2ND BUT COULD BE RETRO				
COULD BE RETROCATIVE TO THE DAY BEFORE IF				
MISSED CWS ON DOUBLEHEADER ON THE 2ND				
DOUBLEHEADERS IN BOLD-Number in order of Double headers				
1-7 in brackets				
MINNESOTA (1)	**W-02**	**1**	**METRODOME**	**TIGERS 12:10 PM**
CH W SOX (1)	**W-02**	**2**	**US CELLULAR FIELD**	**ATHLETICS 7:11 PM**
HOUSTON	T-03	3	MINUTE MAID PARK	DODGERS 1:05 PM
CINCINNATI	F-04	4	GREAT AMERICAN BALLPARK	PADRES 12:35 PM
ATLANTA	S-05	5	TURNER FIELD	**ASTROS 7:05 PM**
PHILADELPHIA(2)	**S-06**	**6**	**CITIZENS BANK PARK**	**METS 1:35 PM**
NY YANKEES (2)	**S-06**	**7**	**YANKEE STADIUM**	**RED SOX 8:05 PM**
PITTSBURGH	M-07	8	PNC PARK	ASTROS 7:05 PM
TEXAS	T-08	9	BALLPARK IN ARLINGTON	ANGELS 7:05 PM
SAN DIEGO (3)	**W-09**	**10**	**PETCO PARK**	**MARLINS 12:35 PM**
LA DODGERS (3)	**W-09**	**11**	**DODGER STADIUM**	BRAVES 7:10 PM
DETROIT (4)	**T-10**	**12**	**COMERICA PARK**	**TWINS 1:05 PM**
CLEVELAND (4)	**T-10**	**13**	**PROGRESSIVE FIELD**	**RAYS 7:15 PM**
CHICAGO CUBS (5)	**F-11**	**14**	**WRIGLEY FIELD**	**GIANTS 1:20 PM**
MILWAUKEE (5)	**F-11**	**15**	**MILLER PARK**	**REDS 7:15 PM**
TORONTO	S-12	16	ROGERS CENTER	YANKEES 1:07 PM

WASHINGTON (6)	S-13	17	**NATIONALS PARK**	ASTROS 1:35 PM
NY METS (6)	S-13	18	**SHEA STADIUM**	ROCKIES 8:05 PM
JULY 14-16 ALL STAR BREAK			**3 DAYS PENALTY**	**DAYS 13,14, 15**
COLORADO	T-17	19	COORS FIELD	PIRATES 7:05 PM
ST. LOUIS	F-18	20	BUSCH STADIUM	PADRES 7:05 PM
LOS ANGELES	S-19	21	ANGELS STADIUM	RED SOX 12:55 PM
ARIZONA	S-20	22	CHASE FIELD	DODGERS 1:10 PM
SEATTLE	M-21	23	SAFECO FIELD	RED SOX 7:05 PM
FLORIDA	T-22	24	DOLPHIN STADIUM	BRAVES 7:15 PM
TAMPA	W-23	25	TROPICANA FIELD	A'S 12:40
BALTIMORE	*T-24*	26	ORIOLE PARK AT CAMDEN	ORIOLES 12:40 PM
KANSAS CITY	F-25	27	KAUFFMAN STADIUM	**RAYS 7:15 PM**
OAKLAND (7)	**S-26**	28	**MCAFEE COLISEUM**	**RANGERS 1:00 PM**
SAN FRANCISCO (7)	**S-26**	29	AT&T PARK	**D BACKS 6:00 PM**
BOSTON	S-27	30	FENWAY PARK	YANKEES 8:05 PM
I COULD HAVE MOVED FLORIDA TO THE 23RD FOR A DOUBLE				
HEADER IF I MISSED THE 6TH NYY GAME(STILL FOR 30-26) ALSO METS 13TH				
THEY ALSO PLAYED ON THE 22ND COULD HAVE MOVED				
NY YANKEES TO MONDAY THE 28TH IF MISSED BOTH				
NEED 7 DOUBLEHEADERS FOR 30-26				
NEEDED 6 DOUBLE HEADER FOR 30-27				
NEEDED 5 DOUBLE HEADERS FOR 30-28				
ABILITY TO RESTART THE STREAK AGAIN ON JULY.09 IF FAILS				
I COULD MAKE UP EITHER MILWAUKEE OR CLEVELAND ON TH 28TH				
IF MISSED				
THERE WAS NO MAKE UP GAME FOR SF GIANTS				
AFTER THE STREAK WAS OVER IF MADE IT ALL				
CASUAL VIEWING	**LIST OF GAMES IN 3RD COLUMN OVERALL**			
	GAMES FOR TRIP			
NEW YORK YANKS	M-28	35	YANKEE STADIUM	ORIOLES 7:05 PM
NEW YORK YANKS	T-29	36	YANKEE STADIUM	ORIOLES 7:05 PM
BOSTON	W-30	37	FENWAY PARK	ANGELS 7:05 PM
NEW YORK YANKS	T-31	38	YANKEE STADIUM	ANGELS 7:05 PM
ST.LOUIS	AUG	39	BUSCH STADIUM	PHILLIES 7:05 PM
	1ST			

CHICAGO CUBS	S-02	40	WRIGLEY FIELD	PIRATES 12:05 PM
HOUSTON	S-03	41	MINUTE MAID PARK	METS 1:05 PM
TEXAS	S-03	42	MINUTE MAID PARK	BLUE JAYS 7:05 PM
TEXAS	M-04	43	BALLPARK IN ARLINGTON	YANKEES 7:05 PM
CHICAGO CUBS	T-05	44	WRIGLEY FIELD	ASTROS 1:20 PM
CHICAGO W SOX	T-05	45	US CELLULAR FIELD	TIGERS 7:11 PM
CINCINNATI REDS	W-06	46	GREAT AMERICAN BALLPARK	BREWERS 12:35 PM
ST.LOUIS	W-06	47	BUSCH STADIUM	DODGERS 7:15 PM
SEATTLE	T-07	48	SAFECO FIELD	RAYS 7:15 PM
SEATTLE	F-08	49	SAFECO FIELD	RAYS 7:15 PM
SEATTLE	S-09	50	SAFECO FIELD	RAYS 7:15 PM
SEATTLE	S-10	51	SAFECO FIELD	RAYS 1:05 PM
			2ND ATTEMPT	
			30 GAMES IN 26 DAYS	
			JULY.09-AUG.03 2008	
SAN DIEGO (1)	**W-09**	1	**PETCO PARK**	**MARLINS 12:35 PM**
LA DODGERS (1)	**W-09**	2	**DODGER STADIUM**	BRAVES 7:10 PM
DETROIT (2)	**T-10**	3	**COMERICA PARK**	**TWINS 1:05 PM**
CLEVELAND (2)	**T-10**	4	**PROGRESSIVE FIELD**	**RAYS 7:15 PM**
CHICAGO CUBS (3)	**F-11**	5	**WRIGLEY FIELD**	**GIANTS 1:20 PM**
MILWAUKEE (3)	**F-11**	6	**MILLER PARK**	**REDS 7:15 PM**
TORONTO	S-12	7	ROGERS CENTER	YANKEES 1:07 PM
WASHINGTON (4)	S-13	8	**NATIONALS PARK**	ASTROS 1:35 PM
NY METS (4)	S-13	9	**SHEA STADIUM**	ROCKIES 8:05 PM
JULY 14-16 ALL STAR BREAK				DAYS 6,7,8
COLORADO	T-17	10	COORS FIELD	PIRATES 7:05 PM
CHICAGO W SOX	F-18	11	US CELLULAR FIELD	ROYALS 7:05 PM
LOS ANGELES	S-19	12	ANGELS STADIUM	RED SOX 12:55 PM
ARIZONA	S-20	13	CHASE FIELD	DODGERS 1:10 PM
SEATTLE	M-21	14	SAFECO FIELD	RED SOX 7:05 PM
BALTIMORE	T-22	15	DOLPHIN STADIUM	BRAVES 7:15 PM
TAMPA (5)	**W-23**	**16**	**TROPICANA FIELD**	**A'S 12:40 PM**
FLORIDA (5)	**W-23**	**17**	**DOLPHIN STAIUM**	**METS 7:05 PM**
PITTSBURGH	*T-24*	18	ORIOLE PARK AT CAMDEN	ORIOLES 12:40 PM
CINCINNATI	F-25	19	KAUFFMAN STADIUM	**ROCKIES 8:05 PM**

OAKLAND (6)	S-26	20	MCAFEE COLISEUM	RANGERS 1:00 PM
SAN FRANCISCO (6)	S-26	21	AT&T PARK	D BACKS 6:00 PM
PHILADELPHIA	S-27	22	CITIZENS BANK BALLPARK	METS 1:35 PM
MINNESOTA	M-28	23	METRODOME	WHITE SOX 7:05 PM
ATLANTA	T-29	24	TURNER FIELD	CARDS 7:05 PM
BOSTON	W-30	25	FENWAY PARK	ANGELS 7:05 PM
NEW YORK	T-31	26	YANKEE STADIUM	ANGELS 7:05 PM
ST.LOUIS	AUG	27	BUSCH STADIUM	PHILLIES 705 PM
	1ST			
KANSAS CITY	SAT-2	28	KAUFFMAN STADIUM	7:05 PM
MAKE-UP DATE FOR DODGERS-GIANTS AND MOVE KC TO AUG.4TH				
HOUSTON	SUN-3	29	MINUTE MAID PARK	METS 1:05:00 PM
TEXAS	SUN-3	30	BALLPARK IN ARLINGTON	BLUE JAYS 7:05 PM
OPEN DAY	MON-4		IF NECESSARY	
OPEN DAY	TUES-5		IF NECESSARY	
MAKE-UP DATE FOR DODGERS-GIANTS WAS AUG.02 AND MOVE KC TO AUG.4TH				
AUGUST THE 4TH AND 5TH COULD BE MAKE UP DATES FOR				
TEXAS IF FAILED DOUBLE HEADER WITH HOUSTON-ALSO MAKE-UP				
KC AND SAME FOR NEXT DAY				
THE 28TH WAS MAKEUP DATE FOR MILWAUKEE, CLEVELAND, FLORIDA IF				
DOUBLE HEADERS FAILED				
NEEDED 7 DOUBLE HEADERS FOR 30-26				
NEEDED 6 DOUBLE HEADER FOR 30-27				
NEEDED 5 DOUBLE HEADERS FOR 30-28				

Game#1 Day #1
The Metrodome
Minneapolis, MN
July.02/2008

The key to making this doubleheader was to have a quick game between Minnesota and Detroit. I flew into Minnesota from Chicago after watching a White Sox game the night before. Why would I do that before I was going to see them on this night? It was something I learned in this game early by meeting the 'Guinness Book of World Records' guidelines of not going to a stadium twice in the same streak attempt. Should I not make my Minnesota to Chicago flight on this day, or not arrive before the first pitch for the White Sox—I had US Cellular Field in my back pocket already. It was good practice for verification as well.

Since I landed had landed at the Minnesota International Airport-(MSP) at eight in the morning, (flying in from Chicago's Midway Airport), I decided to check out the 'Mall of America.' It was also a good chance to check out the subway transportation that was going to take me to and from the game later at the 'Metrodome.'

I was happy to see the close proximity of the 'Lindberg Terminal' to the airport. It is one of only a few cities that have a light rail service directly from the airport to a stadium. To help matters even more I noticed they had a security clearance for travelers that only had carry-on luggage right out of the terminal. There was little wait for this line and the people were moving through at a fast pace. I, of course, had some of my luggage stored at a hostel in Chicago's Downtown core where I was staying anyway, and the biggest amount of luggage was stored at my brother's house in New Jersey—where I would be doubling back to collect several times throughout the journey. All I had that day was a coat, my cell phone, and a digital camera to document each ballpark visit.

I had a sheet with all the subway times for the '55 'HENNEPIN/MALL OF AMERICA HIWATHA LINE SCHEDULE.'

I made it to the Mall of America at about 9 AM in the morning, but was way too early to have most of the shops open. So I had breakfast and walked around the entire mall once to at least say I have seen the place. I was very tired from already watching baseball games from McAfee Coliseum, Shea Stadium, Yankee Stadium and US Cellular Field for 4 straight days in a row. I decided to rest on one of the comfortable bean bag chairs in the foyer of the mall.

The next thing I knew I was being poked by a security guard of the mall telling me I could not sleep there. I almost jumped up parallel out of that bean bag chair because it was already ten minutes to eleven—had that security guard not woken me up I would have probably missed the first game. Still I ran to the subway station and met up with about a hundred other 'Twins' fans-who were also parking at the mall to take the subway in to the game.

I was mad at myself for the decision to be so far away from the ballpark, and at that point decided no matter what I did from there on in any city, to always be within earshot of each ballpark. I did know I was going to be in okay shape to make it for 1st pitch. I still had to wait ten minutes at the station for two trains to pass before I could board a train.

I made it to the game at 11:45 AM

It was a muggy day outside so I was glad I was indoors. Since I wanted to have a comfortable seat, I bought a twenty dollar ticket to sit at the home run porch area in left field.

I have a soft spot in my heart for the 'Twins' and the 'Metrodome.' I have always liked the Twins since the days of Kirby Puckett. He was one of my favorite players growing up, and I actually read his novel when I was a teenager, (it was one of three other books I had read in baseball at that age. I also read books by Rickey Henderson, Paul Molitor and Pete Rose.) Throw in the players Don Mattingly, Dave Winfield and George Bell and were talking about all my favorite ballplayers at that time.

The 'Metrodome' was opened in the early eighties and was considered a 'state of the art' building when it first opened. The white 'Teflon roof' is easy to pick out from far distances in the city. The 'Metrodome' looks far better from the outside then the inside. When you looked at the roof from the inside you see silver coils and bright white, you also wondered how any ballplayer ever saw a white ball that was ever hit?

The tickets themselves were very well priced to see an entertaining product on the field. I was happy to see that they even had a Canadian Flag hanging from the rafters in the middle of the Field. I wondered if that was placed there to appease the Canadians: Justin Morneau and Jessie Crain that were on the team

I sat in my seat and listened to the opening line-ups being read out. The place had the worst sound system in the major leagues by far. They really should have turned down the audio.

I also bought lower level seats because you were not allowed in the lower levels if you have upper deck seats. I hate ballparks that do this, it would be one thing if all major league parks adopted this policy but they have not. The previous year, on my first visit, I had found out how high the general bleacher seats were for your seven dollar fee, and had no plans to ever sit that high again. Being lower was definitely the way to go at the Metrodome.

I do give to the Twins players for their generosity to kids in the way a lot of them donating private boxes—out of their own pocket—to the games. Whether it is "Morneau's Mounties, The Crain Train, the players are at the fore front for the community. I also liked the Wall of Fame with pictures of Kirby Puckett, Frank Viola, Harmon Killebrew, Carew, Kent Hrbek, and Rick Aguilera. I watched every inning of the playoffs on TV of both the 87' and 91' playoffs in which they won the World Series. Even though the '91 series is considered a better series I remember the '87 series with the Cardinals a lot more because I watched it entirely with my 3 brothers and father at the age of 11.

I bought a few hot dogs, a coke and watched as the mascot 'T.C' zoomed around the outfield on an 'ATV.' He stopped right before our section and scaled the fence over to high-five some fans. The fence in left was not very high. T.C is probably the best all around mascot in the game, he hits batting practice, hugs kids, dances, drives the ATV around and comes into the stands a lot more then any mascot I have ever seen.

The game started on time and my quest had begun. It was a new way to watch a game. Even though I was cheering for the Twins over the Detroit Tigers, I was cheering for fast innings and outs more than anything. For certain I did not want to see extra innings at all. I had to catch the subway back to the Airport—and catch a 4:56 PM flight to Chicago that landed at 6:30 PM— for a 7:11 PM start time at 'US Cellular Field. It was now 12:10 PM at first pitch.

Much to my delight, the Twins put up a five run bottom of the third to take a 5-0 lead. I loved this because the home team winning also meant a half an inning less. The way I figured it, I hoped for 15 to 18 minute innings, this would mean a game that would last two hours and 15-45 minutes long. So I started watching for innings that lasted this long. I soon learned my new best friend was the double play ball. I was constantly doing the math in my head, 50 minutes for 3-innings was about a 2 hour and 30 minute contest. I looked at the scoreboard of the Twins directly behind me to see the totals.

For such a big facility, the screens showed replays at other ends of the Dome were pretty small. The fans in the ballpark were quite loud when the Twins were winning and it reached high levels

19

on the old wavelengths of sound. There was definitely a reason why the Twins always had one of the better home records.

The Astroturf back then—turned into Field turf later—led to seeing-eye singles more then any other ballpark in the majors. You also had to love the uniqueness of the 17 foot baggie in right field-it was often compared to the 'Green Monster' in Boston but only for size, it was surely not as attractive.

Another negative towards the ballpark were rats in the 'press box', the roof deflating a few times to accumulated snow(caving in during the 2010 NFL season) and players that suffered knee injuries as a result of the concrete underneath the playing surface more so with the Astroturf of course before the turn of the millennium.

I was standing for the final pitch with much jubilation as the Twins won 7-0 in front of 30,120 fans (including me) in a game that lasted 2 hours and 30 minutes. It was now 2:40 PM in the afternoon. I documented the end of the game with pictures, video, and had a Minnesota Twins usher sign my log book and raced out to the subway train station. What I saw outside made me panic. There must have been a few thousand people lining up to take the train. I asked a guy the approximate wait time for a line this big from where I was? He said "about a 40 minute wait."

I figured this had me to the airport at around 4:00 PM at best. It was very risky to make the 4:56 PM flight-but it would not unattainable. I thought back to a trick my dad always did at stadium visits. I ran up to the next station about a mile up the road. There, there was no line-up at all. All it took was running to beat the crowd. Chalk one up for dear old dad teaching me well as a kid. With no line-up I stood on the twenty-minute train to the 'Lindbergh Terminal', whipped out my boarding pass that I had printed several hours earlier—and went through the security gate without any bags. I made it to my gate at 3:45 PM. I had a solid opportunity to complete this doubleheader. One game was done. Had I missed that flight I would have been taking a Greyhound Bus all night in order to arrive at 3:00 AM-only to grab my stuff from the hostel and turn around for a flight to Houston from O'Hare Airport.

Game#2 Day#1
US Cellular Field
Chicago, IL
July.02/2008

I had a tip from my brother Trent early on in the planning stages, that .the United States airline companies often 'sand-bag' their flying times to destinations to take jet-way delays into consideration. More often then not, the airlines are able to beat the scheduled arrival time by many minutes. I actually used a tool on the internet called 'Flight Tracker' to watch the very flight I was on to see if this was a correct statement. I watched this exact flight land 4 weeks in a row, all approximately 15 minutes earlier then the 6:32 PM time it was supposed to arrive on that day. That day I was not as lucky. It was after all a 'Chicago Airport.' Still at a 6:30 PM arrival-I had about 40 minutes to first pitch. I had called in a sedan service to pick me up from 'MIDWAY'.

True to their word, there was a young guy in his twenties waiting for me in the arrival gate and he escorted me through to the limo stand at a running pace. I saw it had started to rain and weather was something I would always keep my eye on during transportation throughout the trip.

Midway Airport is 9 miles from the airport to the ballpark in heavy Chicago 'traffic.' The trip was said to be around 15 minutes on the map, but I knew that would be doubled with the traffic on the '55 Highway,' and it being game day. The driver was fast and weaved his way through the rain. We arrived at the ballpark in thirty minutes. It was 7:03 PM. The limo driver turned on the radio a few minutes before arriving to listen to the pre-game show. I heard the broadcasters say there would be a rain delay to start the game

Was this good or bad news? The forecast did not look good, it was supposed to rain all night. This led me to another rule set forth by the "GWR".

There was an inherent risk to any game I went to. Since the rule states I can not go the parks twice during the same streak, what if there was a rain delay midway through the game and they called it? I read the rules again. I had them stuffed in my coat. It says I could not go back to the ballpark again-(during that given streak) in case of a rainout if I watched one pitch. Now if it were to be suspended for any reason, I could complete the game whenever it was resumed. But this posed problems because they would have to have resumed it after the last game of the streak for it to count for me. This meaning under the current attempt my last game was to be on the 27th of July. I would have needed this game, (should it be suspended) to be resumed on exactly Monday July.28. I already had the previous nights game in the bag and could retroactive the streak to it if I wanted. This would mean the streak would become a 30-27 attempt instead of a 30-26 attempt—but I would not have to worry about the weather.

I did have a chance to re-schedule a Chicago White Sox game on the 18th of July. To give myself that option, that was why I was flying to ....Indianapolis.... on the 4th of July morning. I could drive to Cincinnati—the original scheduled game, or drive to St. Louis instead—in case of switching Chicago White Sox to the 18th 2 weeks later. All I had to do was switch a flight to Cincinnati for the 27th and move Boston back a day to the 28th. My flight on the 18th was a 2-parter. I flew from Denver, Colorado in the morning, and then had a flight from Chicago to St. Louis scheduled—with a layover in Cincinnati. This gave me all three cities with an available game on that date for me to see.

I knew this upon reaching US Cellular Field on that July.2nd game. I decided to walk into the rain delay in Chicago. By doing this I needed them to play an 'official game once the 1st pitch was thrown or this streak was dead in the water! I only ever wanted to use the July.1st game in Chicago in case I missed my flight in from Minnesota.

From the moment I walked into US Cellular the rain let up. I was sitting in the 500 level, so there is a nice long elevator to take up to that level. Much like the 'Metrodome,' you are stuck to the level the ticket says you are at. This bugged me almost as much as the 21 dollars shelled out for what is the equivalent of a 'nose-bleed' seat.

I also remember the year before when I brought my wife, when we paid 22 dollars for parking, yikes! Chicago is not a very value priced ticket. They do have great hot-dogs though.

Outside the park, there are many street vendors that carry tones of paraphernalia. There are various bands playing outside the stadium usually before the games—which is a nice feature you don't often see at ballparks.

The White Sox also pay good homage to their heroes of yesteryear. There are many bricks, pillars and statues of greats like; Carlton Fisk, Harold Baines, Frank Thomas, Nellie Fox and Luis Aparicio. Inside the park is very similar to the Indians 'Progressive Field.' It was also built around the same time as Orioles Park at Camden Yards, and the above stated Jacobs Field as it used to be called.

During the game, the scoreboard in centerfield will shoot fireworks through 7 candy-cane style colored pillars—on top of the big scoreboard—and the pillars illuminate to their painted colors. It is a nice spectacle.

In addition to that scoreboard, there is another scoreboard under the main one—near the grassy back drop in center field. This scoreboard is used for player stats. In left centre field is the official score-line scoreboard.

As it goes for the stadiums, The 'Cel' is probably the best to see what the score is from any angle in the crowd.

The concourse in the outfield is designed so that you can walk around freely. I like the stadium as the top half in the league, but the value for the overall experience is suffered by anyone who wants to drive to the park.

The previous night I learned the 'CTA' (Chicago Transit Authority) schedule very well. After the game that night I was going to take the 'Red Line' sub headed towards Howard, to head back towards downtown Chicago, were I was going to go back to the hostel, have a quick snooze and hop on the 'Blue Line' Train that would take me from Jackson and State Road all the way to O'Hare Airport. Once I learned these subways I decided never to drive in Chicago again if possible.

The game started at 7:35 PM, and the clouds had subsided for the time being. It is never fun to sit in a seat after it has been rained on. The smart ushers—(I have seen Cincinnati and San Diego ushers do this) carry towels and dry off your seats as they escort you from the concourse. Most of the parks ushers are not even adept in walking you to your seat as a sign of good service.

I thought I was in the clear at this point from any future weather that night, boy was I wrong. Let's get back to the game first.

The White Sox took a 5-4 lead into the top of the Ninth. That is when the rains started to come down in a hailstorm. I could not take the constant pelting and went into the 500 level Concourse with a bunch of other Chicago Fans. Since it was wet, I was worried about picture/video recorder being affected. On a TV, I watched in dismay as Grady Sizemore hit a solo homer of Scott Linebrink to tie the game at 5. The rain came down even harder. I was petrified the umpires were going to call a rain delay—or even worse to suspend it outright. All of a sudden my decision a few hours earlier could have come back to haunt me. All I heard about the last 48 hours had been the upcoming rain. Man I was sweating it out. After all the planning and leg work for the trip, it could all come to a halt in the first attempt on the very first day!

I would have to start again the next day at zero. Yes there was a contingency plan to it, but because of a limited home schedule in Minnesota for the coming weeks, it would be easier to re-schedule the attempt for a July.09 start. Houston was even worse for re-scheduling the next day. With the 4 doubleheaders in 5 days to start off with beginning July 9th, I would be able to shoot for a 30-26 chance again. It was finish this game right now or I would restart the next week. I was worried.

The Minnesota-Chicago doubleheader is not what most people would think for doubleheader chances. I would be really disappointed if it was stalled because of a suspended game. The roundtrip plane ticket to and from Chicago was one of the higher plane fares at about three hundred dollars round-trip. The sedan service ran about 70 dollars. You add in the car rental in Chicago the previous day, and two days at the hostel—and it would mean about 500 dollars spent on the first day without any games to show for it should the game be called now.

The bottom of the ninth was scoreless. More rain came down.....

The top of the tenth proved to be awful viewing in watching the hitters try and locate the ball even to swing.

I umpired for ten years growing up. I was convinced they were going to call the game. There was no end to the rain in sight or forecast.

A.J Pierzynski then came up to bat in the bottom of the 10th. I was pacing around the walkway to the 521 section. I decided to stomach a few glances at the field from the outside again. I had been up since 3 AM at that point. The Cleveland Indians pitcher Kobayashi leaned back and fired a fastball—A.J cranked a 'thunderous' shot headed into the night towards left field. I never even saw the ball land in the stands, but when the fireworks shot off from the scoreboard the place went ballistic. The White Sox fans I had been watching the game with, burst outside of the Concourse—and all of them were high-fiving each other and I joined them. I was just as happy as they were—albeit for an entirely different reason—I had completed 2 games in my first day! A.J Pierzynski will be favorably remembered because of that walk-off homer.

The hour and a half it took for me to catch a train back to the Hostel did not bother me in the pouring rain. I had my camera tucked into my pocket deep with my verification of proof I had been there.

Game#3 Day#2
Minute Maid Park
Houston, TX
July.3/2008

I couldn't sleep after the previous night's game at Us Cellular Field; so much of the streak scenarios had been running through my mind. I had nailed a doubleheader with a flight involved between cities. It was a remarkable accomplishment with planning. I took the 'Red Line' subway train to my hostel room on Congress Parkway. It was an only a twenty-minute trip.

The hostel was sponsored by 'Hostelling International.' So they had a student work center with internet and vending. I should have probably slept but I was too fired up—and thoughts of oversleeping could not be erased from my mind.

I made the decision after an hour that I would forego taking the hour long subway to 'O'Hare Airport'; instead I opted to take a taxicab.

The plan was quite simple, I had a flight that left at around six in the morning and would arrive in Houston at 8:30 AM. I had one of my free car rental days waiting at 'Thrifty Car Rental' at 'IAH' airport. It should have been easy enough to drive to the ballpark—'Google maps' said it would take about thirty minutes or so to drive there. It was my first new ballpark during the trip. It was my 20TH ballpark overall.

O'Hare Airport was one of the first airports to have internet services and I really enjoyed having the option as I was waiting for that morning flight. I was flying with 'Continental Airlines' that day.

The skies were blue and everything appeared to be normal when I made it to the gate. I was traveling with only my briefcase that carried all of my travel information. I had one bag checked to be picked up upon arrival. I was 60 minutes until boarding.

There was a momentary pause before the sounds of the speaker came on. The flight had been delayed by 3 hours now by virtue of the flight crew having arrived in late the night before due to inclement weather. I did some quick, mathematics in my head. We were now flying out at 9:30 AM in the morning, and arriving in Houston just after noon time. This was not good at all. I felt uneasy about the whole transportation. I had never been to Houston and I could be delayed a long time in just waiting for the rental car.

I called Thrifty to cancel the car reservation with enough notice to not have them charge a deposit against my visa. Luckily for me I had my phone numbers list and called my limo driver for the next month's game I was going to attend after the streak was supposed to have been over.

Much to my dismay, my sedan driver would be unable to help drive me to the game due to a previous commitment. I was frantically searching on the internet until I found a limo service and called it with 'my air miles long distance number.'

It was nice to have discovered a free way to acquire long distance minutes just by cashing these Air Miles in from shopping at Safeway. After three phone calls, I secured a driver to pick me up from the limo area just after noon. I needed the same service back to the airport after the game to catch a 7 PM flight to 'JFK.' The next day's travel day was even more intense.

The cost for the 2-way sedan service this day was only $110. This of course was definitely a good alternative to use in the city of Houston. Normal car rental rates plus insurance and gas—and parking at the game would almost have equaled that amount anyways.

"Damn!" I whispered while drinking a coke and intermittently biting a cold sandwich to fill my stomach up till game time. I had just digested the cost of altered travel plans when I was presented with a new problem, "what am I going to do with my checked luggage?" It was full of just ordinary clothes at least so I decided to just ditch the luggage parcel and try and retrieve it later in the day. Again every time problems arose throughout the trip I would re-evaluate the rest of the trip with the gained knowledge. Somewhere in the back of my mind I had considered this scenario and was happy to have disposable luggage in the event I was not able to recover it later. There would be no further delays in going to Houston.

My sedan driver was in his middle forties and was well dressed with black slacks and a sports collared shirt with a purple tie on. He had gone the extra mile to meet me in the meeting area with a white sign that read my last name.

"Mr. Booth, right this way, you are in no danger of missing the first pitch, I will have you there within a half hour."

This put my mind at ease. As part of my original planning I had a different schedule of dates which included extra sets of tickets to the Astros later in the month—I offered them up to the gentleman immediately. I was trying to sell them online but with no success. It continued my good will acts during the streak. I made it to Minute Maid Park within the half an hour as the sedan guy had said. I then walked up to the corner of the building. It was about Ninety-Five Degrees out.

I was happy to not have fought with real parking and navigation at this point anyway. I immediately was impressed with the cleanliness outside of the ballpark.

Upon entering I saw the homage to past players on the wall of Craig Biggio and Jeff Bagwell—the wall I liked the best was of Craig Biggio's 3,000 hits wall. Past that was a 'HOMERUN PUMP'-gas pump---I actually prefer to watch the game along this area. The Train in the left field bleachers goes off every time there is a homerun hit.

I noticed that with most indoor stadiums that they are tougher to take clear pictures. I had only brought my silver digital camera and had left my briefcase in the sedan because I was not sure of the park's policies when it came to what you could bring in. I walked around the concourse and was impressed at the sightlines. The hill in center just adds to the character of the park. The sunlight still shines through the windows past the field, which makes it somewhat bright.

I made my way to the concession stand and purchased a soda and pizza—which was awesome. I sat in the four hundred-section while I ate. I met a nice usher who signed my book itinerary and I explained my situation of having to be there for every single pitch. He was nice enough to radio a fellow usher near the exit later in the game to help sign my page that I was there for the last out. It would have cost me a few minutes rushing down the escalators from the fourth level.

There was a nice tribute to the soldiers from overseas being a day before the 'Fourth of July' on the big scoreboard. This would be a repeating theme of baseball games that made me proud to visit these stadiums. Respecting the fine men and women that were protecting the country through baseball was high on the list of MLB. With Thirty-Six Thousand other fans I saw Houston win 5-2 over LA Dodgers in 3 hours.

I liked that during the seventh inning stretch the Houston fans sang "Deep in the Heart of Texas." They also loved playing the "Sesame Street's version" of 'get playing' baseball—as it promoted kids playing baseball and it was quite entertaining.

I actually prefer not having the sun beating in my face while watching games so I was happy to watch the game indoors.

Minute Maid Park has lots of little scoreboards in the lower levels so you always know what the score is. Their big score board is easily seen in the right center field wall and is great for viewing replays. There is also plenty of concourse room to walk around each level.

The Staff at Minute Maid Park are always courteous and were there to help in anyway. I would not say there is an abundance of different food but what they have works. The pizza was sensational and the ballpark hotdogs are good and well priced. It is a good park to come and go from for when it comes to park accessibility. They also open up the ballpark roof after everyone leaves to air it out.

Since the ballgame was over in good time I was able to race to Congress Street and Crawford. It was a perfect sedan pick up.

Now came a little bit of worrying. I had some time to locate my luggage. I walked to the baggage area of security and explained that I was in pursuit of a world record and that I needed to make it to the park on time for the game and said I did not see my luggage ever come down the ramp. Of course that was a lie-but what was I going to tell them? They could not find the bag at the airport and I was re-routed to a more secure part of the airport for more screening and analysis. I was not seen as a security threat—they just needed to locate the bag by asking itinerary questions.

A few more minutes and I would be okay with the idea I was not receiving the bag back—there were inherent risks to the streak chase. Just then they told me "Continental Airlines had re-routed the bag to JFK already—this actually looked good in my favor because it looked like it was their fault all along. I would meet up with my bag in New York City.

My day was not over yet. I did a radio interview with "CBC Radio" back home for five minutes live with reporters I still can't remember the names of. I explained them the day and then told them the "Jim Maclaren story." The lady host began to cry on air, and it was then I fully understood the magnitude of the streak now gaining momentum, it was my third radio interview already and back home the 'Associated Press' had picked it up in all the newspapers.

The very next day I had another radio interview some where between Indianapolis and Cincinnati when I could spare a few minutes from the road. I had also been communicating non-stop with the 'Detroit Free Press- who were going to follow me around the ballpark all day when I arrived there the following Thursday in Detroit-and about nine days into the trip.

During the radio interview, my gate had changed to a different area and I only realized it at the last minute-scurrying about as fast as I could. I was going to keep tabs on every last detail in order to break this record. I noticed the Houston Airport has more carts transporting people then any other airport in the USA. I wanted to have that option available but it was not meant for healthy free-bodied people. I managed to sleep the whole flight to JFK. It then took me about thirty minutes to find my rental car in the parking lot. Again I needed to be sharper from that point forward.

I drove back to my brother's house in Sicklerville New Jersey and would only be there to shower before heading to Philadelphia's International airport for an early morning flight to Indianapolis en route to Cincinnati.

Game#4 Day#3
The Great American Ball Park
Cincinnati, OH
July.04/2008

It felt wrong from the time I made it to the Philadelphia Airport. It was a tough shuttle ride from the parking lot to arrive at a full security checkpoint-even at an early time of a 5:45 AM flight. I had flown out of PHL before-just never the dreaded 'F' gate. The fact you have to wait in yet another line for a shuttle to the gate is brutal. This caused me even more panic. I had to catch that flight to Indianapolis on time to make it to Cincinnati on time. One of the things I learned when booking all of these flights was that Cincy's Int'l Airport (CVG) completely rips you off for fares to and from its fine city. I was at an all time frustration when I became the last person on the shuttle—and virtually sprinted to the jet-way to make it 2 seconds before they closed the security door for my Us Airways Flight from Philly.

Landing at Indianapolis Airport I knew once again that it was going to be a long day. I first had booked this trip that did not include a record chase—rather I was going to see all 30 Major League Teams—and the 1st 48 States in 45 days. So this date included a matinee game in Cincinnati—then a massive drive to the Alabama border before driving back to Memphis Airport by way of Mississippi State—and by taking the bridge that takes you into West Memphis Arkansas—before taking a u-turn in order to head back to Memphis Airport.

This would be a challenge.

I was surprised how fast I received my rental car in Indianapolis—I was to start driving on the highway 74-E. Wouldn't you know there was a massive traffic accident grid-locking the highway for hours on the 4th of July near Greensburg, Indiana, so for that reason alone I decided to drive up the Hwy-70 —and then onto Hwy 75-South from there as I could make up some time driving the extra distance it would take with the detour.

It was going to be challenging but I had done the trip down I-70 two times in the last eighteen months so I was confident in driving that way.

I did my radio interview on the road and was making great time on the highway. I was on course to make this game after all. Despite it being a holiday, the roads were not that bad. I know there was probably a faster way to make it to the game-but I knew this way better.

The interview lasted ten minutes and I hung up my phone before I started looking for my button on the camera that broke off in the Mall Of America-so much so that I begun swerving on the highway near Eaton, Ohio, then there were police sirens in the background. Good lord!

The officer was a behemoth at well over 6 ft. 5 and weighed over 250 pounds would be my guess.

"License and registration please sir?"

I was mad at myself for not waiting till I arrived at the park. It was best to be as polite as I could be-I needed for this to be a quick ticket. I was wearing shorts and a brown rugby shirt with sandals and no socks. I watched the clouds roll in almost simultaneously as being pulled over and it rained hard.

The officer came back to the car, "son you need to step into the back of the police vehicle?"

"Wow, officer is that necessary?" At this point I was so tired from the first few days I was oblivious to this being some sort of safety measure.

"No, you are from Canada and I need to take some more details from you and there is no room in the front passenger seat." Rain was pelting off my hat as I made my way to the police car.

I was relieved he knew that I swerved because I was looking for something as opposed to drunk driving or something. "Officer, I am actually driving to Cincinnati for the game as part of a record streak to see all the major league games in the least amount of days, I was stupidly looking for a piece to my camera, that is why I swerved. Is there any way to pay this thing immediately so it can be done faster, I mean I was at fault I know I was wrong?"

"Sir, this will only take a minute," he replied nicely.

Yeah right, it took 20 minutes. I was behind schedule and hoarding a wreck-less driving ticket worth a couple hundred dollars. I was finished for making first pitch, I hit major traffic coming down the 75-S, and knew I would not make it to Cincinnati until at least after 1:30 PM-and the game was to start at 12:35 PM local time. Back a few hours ago I was singing the praises of driving a 'Dodge Charger' with a Satellite Radio.

Now I still held hope of maybe the game would be delayed for rain or something. The announcers on the radio had said the weather was okay and they were starting on time. I was still 40 minutes outside the city!

"Were back with opening pitch," the man said from the radio.

"Well, that just completely blows," was my response.

I had not even contemplated missing this game. I was going to have to restart the streak on July.9th for my 2nd attempt. I always had that in my back pocket should I need it. I knew this might be the case, it was my belief that it would happen through a collection of double header misses—and not because of traffic and cops. It would serve as another reminder of things not to do in the future—Fourth of July travel. This was always tough when scheduling as Cincinnati had limited home games that month and I needed Atlanta the next day.

The announcer microphone was back on the radio, "well folks, it seems we are going to be delayed for a few hours as we are being ambushed by some rain now and they have put the tarp on the field. The weather reports say it will clear up so tentatively it looks to start about 2 PM."

"Yeeeeessssss!!!!" I screamed. I still was going to be focused in on getting there. I drove the car nicely through the rest of the drive and parked at the closest spot to the entrance on Pete Rose Way—and ran into the park. I was saved by a rain delay—I never thought I would benefit from such an event. I was good to resume the streak.

I met some really nice people in the stands once I walked up to my seats. I ate two hot dogs as fast as I could because I was starving. I then announced my name and what I was doing—since the game was about to start (and there were no ushers present), I had fellow fans sign my log sheet that I was there for 1st and last pitch.

I was happy when Ken Griffey Jr. came up and smashed a ball over the right field fence, causing a fireworks blast from the boat seats.

The Great American Ballpark is one of the best parks in the majors for scenery outside the yard. You get a close personal view of the Ohio River. The park also features the 'Cincinnati Reds Hall Of Fame" that is directly adjacent to the park—great place to check out the 1st Major League Baseball Club. Particularly if you are a Pete Rose fan, you have to visit this Museum. Pete Rose is nowhere to be found at Great American because of his lifetime ban—but his career is nicely chronicled inside the doors of the Cincinnati Reds Hall of Fame.

The concourses at Great American are spacious, clean and the workers there offer the nicest hospitality. There is not a bad seat in the place. Cincinnati's fans are amongst the smartest in baseball and have been faithful to the team's struggles of late.

I was fortunate to sit in the right field bleachers during my first visit and watched Ken Griffey Jr. talk to all the fans throughout the game. They have 3 mascots still in use that walk the field in: 'Gapper,' 'Mr. Redlegs' and of course 'Rosie Red,' a truly great experience for the kids. The fireworks display on Friday nights in the summer are incredible against the back drop of the Ohio River.

I was happy to have the game end in 2 hours and 20 Minutes in real length— and nearly four hours with the rain delay to start the game. The Reds won 3-0 behind a brilliant pitching job of Bronson Arroyo.

After the game I was treated to a drive of a lifetime, and while I never made it to the State of Mississippi because of rainy weather and time concerns——I highly endorse taking a long drive south through the State of Tennessee on the Fourth of July. I watched four straight hours of fireworks as I drove south past the city of Nashville, and all the way to the Alabama border.

It was an eleven hour drive I accomplished before driving the car rental back to Memphis Airport. It was so dark when I returned the car rental I left my camera in the car by accident. I actually phoned 'National Car Rental' from the airplane, and they made arrangements to send the camera FED-EX to my brother's house that very day. It would be there when I returned the following day. I had escaped a major travel day of adjustments. It was only three days into the trip and I loved the constant adrenaline rush.

I routinely called my family and friends back West-from the Eastern Cities-in order to get revved up for the games. So I wouldn't miss flights, or over sleep alarms, I had many friends text me or call me as a precaution. I was fortunate to have friends from newspapers that are up at all hours in the night—to have helped me with this. I boarded a Memphis plane onward to Atlanta for my first visit to 'Turner Field.'

Game#5 Day#4
Turner Field
Atlanta, GA
July.05/2008

It was a non-eventful plane trip, and I was happy to make it to 'Turner Field' with plenty of time for game number five. I had never been to the ballpark here yet, and was impressed with some things and yet other things were left unclear. There was a good turnout of 37,000 people to watch an Atlanta Braves team that was struggling. I was left to ponder why the fans would not sell the park out in the playoffs?

Turner Field has the most interactive pre-and post game interviews at their broadcast pavilion near the front entrance. I was amazed at how close the fans got to the announcers. After the game I watched that night there was a post-game concert with the popular band Arrested Development'. The stage in left-center field after the games is a nice venue to keep the fans entertained even after the games.

The park is quite monstrous with the levels, but it might have been better if the seats were cascading up and down over the field. The staff at the park is below average, and if you are in the upper seats you virtually have no help.

Then we get to the "Tomahawk Chop.'

The chop is really the most absurd tradition in baseball or sports for that matter, but the fans do it religiously. I was astounded to see groups of fifty people and upwards doing this tradition in sync. I will give them credit for being dedicated.

The outside of the park is not the greatest area of town but the red brick building stands out largely. I like the historical pictures, plaques and statues of all the greats like: Hank Aaron and Warren Spahn. I think the fourteen pennants have spoiled the fans to the point where the regular season does not matter and this it too bad. I am sure in time the history in the park will be so much greater when: Chipper Jones, John Smoltz, Bobby Cox, Greg Maddux and Tom Glavine all get their due.

There are large concourses, but it takes forever to reach the upper decks, and it seems so far away from everything once you are up there.

The game was a dud from the get-go. Houston pasted the hometown Braves 6-2 with Mark Loretta doing the most damage collecting four runs batted in. The game was over in 2.5 hrs. The best part of my experience was the concert afterwards. Maybe it was because I never liked the Braves being both a Yankees and Blue Jays fan growing up.

Atlanta was easy to navigate around with the rental car and I stayed at a 'Quality Inn' I bargained for on www.priceline.com. I paid $10 to park at the game and another $15 over night at the hotel downtown. The experience was all right, but then again I left this ballpark for the very end of my chasing for a reason. I caught up on sleep and had an early morning flight to Philadelphia. It was nice to have a stress free travel day.

Game#6 Day#5
Citizens Bank Ball Park
Philadelphia, PA
July.06/2008

On the drive back on the Hwy-76 W-I started to get cocky about this whole trip. My dream of 30 games in 26 days was on track. This day upcoming I had scouted more than any other doubleheader scenario. It was 8 AM-and I was driving back to my brother Trent's in N.J for a visit and breakfast before returning to the Park. I planned to park at the 30th street station with my rental car and take a cab to Citizens Bank Ballpark afterwards.

From there I was going to see a game between the Mets and Phillies. Around 4:30 PM, after the first game ended I was going to take a cab back to the 'Amtrak Station' on 30TH ST.

I was slated to take a 5:10 PM train that would get me to 'New York Penn Station' at nearly 7 PM. From there I could take the subway to Yankee Stadium. It was a Sunday night game—so the starting time on the New York game was 8:05pm. Using Amtrak was the way to go—the previous year my brother Trent and I did a doubleheader with 'Shea Stadium'-and 'CBP.' You are able to skip the traffic and Tolls for a little more money—but way more convenience.

If I made this doubleheader it would be 7 games in 5 days. I was stoked to have a chance to see Yankees vs. Red Sox as the second half of the doubleheader.

I did some laundry at my brother's house, and then left for the park to arrive around noon for a 1:35 PM start.

Citizens Bank Park is one of the best parks to watch a game now with the bustling crowds and hardcore fanatics that are Phillies fans. I was not happy to see rain clouds surfacing the sky when I arrived. The weather report had called only for clouds. I noticed when walking in for my 1st day game that Citizens Bank Park is really accessible for everyone including special ramps for the handicapped. The park outlay is nice.

The 'Tony Luke's' area surrounded by 'Ashburn Alley' is my favorite place to watch the games from.

I don't like spending lots of money for any game—so "Standing Room Only" seats are perfect for me.

I walked around the park before the game and took some nice video. The 'Sports Complex' that CBP is part of with: "Lincoln Financial Field, The Wachovia Center and the 'Old Spectrum', make it a sports goers dream in solving any driving issues. The mere fact the airport is so close by really gives the park even that much more credibility.

Being at Phillies games you must watch the 'Phillie Phanatac,' who is probably the most entertaining mascot in the Major Leagues today with apologies to 'T.C. from Minnesota" and the 'San Diego Chicken.' This mascot loves to aggravate the umpires and opposing ball teams by all sorts of shenanigans.

I ate a Phllly Cheesesteak as soon as I got in the ballpark—again is the best singular food all time at any ballpark.

I was seeing the New York Mets for the 3rd time in a week. I had seen them play in Houston 3 days before that, and the previous Sunday before the streak had started. I was lucky enough to see a Yankees/Mets game at Shea Stadium. I have always hated the Mets—even more since they got rid of Daryl Strawberry and Dwight Gooden. I had cheered for them in the 86 World Series only because they were playing the Red Sox.

I was happy in one way to see the game progressing along at 1-0 Mets in the eighth inning while I was keeping a watchful eye on the rain at all times. They were throwing pounds of sand on the field between every inning. It was only nearing 4 PM—and the game was eight outs for being finished. I had talked to all of the security guys about signing my time log sheet and had the best route to hailing a cab directly after the game ended.

Ryan Howard was up to bat and the umpire was checking out the rains with his fellow crew huddled up. The motion was made for the tarp.

"Damn," I said, knowing the rain was not going to let up. I could have taken about a 40 minute delay or so and attempted the 5:30 PM train—to have a chance but it was not to be.

Not only that, but the rain was coming down even harder. Since the parks are a hundred miles apart I was thinking about a Cincinnati scenario where the Yanks/Red Sox could have been delayed in my favor.

It was now turning into me hoping they would call the game because it was 7 PM at night. I was with a lot of fellow fans that had been crammed into the covered areas of 'CBP'. The Mets were up by one run—technically it was a game, although I did not really want an asterisk of a shortened game as part of the streak. I had come to the realization that I spent a lot of money just to miss that Yankees doubleheader on that Sunday. The worst was that the chain reaction of that missed game would mean the return game at Fenway Park, between those two clubs three weeks from that Sunday would be missed as well.--$300 in tickets completely eaten.

I was feeling really down until the 'Phillie Phanatac' stole the ATV from the grounds crew and peeled around the rain soaked field with the field crew chasing him for ten minutes. It was an awesome release from the tension I was feeling. With only one game missed I could still turn in a 30-27 trip. My Boston game as the last game was also strategic. I needed to move Baltimore from the 22nd to 27th and move the Yankees into Baltimore's 22nd slot—and then Boston could be moved to the Monday 28th game. The flights I had actually worked out because of my 22nd flight had me arrive in New York early in the morning. Gone also was the possibility of hitting all doubleheaders before the 22nd of July—where I could have skipped the hard to make 23rd Tampa Bay-Florida doubleheader attempt and used the Florida game on the 22nd—and push Baltimore to the 27th as the final game for a 30-27 attempt.

To add insult to the length of game, the Phillies tied it in the bottom of the Ninth at around 9 PM—and the game ended at 10:54 PM at night. The Yankees game actually ended about the same time as the Phillies. I took a cab back to my parked car at the 'Amtrak Station' and drove back to my brother's house again. I needed to drive to Pittsburgh the next night before driving back the day after that to New York City. Things were just beginning to spiral downward.

Game#7 Day#6
PNC Park
Pittsburgh, PA
July.07/2008

It was not my first time to see the Pirates play at 'PNC', the previous year I watched a doubleheader featuring Barry Bonds last games to be played in Pittsburgh— for awhile I was thought he might pass Hank Aaron for the all time Homer list for the games I was attending. Barry had surpassed Aaron a week earlier but I was still glad to see him in the starting lineup. Now I was back less than a year later.

I was ready to rebound from the day before. I drove 340 miles from my brother's house in New Jersey—to arrive in Pittsburgh with lots of time to spare.

I parked in a business building across the "Roberto Clemente Bridge." PNC Park is very convenient for parking, as they close off most of the bridges directly nearest to the ballpark. The park looks immaculate from the bridges and especially in reverse from the park where you can see the bridges.

Pittsburgh is a blue collar town but it a beautiful city downtown. The crowd was not bustling that night. There were 13,223 fans for the game and half that many were there when I arrived.

There may not be a better new ballpark when it comes to respecting the history of their team. There are statutes for just about any significant member ever associated with Pirates. There is a great amount of history of the World Series Runs of 1971 and 1979. The area my ticket was in was the left field bleachers section for a $9 price. Quite simply it is the best value in the majors considering it is general seating. You are right on top of the left fielder.

I made it over to "Greentree Pizza"—located just behind the huge scoreboard. I was staving so I ordered the large fourteen inch Pepperoni Pizza. It is made on a light thin crust and is one of the best singular foods in the majors.

Around the park, people were texting each other on their cell phones as the Pittsburgh Pirates display between every inning on their scoreboards. This is a fun thing to do—and very fan interactive.

They have two mascots that are running around the empty park. 'The Pirate,' (who will steal your food if you are not looking and/or opposing team ball caps that fans wear) and 'The Parrot,' (who is a lot more kid friendly and usually can be found occupying seats in the empty lower bowl.). I was pleasantly surprised that the ushers were so nice to me when I told them about my record streak. The lady talked to me for thirty minutes about the ballpark and even asked if I had time for a tour while in the city, she said she could call her boss if I wished. I politely declined as I had a long drive back to New York City. It was then I realized I actually needed a quick game.

It was one of the plane fares bought before the trip started and impossible to change because it was too costly. I would have about six hours to drive back to New York for a five and a half hour drive. There was not much wiggle room

were available seats. 7 seats was a lot for a 9:00 AM Flight. It would have been different if it was the flight I had just missed. I had to try it. New York traffic had swallowed me up that morning, maybe it would swallow up others. "Print me the pass, I will try."

"You never know sir you might also get a family that does not want to fly separately. You are a single traveler so you have a better chance than others."

I grabbed my new boarding pass and headed trough security, and pressed onward to the gate. There was not much open for breakfast so I was happy to have polished off that huge pizza in Pittsburgh the night before. I needed to call the airlines to see if I could arrange other travel arrangements to Dallas.

I searched for the internet at 'LGA' which was non-existent at that time. I called every airline up. It was going to be $600 or $700. Day of flight's prices sky rocket on same day sales. My plan was simple now. I would see if I made the next flight before another decision was to be made. I called Visa in the meantime and I was appalled to see that I had little credit left with all of the pre-authorizations against the car and hotel rentals. I was awaiting a payment to go through as well. I had $450 left. I was stuck. Not only was I in danger of missing my game in Texas—but my streak reset needed to start over in San Diego the next day.

It was a lost cause at 'LGA' and I left the airport at 10:00 AM-by boarding what I thought was a charter bus in between 'LGA' and "JFK." I wanted to be at JFK incase I was stranded-since there were more amenities and late night domestic flights. At 10:30 AM-the charter bus let me off downtown in Manhattan.

"Wait a second I purchased a bus-ride all the way to JFK." I said to a heavy set German fellow.

"You boarded the wrong bus." The man replied.

"No I didn't." I was right--the man had forgotten to switch the template on the bus signage based on what I had seen back at 'LGA'- he had deceived me.

"I paid for a ticket to JFK, and that is what your sign said. I know you are going to try and stiff me," I was being rude back to the rude New York people now, "so why don't you tell me how I get to JFK, it has been a brutal morning."

The man radioed a bus a block away, "hold the bus for a minute, I need to drop a passenger for you to take to JFK, I made a mistake, no charges either." The man actually smiled and nodded at me. I was relieved but knew that New Yorkers were good at nearly breaking you and then surprising you with doing the right thing.

I made it to JFK at noon in the hot heat, it was approaching 90F. I was still not ahead of the game. Like LGA-JFK did not have internet accessible terminals anywhere. I was running out of options. I called my buddy Dan Dion

Dan Dion and his brother Justin had given me the time off delivering newspapers for the trip. I had known them both for eight years. Justin was doing one of my routes for me while I was away. I had to forfeit the second route because of the timing, but was promised a different route when I returned in August.

Dan was in Langley, British Colombia, and was in front of his computer.

"Dude, It's me, missed my flight to Dallas because of an idiot car rental worker and a bridge closed for construction, I need your help, are you online?"

"Ya, I am online right how. Where are you?"

"I am on the Air-Tram at JFK circling the gates and don't know where to go because I don't have a plane ticket yet, I need you to go to the site www.kayak.com."

"10-4 man."

"Man, I am glad you are home. Okay click on the flights icon and then enter JFK letter into the: 'from part'-and 'SAN' letters in the: 'to' part, and don't forget to make this a one-way flight."

"How is it in the big crapple?" Dan was laughing and typing at the same time.

"Dude, this is a brutal city sometimes, good thing I always had the reset option, knew I was probably going to need it after that Philly/New York doubleheader miss anyway." Some girl left her tote-bag on the seat next to me and I was going to hand it in.

Some old man freaked out on me saying I was stealing it. All this was happening while awaiting results.

"Cheapest flight is $545."

"Not good, okay try LAX from JFK, I need to return there tomorrow night anyway so it will work for a car rental." The man scoffed a look of disgust at me again. If I was not on a good will ambassador tour I would have sworn at him for his ignorance.

A few seconds elapsed, "Dude, I got an American Airlines flight leaving at eight your time arriving at just after eleven in LA-price is $160."

"That is awesome, book that dude, click on it for me and I will give my credit card number to buy it-and then you can give me the confirmation code, then I will need to hit Budget Car Rental's site next."

Dan helped me for the next fifteen minutes and I was now going somewhere again. I had several hours before the flight to kill. I was fortunate enough to have the reset option. The new attempt was still 30-26 days. I had a grueling stretch of 4 doubleheader attempts in 5 days: SD Padres-Los Angeles Dodgers, followed by a Detroit Tigers-Cleveland Indians attempt; followed by Chicago Cubs/Milwaukee Brewers; then Toronto isolated by itself before a Washington Nats/New York Mets attempt to hit the all-star break.

If all were hit all games I would be at 9 games in 5 days, even with the 3 day penalty for the all-star break I would have a chance on the other side of it. I arrived in LAX without a hitch.

I had just enough credit on my visa to rent the car and I had $150 cash. I knew there was lots of deposit money coming off by the next night at midnight eastern time. I had to make it the next 24 hours with the money I had. There was $30 for parking/probably $20 for gas and $100 left for food and shelter. I drove to San Diego right away. I tried the Motel 6-but no there was no vacancy. I wish I would have known about the hostel downtown then. I decided to keep all my money. I had an idea to shower at a 'YMCA' in the morning. Besides I had to spend money on batteries for the digital camera-plus I needed some health and beauty aids.

I ate 7-Eleven food for dinner and drove around San Diego for a few hours before resting at a 'Rite-Aid.' I slept for a few hours and finally it was open.

A homeless man was outside and needed some money bad to eat. I only had $60 left after the drugstore but decided to give him $5. He was so thankful. I talked to him about my day in New York City.

He informed me that my day was about to change for the better. After I drove away somehow I finally believed it.

Streak Attempt #2
Game#1 Day #1
Petco Park
San Diego, CA
July.09/2008

After watching 11 games in 11 days-that were both before-and during the 1st streak attempt-I was back to square one. At eight in the morning I had made my way to the YMCA, during which I did some light jogging and then had a much needed shower and only had to pay $8. I was happy to see the sun was shining so for once so weather would not play a factor.

It was my third ever game to the San Diego's Petco Park. I parked for $12 in a nearby garage-surveying the street to see which way I would exit onto Highway 5 North after the game. I made my way with over 31,000 fans that day to watch the Padres play the Florida Marlins.

Petco Park has the color blue all over the stadium for seats and there are intermittent breaks in the background for the downtown buildings to be displayed. 'The Western Metal Supply Building' is on the third base foul side of the park, this is where the banner hung for all of Trevor Hoffman's saves. It seemed to have bolstered the loudest and craziest fans of the yard.

I particularly liked sitting in the left field bleachers because you are kind of isolated all by yourself in the area. The center field area is an open area to walk past the fences that feature a park in right center field to watch games at but there are no direct bleacher seats from left center field all the way around.

Petco Park is definitely the most dog-friendly park in the Majors which is a real big surprise right? You can buy tickets for just the park access to watch the game for under $10. The 1st base side second deck has a big overhang on an angle over the lower section. Open space is a nice quality to a brand new ballpark.

I was sitting in the grandstand seats along the 1st base side. I had purchased seats to the game back in March-so I had received 50% of the face value price. What was a $40 ticket became $20. On this visit, it was $1 hotdog and pop day—Petco Park is home to 'WienerSchnitzel hotdogs' which are really good. Maybe only New York and Los Angeles have better hotdogs.

CARL'S JR. is a tasty alternative for burgers and fries-and Petco Park probably has the best Ice Cream Parlor in the Majors on the second level of the 1st base side. I also love the 'frozen Minute Maid Lemonades,' the vendors sell as well.

One thing I noticed upon entering is that there are little scoreboards in the grandstand which reveal the score and amount of outs/inning. This is a must for any new ball park. I was watching the players warm up when my cell phone rang—it was 'Stub-hub'—they were concerned I had not sent a ticket to a buyer that I had listed with them, to a future 'Phillies game.'

It turned out they had sent me a wrong bill of lading with the call letter of CA for California instead of Canada. Since I had them on the phone I began to ask them questions.

"Wait a second. I have listed like forty tickets with you guys and I wondered why my tickets have not been selling since they were about 40% of the face value," I was afraid of the answer because I knew it right then. "Since I am a Canadian do you charge American buyers the International shipping rate even though I go across the border to send them via FED EX?" I crossed over to Washington State all the time to send tickets by mail since it was cheaper.

The man cleared his throat and the other line, "Yes we do, we charge $26.95 per ticket."

"Jesus Christ," I blurted out, again not proud of it but it was a stupid error on their part that was killing my ability to sell these tickets. "That is so brutal. I liked you guys up until now, don't you think you should have had some disclaimer mentioning this when I listed my ticket as a Canadian seller."

The man fumbled for an answer.

"Had I known this I would have donated all of those tickets to charity, seriously man that is a major mistake on your company's behalf. You should really change that in the future because it would be nice to know." I was infuriated and the baseball game was about to start and I had to let this guy go but it brought the streak hardships to life. No matter what is going on your life you have to leave it on the outside. I had to learn to let go. It is much like a baseball batting average, in that you have to fail a lot of times to succeed. There were many financial expenses that I could not control and would fall on my lap as this chase continued. I was able to breathe after talking myself down.

On the polar opposite of Stubhub were my Air Miles ticket vouchers for the Toronto Blue Jays. This side business was providing to be a godsend, averaging $250 US Dollars a week—even while I was on this chase. It had turned out to be a great idea to cash the Miles in for these tickets as opposed to using all of the miles for 'Best Western Hotel Gift Cards' as was the original idea. I was able to be paid through 'Pay-Pal' and then make a payment directly onto my credit card. It saved my bacon one more time at the end of the trip which I will describe later on.

The baseball game moved as smooth as the games do in the National League. I was learning the value of the games in the 'Senior Circuit' being extremely faster with the pitchers spot in the lineup killing rallies. I watched Hanley Ramirez and Mike Jacobs hit moonbeam homers off of the Padres pitching in rolling to a 5-2 Marlins win—in a game that was over in 2 hours and 41 minutes. I was in great shape. It was only 3:15 PM, so I had four hours to arrive at 'Dodger Stadium. The traffic was heavy at times but I made it to the park at 6:00 PM sharp.

Game#2 Day#1
Dodger Stadium
Los Angeles, CA
July.09/2008

I must be one of the only people who like the set-up of the parking at Dodger Stadium. Yes it is traffic laden and takes forever to merge onto the I-110 OR I-101 but it actually is nice for someone out of town to not have any options to park. I first had been to the park on my birthday in 2006.

That day I took a bus from 'Disneyland' for two hours in order make it to the game on time. I also had to leave in the 7th inning-in order to catch the last bus back to Anaheim. It is a hard park to get there, but I had a car on this day and didn't mind at all.

I walked up the many stairs it took to reach the 'Top Deck Level' stairs. There were pictures of all the ballplayers on the wall and fences surrounding the entire park. The same can be said inside as all of the current 25-man roster have full photo's in the concourses. For such a huge stadium, the space serves the baseball club well with an intimate setting of the mountains. I honestly would rather sit on the top level in order to see everything that I possibly could.

I bought yet another 'Dodger Dog, and a 'Super pretzel' before game time, I remembered the previous year about how long it took to order concession food once the game started. When they constructed this park in the 1950's they were smart enough to limit the rows of seats to between 8-12 on the lower levels and this about the same up top.

For this reason alone it is rather easy to access your seats without asking people to stand up for you.

I watched as 6 beach balls were being bounced around the park at the same time while batting practice was going on. When the game starts, the ushers steadfastly go after the beach balls. Each security guard actually cars a sharp object to obliterate the balls once they catch them. It turns out be an endless battle all game long between the fans and the parks staff.

I polished off my food and asked the security guard in my section to sign my logbook sheet before the game started. He ultimately refused. I was astounded. I asked if they had a customer service window to ask if anyone on staff could vouch for my existence at the park that day—still no help. I took an elevator to the lower levels and actually passed the historic announce of booth of 'Vin Scully.' Finally a nice young lady signed my book and asked me to return after the game to get the next signature from her as well. It took me 10 minutes from the time I left my seat, but I was happy to have seen more of the stadium.

I still needed a relatively quick game. I had a 1:30 AM flight out of LAX to Detroit city and figured I had about an hour drive to the airport when you accounted for traffic.

I was in decent shape—yet the last time I was at this park the Cincinnati Reds battled the Dodgers for 16 innings. I actually made it back to my hotel room in Anaheim to see the last inning after leaving in the 7th inning. The subsequent 2 hour bus ride back I had listened to the game on a hand held radio. I wanted this game to be over by 10 PM tonight.

There is something to be said about seeing new things at the ballpark you have never seen before. This game actually did not produce a hit until 27 outs were recorded-and after the 1st hit— the game was still scoreless in the middle of the 6th inning. These were new to me. Derek Lowe of the LA Dodgers took a perfect game into the seventh. Tim Hudson of the Atlanta Braves retired the first 12 batters he saw. I was the beneficiary of all of this. The game was only an hour old when it was in the 6th inning.

I saw the best and worst of the Dodgers fans in one plate appearance by fallen superstar Andruw Jones.

He was booed continuously every time he came up for his year long slump. Then the fans went ballistic for him when he hit a seeing-eye single for the games 1st lead and later broke up a double play by sliding really hard. They gave the man a standing ovation just for his effort. No building has ever been as loud in any game I have been to when Dodger Stadium is full. The game was over in two hours smooth. I made it to the airport by 11:30 PM. An all night flight would be a good spot to catch up on sleep. It was a good first day of the second streak.

Game#3 Day#2
Comerica Park
Detroit, MI
July.10/2008

I had talked to Alexandra Bahou multiple times over the 1st few weeks of my trip. She was a freelance reporter for the 'Detroit Free Press'. It was one of the many media outlets I had reached out to before the trip started. Alexandra was very thorough in her work and had researched every detail about the 'Guinness Book Of World Record' claim rules. Of course I had told her about the criteria.

—I had submitted a list of the scheduled dates on a master grid that read as a depth chart for each day I was on the road.

—I filled out an official application for the attempt which needed to be faxed to the headquarters of 'GWR' in the UK.

—I had to list why I was trying to achieve this record and for what charity.

When that was all accepted the 'GWR' sent me a list of all rules and lists of evidence I needed to turn in once the attempt was completed. I had studied them very well. The key points were;

—For any sporting event for it to be valid you must attend every single play for the duration of the event. This meant you had to be on the buildings property for 1ˢᵗ play until last-and have someone be able to document that you were there. This included video and pictured evidence to back up the personal witnesses list. Any delays due to inclement weather or any other act of god would not give you the ability to leave early at all. Also with this you must be in the venue for the entire match. You could not come in for the 1ˢᵗ play and then leave the facility until the last portion of the event. If the contest was suspended for any reason you would need to come back whenever the event was to be completed and it would still be retroactive to the start of the game.

—You were not allowed to enter the same venue twice within the dates of the intended attempt. You must complete all other venues for the other teams 1ˢᵗ before returning afterwards. An example of this would be if I were to already have gone to a baseball game in Milwaukee and then watch a game in Chicago on another day---I would not be allowed to watch any play at all in Milwaukee even though I could physically for time wise have done it. This was quite prominent in that Chicago game in the 1ˢᵗ streak attempt when it was raining while there was a tie score of 5-5-before AJ Pierzynski hit that walk off in the hailing rain.

Should I have attempted to make the second game of a doubleheader and not made it for 1ˢᵗ pitch-I would not be able to enter the building because I would not see every play. Just like when I stayed for the entire Phillies game with the rain delay. I could not even leave when they had finished 9 innings tied.

I actually asked if I had watched every play at the all-star game at Yankee Stadium that year if it would qualify for a one of the 30 baseball stadiums—since it was within the calendar of my streak chase. I was denied this request as it is still to be every single baseball club's home team in MLB. It could not even be an instance—where the same two teams were playing a makeup game at a different venue—even though they alternated being the home team for the doubleheader.

You better hope your all stadiums are in operation when the attempt starts (anybody remember Olympic Stadium and the Kingdome?). I would have been out of luck when Montreal Expos played in Puerto Rico also—since that was not considered their home park because they only played 20 games there.

—You were not allowed to break any law in order to carry out your record attempt. Not that it mattered anymore-but my wreck less driving ticket might have played a factor into the attempt now that I look back on it. This meant you could not speed while driving. Of course the terms were subject to negotiate.

By the time I reached the parking lot it was 12:37 PM. The forced construction zones almost cost me the 1ˢᵗ pitch. Alexandra was ready for me as I neared the entrance to Comerica. She was well versed on the angles of the park and had been instructing her cameramen before I reached there.

"Wow, you were really close to not making it on time Chuck." Alexandra extended her hand out for a shake before retreating.

"Yeah it should have been a 20 minute drive. Anyways I am here and ready to go." I noticed her press credentials, and she was similar in appearance to how she sounded. I was dead tired with the stress of missing 1ˢᵗ pitch. I knew the Detroit highways fairly well having been in and out of the city 4 times within a year. It just goes to show you that you can never bank on a smooth ride to the park.

to the car. It was only 3:49 PM. This was doable. I watched in disgust as Casilla singled in the tying run. I was elated the next batter Kubel singled for runners on 1st and second. Then Justin Morneau walked and bases were loaded with 2 out.

While I was not happy to lose 15 minutes or so in the process I was hoping that the Twins would score and Joe Nathan was to close the bottom of the Ninth.

Instead the next batter did not make contact-and the game went to the bottom of the ninth tied. The time was 4:03 PM. This was all too familiar. I knew when the Detroit Tigers did not score in the 9th I was cooked for the double header.

Justin Morneau mercifully ended the game in front of 41,500 fans in the 11th at 5:07 PM. I had failed yet another doubleheader attempt. It hurt. I knew the new streak would have to be altered. I spent 4 hours at a hotel nearby freeloading free internet in order to make the changes. I had to spend an additional $300 on 3 flights to change the trip. I switched the Cleveland Indians game to a make it up on the 28th. It was not the end of the world. I moved the intended Minnesota Twins, Cincinnati Reds, Kansas City Royals and Chicago White Sox games also to make it happen. I had researched this probability all along so I could absorb it. The streak could only be 30-27 now.

I email messaged everyone I had to and drove on to Milwaukee. I would have been doing nearly the same drive back west from Cleveland that I was doing going east to Milwaukee. I was tired and rested for a few hours when I reached the Wisconsin border. I had a big day ahead of me the next day. I could not suffer another doubleheader set back.

Game#4 Day#3
Wrigley Field
Chicago, IL
July.11/2008

I had been on the road for 3 days without being at a hotel or sleeping in a bed thanks to that New York fiasco. Thankfully that night I would have a hotel room in Milwaukee to sleep in for a few hours after the Cubs/Brewers double header attempt.

Before I had reached the Wisconsin border—I had to take the Detroit car rental to O'Hare Airport back. At 5 AM in the morning I could pick up the new rental in Chicago, and then had to bring that specific car back the next morning at 5 AM. It was a continuous cycle of 24 hour rentals to consider as to not be charged for a second day. In my planning stages of the trip I had discovered a 'loophole' in Kayak's car rental prices. A one-way car rental fee usually runs extremely high charges from city to city—so here was way to the avoid the excruciating fee by circumventing the rules.

You just needed to rent cars from the one city's airport-and return to another city's airport within a 24 hour time limit. The fee was 10-15% higher then a daily rate, but so much less then the usual one way drop fee.

If you booked the car one minute past 24 hours the second day would retroactive the 1st day back to include the huge fee for a one-way rental and lump both days with that high drop-off rate, meaning hundreds of dollars difference just by one mere minute. Time management was vital to saving money along with scheduling.

I arrived at the 'Amtrak Station' right near the Milwaukee Airport (MKA). I had scouted this route of travel. I was tipped off how to elude traffic by a member of the Chicago Cubs PR staff. Amtrak was the way to go. After further investigation I discovered this itinerary.

Leave Milwaukee via train at 11:10 PM

Arrive at Chicago Union Station at 12:29 PM.

Walk to the 'Clinton Station Blue' line towards 'O Hare' 12:35 PM

Arrive at Monroe Station to transfer to the 'Red Line Howard' train. I made it to this station at 12:46 PM.

I waited 6 minutes to board the train and make it to the 'Addison' Stop at 1:11 PM-which gave me 9 minutes to first pitch.

I was supposed to have made the train 3 hours earlier but I needed to rest. The car was nicely parked back in Milwaukee at the Amtrak Station for a quick getaway after the return train. Sedan car service was to pick me up after the game at Wrigley before driving to Union Station in Chicago.

The return trip was as follows:

I needed to make it the 'CHI' train station by 5:00 PM-to board the 5:10 PM train-to arrive back at the airport station in Milwaukee by 6:35 PM. I would then have 35 minutes to make 1st pitch at Miller Park.

Since I had a few hours to kill in Milwaukee that morning I did a trial run to the park from the airport station following the directions of what I had learned from my 1st trip to Miller Park. National Avenue was the best way to drive off of HWY 94-E right to the ballpark.

It was now 1:11 PM-and like exact clock work I entered the historic ballpark of 'Wrigley Field.' Just like the 1st time I was at Wrigley Field I was in complete awe of the park. The 1st thing you notice is that there is no signage on the field at all. No billboards. There is the classic scoreboard past the 'Green Ivy Fences.' Recently they have put in a Replay Monitor in connection with the scoreboard. I am always surprised on how small the park really is in the stands and in the concourse. It is hard if you are a big guy like myself but the park makes up for everything.

I will put up with the high prices for parking and tickets for the pleasure of watching the game for its true essence. The stores inside the park have something for every budget demographic to always take something home from this park when it comes to souvenirs. The food is reasonably priced and there is never a shortage of vendors roaming the stands with hot dogs and drinks.

'Wrigley-Ville the community" is how this franchise has been able to maximize their earning potential without having a modern amenities park. There is basically a whole community around the ball yard that is dependant on the club to build its revenue streams and vice versa. Since the baseball park had no more space for fans—neighboring buildings created their own stands by adding seats to their buildings. Soon after that, pubs and restaurant sprung up in high rise form and the Cubbies are able to make money from all of it. The crowd control is managed by cordoning off the streets nearby—to let the ball park fans walk around freely and safely within these buildings.

Chicago's fans are the most loyal in baseball. The team has not won a World Series in over 100 years and the home games are always sold out. It is the biggest draw in the majors when it comes to events. The baseball game is almost secondary. Again this is not to suggest that the fans don't care because they do. They are knowledgeable and follow their players religiously. It just means that the park is so gorgeous that a day at the park is still awesome if the team loses.

The scenery is fantastic. Since there is not a lot of signs and such, I found the foul poles to really standout. I like sitting underneath the 'Grandstand' to watch the games. You should really take a full day to experience this community. I am going to return one day to do this very thing.

I had to make sure I was focused on today. While most people were soaking up the entire day, I was hoping the game would end fast so I could leave Wrigley Field in enough time to make my train. I truly wished that is was the other way around—that I would have started the day in Milwaukee and ended up to see the Cubbies play at night. I was here now so there was no turning back. At least I had soaked up a lot more of the atmosphere the previous year.

The Chicago Cubs were playing the San Francisco Giants. Jason Marquis was pitching versus

Matt Cain. It was all the makings of a quick game. I really preferred the 'NL' teams because the pitcher had to hit. Sure enough I was right, after the top of the 7th inning—the game was going fast, but there was a problem, the game was scoreless heading into the seventh inning stretch.

That event, made famous by legendary broadcaster Harry Caray is best watched at Wrigley. They now have a guest singer for every game now that Harry is no longer alive. You can feel the love and presence of his ghost somewhere as the crowd galvanizes in this tradition.

The game was going along fast. It was only 3 PM. Heading into the bottom of the eighth there was still no score. Matt Cain, who had given up only 3 hits, was lifted in the 8th inning. Tyler Walker entered the game for the Giants and proceeded to give up 2 hits before Aramis Ramirez destroyed a 3 run-homerun. I was elated at this turn of events. It was 3-0 Cubs. As much I was happy I would reserve complete judgment until last pitch considering what had happened in Detroit the day before.

"Here we go again," I said as Kerry Wood came into the close the game and gave up an 'RBI' single to Bengie Molina. I could not take the nerves, at one point I turned away.

Kerry finally shut the door down-and I was treated to a rendition of 'Go Cubs Go.' It is a song they sing after every Chicago home game which is as much of a tradition as throwing back an opposition's baseball after a home run. I was caught up in the moment. I took my pictures for verification and was set to meet my sedan driver near the 'McDonalds' outside the park. The game was over so fast I called my sedan driver to see if I could be picked up early.

I was swept with the flowing traffic towards the exit. It was one thing I really hadn't accounted for. Wrigley Field is probably the hardest to exit after a game. It took 15 minutes to arrive at the fast food restaurant after leaving. A group of spectators had assembled around a man name Ronnie Woo Woo.

For those that have not met this long-time Cubs fan Ronnie, you have not been to many games. He had been going to games since the 1940's and is famous for yelling "woo! woo! Ronnie has had written and video documentaries that detail his life as a long-term fan of the ball club. The other fans love him dearly and often pose for pictures with him. I was happy to have met this man briefly while waiting for my sedan driver and how Ronnie 'embodied' what it means to support your ball team. Ronnie said an encouraging word to me and I finally received my phone call from the sedan driver. He actually saw me from a distance talking to Ronnie. Thank-You Ronnie!!

We sprinted to the car down the road. Chicago traffic was a nightmare during Friday traffic and I was glad to not be driving to Milwaukee from the Chicago Area.

The sedan driver was the same fellow who had picked me up from Midway Airport the previous week to complete the Minnesota/Chicago White Sox double header. I watched the clock as the guy veered in and out of the traffic, making the subtlest of moves just to move one car ahead. I finally could see 'Union Station' and signed my visa bill for $61. I ran down the escalator to my boarding train flashing my ticket the whole way down. I made it!

I had to stand, I was sweating profusely, I was much in need of a towel and a drink, but I made it. There would be no traffic to contend with, I could sit when someone would get off the train at future stops.

Since it was Friday afternoon, there were business men going home for the weekend, families heading to Milwaukee for the weekend, others were going to a nearby town in the same manner as me in avoiding the traffic. I had spent $39 on my 2-way ticket. I would have had to park for that much near the park. It was a 100 miles from Chicago to Milwaukee, along the drive I did I was dinged for around $8.00 worth of tolls collected at various parts along the way. Some were 80 cents, some were $3.00 and some were only a few miles apart. I was looking forward to Miller Park.

Game#5 Day#3
Miller Park
Milwaukee, WI
July.11/2008

After a snickers chocolate bar, that had chased 2 awesome hotdogs at Wrigley Field, I was filled with energy to complete my drive to Miller Park. The trial run had proved to be effective. I drove from the airport to the park in 20 minutes. What was even better was the parking lot at Miller Park was full so I got to park right on the street headed towards Miller Park. I parked, grabbed my camera and ran to the park with 7-8 minutes to spare from 1st pitch. I bought tickets to the 'Bernie's Dugout Section' but was in no hurry to go up to the 4th level.

Miller Park's baseball park staff—(throughout all of my travels to parks,)--have demonstrated the best attitude with their fan base. They are so kind and friendly they make it feel like you are guests in their home. I was privy too it when they hosted that series between Cleveland and Los Angeles in 2007 when Cleveland's home park Progressive Field was buried under a foot of snow. Miller Park's staff shined without little notice. From the other chasers I have spoken with the echo these sentiments exactly. They are one of the only baseball teams to not only allow tailgate partying—but actually promote it by giving away a beer fridge from 'Miller Lite' to the party that demonstrates the most team pride through their surroundings.

The ushers are a proven commodity over and over. Not only did the staff sign my logbook, they provided home numbers, they also asked for my online websites to promote the streak.

The general manager of the Milwaukee Brewers staff learned of my campaigning for charity and actually took up a collection to send off from all the ushers who wished to participate. I truly thank all of the kind people and staff from this park for all the continued help and support for me.

Miller Park is perfectly located where it is. There is lots of parking for $10—and it is easily accessible from the main roads. There are many physical qualities inside the building. Much like Safeco Field, it is an open-air-retractable roof--that lends fresh air--and shields the fans of Milwaukee when weather elements would otherwise tarnish their fan experience. The 'Miller' name is all over the park. Bright neon signs are located in right field with a beer clock. The scoreboard in centerfield brightens up the background of glass windows in the back drop. In left field, and in the upper deck, there is Bernie's Dugout. Above the dugout are the stairs that lead Bernie to the top of his yellow slide he burns down when the home town hits a homerun over the fence. In the intermittent times he is flanked by two cheerleaders on either side of him—in his dugout dancing, interacting and urges with the fans to participate in cheer.

The parks levels are easy to maneuver up and down with spacious escalators. Don't forget to watch for the famous sausage race in the game! Milwaukee's fans are also exceptional. I have never had so much fun watching a game as to one of those hosted Cleveland and Los Angeles games. The Milwaukee fans are known to crazy waves to have fun in the stands. They start off with a slow-motion wave, where it is a normal wave, (with about a quarter of the speed)-and then they have an ultra fast wave to show the other side of the spectrum. It is unique, fun and I give the city full marks for initiative.

What I liked is that everyone seemed to know this tradition. The crowd also sings the song 'Over the Barrel' during the seventh inning stretch right after: 'Take Me out to the Ballgame.'

So I made the double header, ate bratwurst and a hamburger for dinner, and watched the 'Brew

Crew' take an early lead but fall later on in the game to the Cincinnati Reds and Ken Griffey Jr. I got to see Bernie fall down the slide, and see the sausage race in the sixth inning. I don't remember who won that race but it was hilarious including several of the sausages falling. What was important was that I had now seen 5 baseball games in 3 days.

I drove the 10 miles and checked into my hotel. I had won a Priceline bid on this given hotel for $17 for the night and it was an 'Extended Stay Of America Hotel" in Wauwatosa. It was ideal for my needs. I had a long hot-shower, completed some laundry and was ready to sleep. It would not be a long sleep however. 4 hours later I needed to be on the road. I was flying into Toronto in the morning for a Saturday matinee versus the New York Yankees.

Game#6 Day#4
The Rogers Center
Toronto, Ontario, Canada
July.12/2008

I was tired, as it had been two weeks since I started going to baseball games and by far this stretch of doubleheader attempts was the gruesome part of the schedule. In the streaks infant stage of planning I had thought about a crazy idea to add a 5th double header attempt in consecutive days-with a Toronto day game and Pittsburgh night game. It wasn't impossible but I gave it a 30% chance to happen. The Toronto game started at 1:07 PM and the non-stop flight left at 5:05 PM. I would have needed the game over by 3:45 PM and have little weekend traffic. Now I do have a priority boarding pass through international security that we call 'Air Nexus' so that was in my favor as well. There was only one thing.

Before I had started this streak attempt the original design this trip had was visiting each ballpark in six weeks---this included watching a baseball game with each one of my blood family relatives. I was going to see 4 games with my 3 brothers and dad later in the month.

This game was set aside for me to watch a baseball game with my mother. I bought her ticket even before I had bought my tickets. The itinerary was this.

8:29 AM—my mom was arriving from Montreal Quebec Canada, she would have to wait at the airport by herself for an hour before I arrived.

9:30 AM—I was to arrive. I had pre-ordered a two way limo service to meet us at the airport and drive us right to the game. My mom was nursing a broken ankle and as such it was tough to move around. This eliminated all worries.

10:00 AM—we would arrive at the Rogers Center and we were to have had a wheelchair provided for my mom. The Toronto Blue Jays had arranged a tour through the ballpark before the game including field access. My Mom and I were going to meet some of the Toronto players. All of this had been pre-arranged for weeks. Also teams that had contacted me about similar tours were: Texas, Boston, SF Giants and Cincinnati.

1:07 PM—The game would start, while I was glad to be with my mom at Rogers Center-we still needed a quick game as we both of us had flights out of town starting at 6:30 PM-with me to New Jersey airport (EWR), while my mom had a flight back to Montreal at 7:30 PM.

I had spent lots of money in order for this day to happen. The Yankees game was a sellout in Toronto, and while I had vouchers and the Blue Jays offered tickets, I had already bought 'Infield Baseline Seats' along the 3rd base side for $60 each. The sedan service was $120 for the roundtrip and the plane fares flying in and out of Toronto were over $700. Flying in and out of Canada is not cheap. What was impossible for me was that I could not rent a car in the USA and bring it across to Canada. This hampered my travel plans by ground so air was my only possibility.

Aside from the rule of Canadians not being able to take the car across the line, everything on the trip was bought in US currency causing many expenses from various financial institutions for me. Each time I made a purchase there was an exchange processing fee.

I was in O'Hare Airport awaiting the flight when I had received a phone message from my step-father Doug. He has explained my mom had missed her flight and was on the next flight to Toronto. This was not a big deal as she would now be arriving at the same time as me anyway. She was just out the $59 fee. It was a rather modest and fair price set by 'West Jet Airlines' in Canada. I had to pay $100, $75 and, $150 in 3 separate instances with the airlines in America for the same thing.

It was another flight out of Chicago-and I was happy to see a clear and wind free day. My flight was to leave in 45 minutes. The plane was at the Jet-way and people were de-boarding the flight. This was way better in contrast to the last flight out of Chicago when I barely made the flight to Houston in time for the game and had to abandon my luggage.

I noticed there were not too many people in my gate area which kind of alarmed me so I went to the 'United Airlines' ticket counter where a customer service agent was.

"Is everything okay for the 7:00 AM flight to Toronto?"

"Oh sir, the airline was supposed to have called your cell phone number and leave a message, are you sure they have not done that?"

I had felt this feeling before, I did not want to retrieve the message I thought had been my wake-up alarm from back in Milwaukee. "Instead of racking up long-distance charges can you tell me?"

The skinny woman was in her late fifties with auburn/grey hair and was nicely dressed. She had a calming voice but I had a feeling it was going to feel like daggers from what she was going to say next. I had my hand propped on my briefcase. I had shaved, put myself into a nice collared shirt and dress pants to see my mom.

"Sir last night the flight crew had some delays flying in from Philadelphia with wind, and ended being delayed by more than 4 hours. This is the same crew that was to fly this plane to Toronto this morning. So I am sorry sir, the 7:00 AM flight to Toronto has been cancelled."

I was floored. I was worried. It was one thing being stranded and traveling by myself, I was now upset my mom was going to be in the airport in Toronto all by herself waiting for her son who was not going to be there when she arrived. She had a broken ankle was all I kept thinking. "What is happening with all the passengers that were flying the 7:00 AM?"

"The flight has been changed to 11:00 AM-which arrives at 1:30 PM."

I was not forecasting this. At least I hoped this kind of thing did not happen.

"There has got to be someway I can get to Toronto, my disabled mother is flying into to Toronto from Montreal to meet me. I am due for a baseball game in Toronto. I am chasing a world record." I was explaining this while the phone rang.

"You can try the other airlines, but all of our flights have been delayed this morning, I am terribly sorry."

I was no longer tired. Chicago had been my nemesis once more, this was disastrous. I was at a crossroads. There was no doubt that I had to fly to Toronto and meet my mom. No record chasing from baseball was supposed to stand in the way of my family visiting. I made that promise to my family members. Maybe if I had answered my message, maybe if mom had first missed her flight I could have persuaded her to meet me another time after the streak but she had boarded a flight to Toronto. The ticket was used.

Had I not been spending the day with my mother I knew what my course of action would be; I would be on the internet right now arranging a one-way car rental from Chicago to Washington. From Chicago, I would drive the 5 hours to make up the Cleveland Indians game first. After the Cleveland game I would drive all night to Washington in time to make the 24 hour exception. I had a one-way rental set-up from' EWR' that I could still cancel. The only extra cost would be gas, parking, tolls and a game ticket in Cleveland. In terms of games, I could have switched the Toronto Blue Jays to the exact date the Indians played. It would have only cost me $150 or so.

Once the weekend was over I had the all-star break to recover and figure things out. There was one other scenario I knew of that I could try should I rummage up enough finances. I knew the ramifications of taking a zero too. I would have to see the Blue Jays at the very end of the streak and add the day. It meant the best I could do (should I keep the present schedule) was to tie the world record. I would investigate possible other scenarios, maybe there was something I missed. I called my step-dad and told him to phone my mom and say I was headed for Toronto.

It was a hug filled with emotion and worth. I knew I made the right decision when I hugged my mom. She started crying because she knew what coming to the airport meant. She was walking with a cane and limping.

"Mom, what are you doing, let me get you a wheelchair."

I foraged a wheelchair nearby and she went in it. "Mom, I am so starving lets go eat some pizza and have the best 3 hour visit ever."

We laughed hard, we ate lots of food, drank lots of pop. All the while knowing what is in the background. My mom, the one who watched me play baseball growing up. The one who helped me become the man I was.

My mom and I had worked on my 2 novels all year long. My mom, who once had a major surgery when I was a teen-and showed up in a blanket in the stands the next day because she knew it was my final game of the season, meant more to me then baseball that day.

I was carrying the 1st edition of my sports book in my hand. The streak was important for some reasons. Part of me would always wonder what would have happened had I not boarded that flight. The majority of me, tells myself that 'it was the best damn decision of my life!!

I said good-bye to my mom a few hours later and boarded my flight to 'EWR.' I also cancelled my trip to North Carolina for the start of all-star break. I wanted to spend it with my brother and his family in New Jersey. Besides, I still had a chance to tie the 'said' world record and/or break the listed-'Guinness Book World Record."

Game#6 Day#5
Nationals Park
Washington, D.C
July.13/2008

I had fallen asleep on my brother's couch. After a few hours of visiting I crashed. It was 7:30 AM in the morning. The game was at 1:35 PM. I was out the door at 8 AM. It said the drive was just over 3 hours and 172 miles to the airport (DCA) I had some finagling to do. I needed to go to the airport, catch a cab to the Nationals game and then I had a sedan picking me up at 4:30 PM for a 6:00 PM flight from DCA—to land at La Guardia in New York where yet another sedan driver was to drive me to Shea Stadium for the Sunday night baseball game. I would be sweating another quick game in Washington.

It was my 1st time to a game in Washington. Once upon a time, when the Nationals were in Montreal, I saw the franchise play at Olympic Stadium in Montreal. Funny enough it was 13 years later and instead of Pascal Perez, it was Odalis Perez towing the hill for the team.

I made the trek down the I-95 S, through the beltway express to Reagan Airport. It was only after noon when I arrived. Of course there was a little problem. I could not find a gas station near the airport. I had no interest in paying $6.00 a gallon to have them fill the tank. I did have some time before the game. 20 minutes later though I began to panic. Then I split the front side of my windbreaker pants when I slammed the brakes in finding a gas station. Now I had gas in the tank and a wardrobe problem. I would find a pair of pants at the ballpark. The key was getting there, and despite it being just around 5 miles from the airport, I wanted to get there. I had my fleecy jacket wrapped around my ripped pants. That's all I was carrying.

I had a return flight in the morning to Washington from New York the next day. This was the origin of my flight to Chicago—on the Tuesday—in order to visit the 'Field Of Dreams Movie Site' in Dubuque Iowa, for the duration of the All-Star Break.'

I took a cab and entered Nationals Park. I searched the park from pillar to post looking for a new pair of pants/shorts only to be denied. I was frustrated beyond belief. I wanted to have a nap from the stress. I still asked and received my usher witness at the ballpark to sign my logbook. I was too tired to walk around the Park after that but I liked what I saw.

My first thought of the ball yard was that size wise it was close To 'Petco Park.' I liked the outfield concourse space the best. The bathrooms in the middle of an outfield concourse are always a good idea too. The restaurant in the center field area looks like one of the best party atmosphere's around. Even though I have never tried it myself, people swear by 'Ben's Chili Bowl.'

The outside is very clean and brand new as you can imagine with Washington. The ticket windows are kind of hard to find but I like the curly W's all over the outside of the yard. The concourse is not ensconced in rich tradition yet but there are things to celebrate about previous teams that were in the Washington Area.

The sightlines are above average. I watched the first few innings leaning my sore back against a pillar. A few different times security guards checked on me. It was blistering hot. It was nearly 100 degrees out. I drank as much water as I could but I was tired. The Houston Astros were the visiting team. Between that club and the New York Mets, I was seeing them in the teens somewhere. If I was a lot more cognizant for the game for the entire game I would have wanted to strangle Odalis Perez. He was so slow between pitches. By the time the 6th inning started I was at full attention. I was brought back from the dead by watching the 'Presidential Race' in the fourth inning. That is one of the funniest things I have ever seen in my life.

Contrast to Odalis Perez was Houston's Brendan Backe, as he was throwing innings with ease. Thank god Houston was up by 3 runs and it never seemed that the game would be in doubt. The game was right around the 3 hour pace. When I scouted this doubleheader attempt it would never be doable during the weekdays because of the traffic, but the close proximity of the ballpark to the airport made it really enticing. On the other end, Shea Stadium was even closer to LaGuardia and I had the beneficial 8:05 PM 'Sunday Night ESPN' start time.

I made sure I strolled around Nationals Park more to see what it had to offer. I liked the big scoreboard—visible from anywhere in the park really. The color schematics were sharp. I think the uniforms were really sharp on the ball club. I don't think you can really go wrong with red. What I like is that they did not build layer upon layer of outfield bleachers to impede the view of the buildings downtown. Put a winning baseball team on this field and the park atmosphere will only be enhanced to match this good looking structure.

I never clapped so hard when Washington finally took Perez out of the game. Houston tacked two more runs on the board and fans had already been mass exiting the park for over an hour. The announced crowd of over 31,000 had dissipated to half of that many.

I was standing at the end gates, which are proudly surrounded by more curly red "W's. I had my sedan driver waiting on South East Capital Street. We were out of there and made the 5 mile journey in 15 minutes. It was now 5:00 PM- with me entering the airport security as the game had ended at 4:30 PM. One bonus of being at the airport earlier was printing my boarding pass—and being familiar with what Gate the 'US Airways.' Flight was.

I was in the process of going through security when I was told to take my jacket off my waist. I then requested a private screening. I could not have this embarrassment in front of all these nice people.

To their credit, the security was very nice. Now I was questioned for a minute for why I did not have any luggage with me but other then that it was all right.

In an ironic and mind puzzling phenomenon, there was a thundershower headed our way at the airport. I knew this doubleheader was in jeopardy.

Game#7 Day #5
Shea Stadium
Flushing Meadows, NY
July.13/2008

We made it to our plane, boarded the flight 10 minutes late, and were on the runway. The captain was about to address the passengers.

"Folks we have some bad news and some good news. The good news is that we are cleared for take off, the bad news is that we might have to turn back if the wind picks up anymore."

Nothing like an adrenaline shot to boost me right out of my somber mood. I have never studied the shiftiness of an aircraft as I did on that flight. I could not take anymore setbacks. Any slight delay could cost me big time. I had a favorable schedule coming after the break. With this game made in New York I had 6 days in a row without a doubleheader attempt. The cities were; Colorado, Cincinnati, Oakland, Arizona, Seattle and Baltimore before a Tampa Bay, Florida double header attempt.

I finally breathed normally as we touched the ground with the aircraft at 'LGA'. My sedan driver could not have been nicer. He made a swift $60 for driving 3 miles-so I can't blame him for being in a good mood.

The worst part about ripping my pants was spending $30 on a pair of shorts with the New York Mets emblem. I am a New York Yankees fans, they would soon be donated to my cousin.

I did not like Shea Stadium at all and was glad they were moving to the new ball park the next year so I would never have to return to Shea again. I watched the Mets mangle the Rockies 7-0. By the time the game ended it was past 11:00 PM. On the way down the exiting the ballpark I came within 10 feet of being right next to ESPN commentators Jon Miller and Joe Morgan' I can't believe in the size difference between the two men.

In a classic way to hit the break I had to wait 30 minutes for a cab after the game to head back to LaGuardia. I needed to save money from time to time by being at the airport for a few hours to await early morning flights —as oppose to wasting the cash for a few hour hotel stay.

'LGA' was not really comfortable. It was probably worth the $35 cab ride, (yikes) flat fee, in order to arrive at the airport safely—as oppose to walking the 3 miles through that neighborhood at night though. The $35 cab ride is non-negotiable for these sedan guys leaving the park. The good news is that most hotels are at least 5-7 miles away from the park anyway.

Game#8 Day#9
Coors Field
Denver, CO
July.17/2008

Fresh off of my 3 days penalty (for the MLB All-Star Break) I was ready to resume my quest at Coors Field. This was a scheduling nightmare in which Colorado was only one of four choices for the streak that night. The other games that night were in: St. Louis, Cincinnati or Baltimore. The Rockies were only in town for 9 days out of the 26 though. This game was a decent shift back to the Midwest to combine with St. Louis as part of the original schedule.

Now I had the St. Louis game booked with my brothers and dad on Aug.01. When I arrived in Denver it was early in the morning. My visit to the 'The Field of Dreams Movie Site' had me well rested for the next stretch of games. Some of my credit card deposits were now coming back to my available balance. I had been paid from both paper jobs and managed to sell some extra tickets to the New York Yankees and Mets that I had purchased dating back to April. I was back in the money game.

The crazy doubleheader scenario I had in mind was for July.31. I decided it was only a necessary evil if I had missed any games prior to July.28th. It was a Cleveland day matinee that started at 12:10 PM-and I had a chance to catch a flight to New York at 4:52 PM-that landed at 'LGA' at 6:24 PM. It was a risky and pricey attempt at a $500 hit but my brothers and dad had my back in the event I needed the extra game. Provided I could hit all of my single games there were 2 double headers between now and then: TPA/MIA on the 23rd and SF/OAK on the 26th. I was really confident in SF/OAK with only 16 miles between those cities. After those two it would be the HOU/TEX doubleheader and that would be it. To tie the record would still be an unbelievable achievement. I could always asterisk it with the 3 day penalty even though there was a tie.

I wanted to keep the legacy trip of Boston, New York and St. Louis with my family. When I activated the second attempt I already cut myself out of the 'Wrigley Field' portion of the trip—because I needed a makeup game.

Coors Field struck a chord with me instantly. The view at this Field is so neat with the mountain back drop. The illusion of open space is so important when a ball park is created. Coors Field is easily seen when you enter the city downtown. There is a huge concourse area past the stands in left center field, where the space can host Thousands of standing room only fans. The seats are nicely sized and painted green. Right Field has 3 decks. The gigantic scoreboard is placed in left center-field with a big logo of the 'Rockies' at the very top of a column of steel. There is a highly visible clock above the Rockies logo.

The scoreboard can be photographed anywhere in the park with its size. The left field and right field walls are not very big in height, so fans have plenty of chances to catch homerun balls. Colorado's mascot is named "Dinger,' and much like Twins mascot 'T.C' you can find this mascot scaling the fence at any moment to fire up the crowd in a cheer.

I bought the cheapest tickets into game. ($4 for the 'Rock pile' ticket) and I parked downtown for $5.

I was excited that during the all-star break I figured out how to work my video-picture camera and this was the 1st day in use. I snapped 20 pictures within being there for 10 minutes. I was happy to have this tool introduced to the evidence keeping. With 8 GB disk of space I could take 1477 pictures. The pictures were of 'HD' quality. I mean I should have had this for the whole trip. I spent $300 on the camera and accessories.

The Colorado Rockies were the reigning NL champions. I played baseball in a lot of the same provincial parks as Jeff Francis so naturally I always liked the Rockies. You can trace that back to the Larry Walker days. Larry also played baseball in the same parks as I did in youth baseball. It is my feeling that Larry Walker does not get his due for being such an awesome baseball player because he played the majority of his career in hitter friendly Coors.

Yes, the park has a lot of grass in the outfield to find if you are not hitting the ball out of the park but how can you argue with a career average of .313 with 383 Home Runs and 1311 RBI'S. The Colorado Rockies have been blessed with some top offensive players. I was happy to see Matt Holiday on this night. Both of the teams had futile records and were not in contention.

Young pitcher Ubaldo Jimenez pitched a beautiful game and I saw Chris Ianetta crush a pitch for a 2 run Homer. The game was threatened by dark clouds for a spell but finished nice and clear with the Rockies winning 5-3 in front of 30,500 fans.

One of the cool traditions is they sing 'Hey Baby' by Bruce Channel right after the seventh inning stretch. This is similar to the fans of Arizona and Boston singing 'Sweet Caroline' by Neil Diamond every game or "New York, New York' by Frank Sinatra being played on an infinite loop at Yankee Stadium until everyone in the crowd has left the park.

I hopped in my rental car and headed back to the airport, it was another quick turn around flight back to Denver. During that morning, before I made it to Denver I was pleased to have my flight to Denver go smooth from Chicago. The next day I was to fly back to Chicago first before boarding that flight to St. Louis. However I was not going all the way to St. Louis—I would never make my connecting to flight in Cincinnati because I was going to a baseball game in Cincinnati instead.

Game#9 Day#10
The Great American Ball Park
Cincinnati, OH
July.18/2008

It was my second trip to The Great American Ballpark, but since this streak was activated on July.09 I was allowed to return to the ballpark. I bought $7 tickets in the highest level behind home plate. Much to my humored self I actually needed a semi-fast game. Sure I had pulled in my walk off the plane maneuver in which I gave myself a few options to fly into—but know I had to be in St. Louis for an early morning flight to Los Angeles.

I used my one way car rental trick and secured a car rental for $56. The flight I had bought was from Chicago to St. Louis with a stop over in Cincinnati, the price would have cost me triple if it was a straight flight. It was a 5 and a half hour drive to St. Louis Airport. This time I would gain an hour—so in actual time it was only a 4 hour and a half drive.

Just in case I had not seen them a lot already, the New York Mets were the opponent. I had seen them in Shea 2x already, in Philadelphia and also in this game. It seemed every day I was watching them or Houston. I had seen Houston in Washington, at home, in Pittsburgh and also on the road in Atlanta. It was not over because as part of my makeup date in Houston I would see them play again. 4 times each was a lot to see a team in 3 weeks— both at home and on the road.

Bronson Arroyo wound up throwing a gem of a game for the Cincinnati Reds—who won the game 5-2 against John Maine of the New York Mets, the game was finished off by an awesome fireworks display. I was in fine shape for the drive. I made it to St. Louis Airport at 4 AM in the morning-and was surprised to see lots of people awaiting the security lines to open for the gates at Lambert.

Game#10 Day#11
Angels Stadium
Anaheim, CA
July.19/2008

It was a flight that I slept the entire time to wake up feeling groggy. I picked up my rental car and drove to 'Angels Stadium.' I was happy to have the game as a 1:10 PM start. After the game was over I had reserved a room at a hostel in 'Fullerton' some 8 miles from the ballpark. I would be able to have a solid night of sleep before an early morning flight to Phoenix. This was a nice schedule for the weekend. I was seeing teams for the 1st time of the trip today in the Boston Red Sox and the Los Angeles Angels of Anaheim. I was totally going to cheer for the Angels today though being a Yankees fan. When I walked into the park, I took a lot of pictures of the big red helmets outside. I really liked my first experience at Angels Stadium back 3 years before that. The stadium had just had a massive facelift under new owner Arthur Moreno. The ushers were dressed in the Cracker Jack Suits with the throwback hats. I liked that idea but they had since scrapped that idea with the staff.

Angels Stadium is pretty well placed in Anaheim off the main streets for the most part. It is easier to access then Dodger Stadium that is for sure. While it is nice aesthetically——it does not possess a lot of the amenities like the modern ball clubs—nor does it carry any type of historical mystique. The park will never achieve the best ranking for appearance or atmosphere but that is not because of the owner's lack of trying.

The Angels are lucky to have Moreno as their owner and with his guidance they have been one of the better run organizations in the last decade on and off the field. I am sure Moreno would like to build a nice ball stadium there just isn't the land available—or public outcry for a new stadium in either city like you hear in most 'MLB' cities. It is the same reason the 2 NFL teams left last decade.

The waterfalls in centerfield are a nice fit with the laid back atmosphere. The haloed 'A' anywhere is very sharp because of the teams colors. There are many obstructed seats that negate the left field bleachers. Still the park looks nice and clean.

. The Angels are one of four teams not to have an official mascot. The others are; The Dodgers, Yankees and Cubs. Although the Angels do have a 'Rally Monkey' made famous by their 2002 World Series Win.

The temperature was overcast for the start the day and I could not have been happier. When you have been on the road for over 3 weeks and are exhausted, heavy heat from the sun is hard to fight off. I could actually sit in the stands to watch the game. Since they were playing the Red Sox, the majority of the fans in the cheap seats were cheering for the visitors instead of the hometown team. In my section for most the game I actually could see the Red Sox mascot 'Wally," making the rounds to all of his visitor fans.

There was a friendly rivalry that was created from these two AL rivals. Boston jumped off to a fast 2 run lead when Kevin Youklis crushed a Joe Saunders pitch over the wall for a 2-0 lead. The game held at that score until the bottom of the seventh when the Angels finally got to Josh Beckett and the Sox by posting 4 runs.

The crowd had some anxious moments as Frankie Rodriguez put a couple of men on base in the top of the ninth before slamming the door. Since I was not in rush for a change I waited an hour before the crowd dispersed. I then located a McDonalds on South Harbor Blvd before heading onto the hostel.

The Anaheim/Fullerton Hostel is right on the golf course. I was able to shower, clean up and do some laundry. I had no real time to chat with the others in there at all. The sun had come out and I needed my 8 hours sleep before heading onto Phoenix via 'LAX' airport. I was developing a strategy in my head should I ever do a streak like this—I just didn't know it yet.

Game#11 Day#12
Chase Field
Phoenix, AZ
July.20/2008

The first thought I had when arriving at 'Phoenix/Sky Harbor Airport' was-"how stupid is this? The car rental facility center was 4 or 5 miles from the airport—which is about the same distance as taking a cab to 'Chase Field would have been.

It was 8:30 AM in the morning. I was chasing a breakfast location with my car rental amongst the number 10 HWY. I was ecstatic to find a 'Waffle House Restaurant.' I had wanted to visit this restaurant since I had seen the movie 'Tin Cup.' All I could think about was steak and eggs. It was already 98 degrees outside. I braved buying a pop earlier in that crazy heat. It was not curbing the hunger.

I ordered the biggest plate of food I have ever received for a portion. Steak, Eggs, Toast and the world class 'Grits'. It is my feeling that there is no place in the United States to order 'Grits' better then the southerner states like: Florida, Mississippi, Alabama, Georgia and Arizona. It was a hearty breakfast for a nominal fee.

It was also a good thing when I had the time to fill my stomach as oppose to buying food at the game. A good meal on a long trip can really hit the spot. Suddenly I felt great again. I hit the highways full of energy as I made my way back towards downtown Phoenix.

Chase Field is easily accessible by Jefferson St in the downtown core. I parked across the street for $7 and proceeded to my $5 zone tickets.

After entering, I noticed the photos on the wall of fame for this young franchise. Randy Johnson, Luis Gonzalez and Curt Schilling highlight all the best time Diamondbacks. There are many good pictures of their 2001 World Series run. I could not help but utter obscenities under my breath while viewing these as a Yankees fan, but it was nice to see. To celebrate the banners, they had big green 'A logo's' on the windows in the left field for the pennant's and division titles.

Also, like other indoor ballparks, the picture taking was made a lot tougher. When I walked the concourse, I noticed that there were several water leaks from the air conditioning. I came to find out later that the air conditioner breaks down all the time—and people are always complaining about a hot ball park. The good news was it was working that day.

I liked the gigantic scoreboard and that was definitely the highlight of all the features of the park. The hot tub seats in right center field was kind of funny—but was kind of a rip off the fish tank at "Land shark Stadium.' To make sure I ate something at the park to put n my report I ate a pepperoni pizza there which was quite tasty. I will give great kudos to their ticketing department and ballpark staff. They are amongst the best in baseball and I have had good experiences with them.

The sightlines are decent from the concourse and it is a very clean baseball park despite the leaking water.

I was surprised to see 39,000 fans were at the game. This was most certainly because the Arizona Diamondbacks had been a good team back in 2007. They were in the playoffs versus the Colorado Rockies. Young players like Justin Upton, Chris Young, Mark Reynolds and Brandon Webb were the main reason there was much optimism for the club to be competitive for years to come.

I took my seat in the 3rd deck and watched the game with a couple of season ticket holders in my section. They raved about the customer service—and how the team had the $400 per seat-season tickets they were sitting in and how there were certain spots they could park for free. This was amazing to me. $5 a game to watch Major League Baseball for a full season would be something I would be up for.

The Diamondbacks took a 4-1 lead into the ninth inning behind an impressive start by Brandon Webb. The Los Angeles Dodgers were floundering in the game against the All-Star Pitcher. I kept talking to this man and woman about the streak, and they were telling me everything there was to know about the ballclub. They told me about D. Baxter—the Bobcat, he was the teams mascot's and kids were flocking to him in droves. I like it when I see young people at the game. Arizona should be commended as they let kids in for free on the weekends when a parent buys a ticket. You have to purchase the tickets before the season, but that is a great deal.

Seeing all the ballparks carry such a diverse audience—especially with the abundance of young people—ensures the state of baseball is sure to grow in the coming years. I have seen hockey games with little kids attending, NBA games are no better. I am not sure about 'NFL' but the general consensus is that they are more of an adult crowd too.

Baseball parks all have cheap seats if you do your homework. A family might have to choose designated games, but at least baseball is making the effort to include 'Joe Family' as part of their fan base. It is a generational sport in which these kids are going to bring their kids. As for the other sports, I think that long term fans are going to dwindle when this generation of kids grow up—not being able to afford the games.

I was astounded to see that Arizona too sings-'Sweet Caroline' like the Boston Red Sox fans do. I can't believe that teams just wouldn't want their own song for a tradition. Then again Neil does have the last name "Diamond' so maybe it wasn't too far fetched.

The season ticket holders called for a blow-up by Brandon Lyon in the 9th inning. They just had seen it too many times that year. I, of course, had no allegiance to any team but wanted to see most home teams win. Well the Dodgers took the lead with a 5-run ninth-only to almost blow it themselves in escaping the desert with a 6-5 triumph.

I stayed at a 'Best Western' about 5 miles from the ball park. It was hot so I wanted to stay indoors. I needed to do some laundry, update my online blogs and sleep. I had a flight in the morning to Seattle. I was meeting my friend Kenji for it.

Seattle would feel like home for me, well at least for a few hours.

Game#12 Day#13
Safeco Field
Seattle, WA
July.21/2008

I made it to 'Sea-Tac Airport' so early that Kenji was to meet up with me at a Best Western nearby later in the day. Since I was spending so much money with 'BW' for the whole summer-I never felt bad about pirating their free internets at all their hotels. I could just flash them a generic hotel room card still left in my wallet from a previous night's room rental. I knew my way around the hotels after a while and fit in. All I had to do at the airport was take the airport shuttle to the hotel which beat a cab fare.

I always tipped the shuttle bus driver $2-3 for the mile they drove me. I was able to kill the time until I was supposed to meet up Kenji.

Kenji and I had been friends for 28 years in 2008. We played baseball in little league together. The years had led us on different paths so we were too busy to visit enough. Kenji even spent two years in 'Tokyo' teaching English. I was jealous of him seeing baseball games in the Tokyodome, 'he had seen Hideki Matsui, Kenji Johjima, and other Asian players play.

For the years over there he was also to follow the path of Ichiro Suzuki's career on a daily basis watching TV. I was also of the mindset that Ichiro was an underrated ball player in the majors. They were so many consecutive years with Ichiro having 200 hits and 100 hits-with 40 plus Stolen Bases. Today we were going to watch him live.

The day was sunny and the business center at the hotel was not receptive enough to the air conditioner just turned on. I had realized on that very morning that I had misplaced my ticket for that day's game so I called Ticketmaster up.

Like so many other things I had done on the trip, I was glad to have done the transaction by credit card so there was a paper trail. The key was to watch the game and then head back to the Airport. The flight at night was just past 12 AM so there would be a little bit of tension for the game to be fast.

I was more confident about Seattle because I had been to over 10 games at 'Safeco Field.' It was only going to be a problem because they were playing the Boston Red Sox. One of the saving graces was that the M's were sporting a 38-60 record so a high turnout was not as expected.

Kenji had called me to say he was minutes away. I closed my briefcase and headed off to the washroom.

I was in there for two minutes when someone had scoffed the briefcase. I panicked and thought I was in trouble deep.

'Hey!" I yelled at a deep manner to the 2 people who were running away with my stuff. I realized at that moment the Kenji had brought my good friends Steve Lees and Rob Blair.

All of us have known each other for 20 years and upwards. Rob was the best man at my wedding. I stayed at Steve Lees's house when for a month when I lived on my own at age 16. These were life long friends and they had joined me on this day. It was a nice turn of events. We all headed to the car to get something to eat.

"Hey Doug," Kenji said as he extended his hand for the streak, "I thought I would bring these balloons for the game." Kenji was referring to Steve and Rob.

I was laughing and coughing. It was my 4th week on the road and it was starting to play with my health. I felt a Froggy throat coming and was eating 'Halls' like rock candy. "You guys are about to be part of history."

Steve Lees had been a small kid who had hit a massive growth spurt in his teens to be the tallest out of all of us now. He had blonde hair and was definitely the most youthful of the group.

Rob Blair has brown hair, with medium height and brown hair. I worked with Rob for 3 years in the pizza industry. Rob was married only a few months before me and is a proud father of 2 daughter's now. He had also driven his car out for the festivities even though he had the least driving experience with the city of Seattle.

'What's up Douger?" This came from Rob, It was my nickname created in my teenage years when I hated everyone calling me D. Booth-and they didn't call me Chuck either like my U.S baseball friends do.

"I'll be a lot better when we eat, I have not eaten a morsel of food all day. " I had slept on the non-stop flight to Seattle and missed the cookies they passed out.

"Yeah, it is only noon, so we are going to drive around 'South Center Mall' until we find a place to eat, maybe get lost and miss first pitch." Kenji said. He too was a father of a young son. His mom was from Japan and his dad from Scotland so he has an awesome sense of humor.

As tired I was, having my friends have my back for this game was going to be refreshing. Company helped the time pass. They had been following the streak back at home picking up momentum. It was an online buzz for the community. The newspaper articles written had been picked up by the Canadian Press in Canada. There was also that Detroit Free Press Article that had been picked up by many syndicate newspapers in the Eastern US cities.

"Whatever I do today, I am not in the mood for any scary moves to be delayed to the baseball game!" The guys were just kidding, but by my seeing that they all laughed.

We arrived at Safeco Field when the gates opened. The outside neighborhood of this ballpark is the only thing keeping this park from being ranked higher. This beautiful ball park has a bunch of rundown buildings—and alleyways that have all of the hard rigors of downtown life. I was trying not concentrate on that. The beautiful brick concrete that is apparent for miles highlight this structure. You can easily identify Safeco's retractable roof from anywhere in the downtown district. Nearby 'Q-West Field' is adjacent to Safeco, and this venue enhances the look of the area.

On Edgar Martinez Way, there is a huge parking lot that is the same height as Safeco and provides lots of parking spaces for a big fee but its close proximity to the park serves some people well.

On my first to trip to Safeco field in 2005, the team still drew at near capacity and the buzz around the outside of the park enabled surrounding businesses to flourish make money. 'Ivens Clam Bake' once had a beer garden and concession stand right across from the park—that was packed with people, and the smell of seafood wafted through the air. This lot was now vacant as the attendance had dwindled some.

This night the buzz was in the air for another reason. The M's were playing the Red Sox. I love cheering against those guys just as I had done in Los Angeles a few days prior.

The staff at Safeco Field were courteous to us as we entered the park, each one of them have nametags with their own hometown and how long they have worked at the park much like they have when you visit ''Disneyland'. It is a nice idea. I took my friends to where we were going to stand for the game and they were happy about the view.

In my opinion, Safeco Field has the best sightlines from any park when you are walking along the main floor concourse. No matter where you are—you can always peek at the action going on. There is an undeniable smell of ballpark garlic from the famous 'Rally Fries'. There is a little section along the left field wall that is a great place to watch the game in which there is a man attended scoreboard underneath. From time to time you will hear the train shooting off past the right field bleachers.

The main scoreboard is in centerfield with the backdrop of Q-West Field in the left center field. The big iconic letters of 'SAFECO FIELD' are also displayed in left field. The most famous area of right field is the 'HIT IT HERE CAFÉ'—which is on the second level—and has nice viewing of the game while eating some food.

The Mariners Mascot is the 'Mariner Moose'. The first time I saw the Mariner Moose, the mascot did the 'Napoleon Dynamite dance and would be seen doing many of athletic moves all around the Field. Unfortunately an accident along the wall one game has caused that Moose to retire in favor of a more 'kid friendly moose'. Somehow the Moose just doesn't seem to be as cool as it once was. I was thinking this to myself as the game started While the day was somewhat stress free I still needed a fast game.

I had a flight that left for a few minutes before midnight. Seattle was always going to be a tough squeeze because it is 1000 miles to the next ball park. Even flights were two plus hours to the California teams. If you left to East of there was the flight time—plus loss of time zones. I would take an all night flight to New York that stopped off in Houston the next day. I had many options from there to go places in case of schedule change. Since I missed games in the streak—I had to fly to New York and then take a train to Baltimore. It pleased me to see Boston pitching Jon Lester and Seattle pitching Jarrod Washburn, two strike throwing pitches, both of whom worked extremely fast.

Any doubt of a slow game was quickly put to rest in the game when Boston took a 4-0 lead in the 8th and then Papelbon put it away quickly in the 9th. I had two hours to arrive at the airport-go through security and board the plane. Since I was quite knowledgeable about the traffic flow the cops use, we were able to strategically park a few feet past were they cordoned off the street, in forcing the cars to travel north towards highway 5. I made it to SeaTac at 10:30 PM, and said goodbye-to my buddies. It was a great to have had company for the day. I was really tired and couldn't wait for the flight. I was not paying as much attention going through the security lines and almost lost my passport having walked away from the area for about 3 minutes before returning to retrieve it.

I fell asleep hard and woke up in Houston.

Game#13 Day#14
Oriole Park at Camden Yards
Baltimore, MD
July.22/2008

I woke up in a fog from the flight arriving in Houston. Much to my disliking we had to de-board the aircraft and switch planes for the flight to LGA in New York. I knew something was wrong from the minute I got off the airplane. When I arrived on the next plane I realized I had lost my cell phone. I could have sworn I placed into pants but it wasn't there. I was already on the next plane. Now it was a cheap phone to begin with and I was not really that upset it was gone—it was just that it was my form of communication and I had some secondary verification evidence for the streak. I asked the flight attendant if I had time to race back to other plane. She said I had 8 minutes. I sprinted to other plane and made it back to my scat on the other plane where I was disappointed to not see the phone anywhere. I had to roll with it now. I ran back to the New York bound flight and made it within a minute of the cabin doors being closed.

I had no phone now. I had a calling card number where I could make calls from payphones if necessary, but my trip just became harder.

It was going to be a tough day. I landed in 'LGA' at 10:30 AM local time. I would need to take a bus to the subway station-and then proceed to make it to NY Penn Station—where I had to exchange my train ticket for a Baltimore bound train. Upon arriving in Baltimore, I would have to check my baggage with the luggage check so I could go to the ball game without my stuff.

During my planning days I had this day set-up for several scenarios so it was not foreign to me to have this occur. The original design was to have gone to Tampa via flight and go to the game as a single, but when I missed the Yanks/Phil's double header it was to become the secondary day for the Yanks, however when I missed my Dallas flight on July.8th I had to reset the trip so now it was the last option of Baltimore. I had a Tampa Bay/Florida doubleheader attempt the next day-and then I would have to fly the next day to Baltimore and then drive the way to Pittsburgh-to re-do PNC Park again.

The negative was that this would be a night where I had to spend four hours at the Amtrak Station over night to catch an early morning flight from BWI-to Tampa. I was becoming an expert of New York City I will tell you that.

This streak was one of several patience times. I was in line for over an hour to receive my new Amtrak ticket. I bought a New York Deli style Pastrami sandwich for much more money then what I should have-and watched the Train Schedule Board. This is a unique experience in its own right.

The board shows all arriving trains and when your train number is up-they flash what gate 1-16 or so you need to be at. It is a mad dash for positioning after that is occurred. From there, you board the train and hope to have a seat. I am not sure how hard it would have been to drive from New York City to Baltimore that day—but at least with Amtrak I took the traffic factor out. For a $45 one way trip—that distance was a good deal. I would have paid $17-25 alone in tolls down the I-95.

I was pleased the train arrived even before 6 PM in Baltimore. Ten minutes later my luggage was checked and I was on a $15 cab ride to the park that had me at the park with 50 minutes to spare. I had time to check out the park, call my cell phone company to cut service off and eat some food.

I had finally made it to Oriole Park at Camden Yards!! It was awesome. I entered from the Eutaw Street. entrance on a sunny evening and headed right for the barbecue pit I had heard about.

The warehouse across from the park was within my sight as I snapped pictures. While I ate a barbecue rib sandwich, with baked beans and coleslaw, I walked around that area for a few minutes reading all the places on the concrete where the players had hit home run balls. I walked into the standing room only area which might be the best in baseball. This park was incredible. When you are in a ballgame in Baltimore you can not think of anybody else other than Cal Ripken Jr. He was a player I admired a lot growing up. I watched the 1983 World Series and saw him talk on the phone with the President of the United States when they won. This is Cal's town. Everything he stands for is prominently displayed at the park. It was too bad the ball club has struggled for so long now and the attendance has waned. The park is immaculate though.

Right in the core of downtown Baltimore, the yard is near everything. Traffic may be a problem, but once you are inside the crowd is there to forget about life for awhile and see a game from an original venue.

I truly had wished I could have had more time before and after the game to soak up this experience but I was ecstatic to be there. I made it to my seat in time for the National Anthem. Wouldn't you know they scream the word 'O' when it comes to the 'oh say, can you see part of it. I love little traditions each park has like this.

I love the scoreboard too. It was really easy to have valid pictures from the size and clarity of the numbers. This was a game I wanted to last into the night because I was in no rush to spend all the remaining time in Baltimore at the Amtrak Station. I watched the Toronto Blue Jays outslug the hometown 10-8.

Amongst my favorite players of all time, I got to see fellow Canadian Matt Stairs pinch hit and deliver and run batted in single. By the time they cleared the park I was the last one out at almost midnight. I did some good planning work back at the station in order to make the next few days go smooth.

Game #14 Day#15
Tropicana Field
St. Petersburg, FLA
July.23/2008

I was more than happy to pay the cab driver the $40 to take me to my hotel early. The flight arrived early into Tampa which I liked. It was now just after 10:00 AM, I had called the 'Clearwater' Best Western and they had agreed to let me check in extremely early. I had not showered in 2 days—and was not looking forward to a hot day in Florida without hitting a fresh-up! This would be a stressful day.

The plan was to attend a 12:00 PM matinee in Tampa-before using sedan service to the Tampa Bay Airport—and then fly into 'Fort Lauderdale Airport'- via a 4:55 PM flight. The plane would arrive in Miami at nearly 6 PM. From there I would have an hour to make it to the ball game.

Once the game ended I had a 4 hour drive back to Tampa to make it to the hotel. Just like the other car deals I had done, I had secured a cheap one-way car rental in Miami by using the 24 hour airport deal. The cabbie dropped me off for 30 minutes at the hotel before returning to pick me up.

It was a nice drive into Clearwater from Tampa, but the trip from Clearwater to Tropicana made me realize why the ball park is so constantly beaten up. There is only one way to arrive at the game. I had set myself up for no expectations at the Trop.

I liked that they had the score board of the starting lineups posted outside the park for everyone to see. I was going to see James 'Big Game' Shields pitch against the Oakland A's. At the very least the Rays were a 1st place club at this point and Oakland was still in contention for the AL West. Of course they had one of my favorite players in Jack Cust in the line-up hitting 3rd.

Once inside, I was actually quite impressed at a few specific things the club has to offer. They have made the 'TROP' very fan and family friendly-with all sorts of interactive baseball games and contests during the game.

Plus since it was summer, they have concession food with a special rate for kids that are there attending camps. They offered $1 fries, pop and hotdogs for the kids. I almost wanted to say I was buying food for a kid to get the deal.

I sat in the 300 section and it felt pretty cavernous up there. They have walking verandas in the middle of the field—way up from the play but these veranda's have actually cost team's games when the ball has been hit up there.

The reflection of the lights all make it tough to take pictures from anywhere inside the park. Still there are pictures of Rays players everywhere. Like every park, I always check out the scoreboard and the Rays have a nice one in the center field wall.

I was impressed with the mascot "Raymond" interacting with the kids long before the game started. If I were not so tired, I would not have minded that plastic thunder sticks were currently being banged by kids.

As for the park, I give the Rays staff good marks for effort, especially when it came to concessions, fan participation and doing the best with what you have. At the very least the tickets were cheap, and it was fully air conditioned in there

When you are expecting the worst and there end up being positives it is a good feeling. I mean really, even at the parks that are not considered the greatest, the game of baseball is being played and that is right up my alley. I sat in my seat with half of the fans being kids and it was a nice feeling.

I always say in the lower end markets of baseball cities that if I lived there I would hardly ever miss a game and it is true. My food, ticket and transportation were well under $50 from Clearwater anyway.

Oakland jumped out to a 2-0 in the second before the Rays put up a 3 spot in the bottom of the fifth. I always liked the home team having a lead in the game because I could eliminate a half-inning by the home team winning. The game was progressing really fast.

At the start of the eighth inning we were barely two hours old. It was looking good for me. In fact, my sedan driver was scheduled for 2:45 PM-at the earliest-and now I had to call him in early. The guy was not answering his phone. I could not sit any longer and watched the game on the main level from near the private suite boxes.

Shields began the Top of the Ninth struggling and put on a couple of base runners. Tampa had tacked on an insurance run in the bottom of 7 for a 4-2 lead. It was 2:15 PM when the inning started. At 2:27 PM there was still no one out, and the A's had pulled to within 4-3 with a man on base. Finally Shields got the first out—and then the Rays brought in Troy Percival.

I was happy at that move, but still pitching changes cost minutes. As long as there was not extra innings I should still be okay.

Should the A's even take the lead then I would cheer for a quick bottom of the ninth inning. I was cheering just for outs baby!

Percival came in and walked the 1st batter, crikey!

I was sweating it now. A tied score would be very bad. I had exhausted all options just to get to this point. The streak could not take one more set back if I were to tie the record. I had always thought this was a hard double header to achieve, but it had potential. I just needed an out.

Troy Percival enticed a ground ball for a double play attempt that failed.

Damn, one out was good, but now the tying run was on 3rd with 2 out.

I could not watch the game from the concourse railings near a section. I was watching it on a restaurant lounge TV through a pane of glass.

Percival was taking a long time. The clock now read 2:44 PM. My sedan driver should be waiting at least by now. I had called him 2 times without an answer.

I heard a cheer from the crowd as I held my head in my hands and watched a ground out. I ran to videotape the celebration and take a picture. I then ran down the stairs outside into the blistering heat. My sedan driver was not answering my calls. Traffic looked to be gridlocked-and all of the buses with these kids were waiting. I was furious with the sedan guy. I saw cabs hauling people out and I made a run for one.

I was running while taping so fast that I asked the cab-driver "hey dude, can you take me to the airport" and it ended up being a woman. I had to make this kind of decision on the go, the sedan guy was late and I had to pay him anyway, so it was my decision to bail and go with this cabbie.

Missing the flight would have cost me hundreds and I could not worry about losing $70 like that if it meant a better chance to make it to my next game.

It was a good decision to have jumped in that cab as we hit major traffic heading towards the airport. I was in the security line-up at 4:07 PM for my flight. There was a decent crowd waiting in front of me-but the TSA was very efficient at the 'TPA airport' that day. I was through in twenty minutes and made it to the gate as they were about to call last call for the flight. I am sure if I went with the sedan I would have missed the flight.

Game#15 Day #15
Sun Life Stadium
Miami, FLA
July.23/2008

Looking back on it now, I was lucky to have flown into Fort Lauderdale as oppose to MIA airport—as it was closer to Sun Life Stadium and consisted of less traffic. Not to mention the car rental facility is right next to the airport in 'FLL', and they send you to suburbia at the airport in Miami.

I still had a tough time negotiating the streets to the park and stopped at two gas stations. I arrived at the park at 6:49 PM-and was able to complete the double header. The only thing that feared me was there were clouds in the air.

Let us be honest here, whatever they call Dolphin Stadium yearly, it still is one of the worst parks in the majors regardless. This is funny because they have a sign in front of the stadium that reads 'EVERY DAY IS FAN APPRECIATION DAY'. This is a football stadium where a baseball game breaks out in—and it rains almost every day or it is reaching 100 degrees Fahrenheit.

You are truly hardcore to be a Marlins season ticket holder! All you can see on the outside is cement. Oh yeah, you can also see elevators that you never need to attend the ball game because 20 percent of the seats only are ever occupied. It boggles my mind how this team has actually won 2 world Series while the Chicago Cubs have skipped 8-10 generations without a World Series.

Inside, the cement is even more presented and there is nothing but Dolphin's pictures everywhere.

I could take more pictures of Dan Marino then any current Marlin. Again, you have to be a true baseball fan to attend this park. I liked a few things about the park.

You could catch a home run ball if you sat in a section all by your self and I also liked the big screen replay monitor. The mascot 'Billy the Marlin' is awesome. There is my theory that the worse the ballpark and/or team are the more present the team mascot is. The Metro Dome always had TC, The Montreal Expos former mascot Youppi was awesome-and he was showcased at 'Olympic Stadium.' I like both of the Pirates mascot's too and PNC Park is a wicked ball park-but the team has been bad for 17 years.

In Sun Life Stadium you feel like you are in a big rectangle once inside the stadium itself. There are not many ball parks that are 80-85% empty when it comes time for the games. Everybody sticks to the first deck. The Stadium is very blue and orange-and has signs of the Dolphins in all corners. You would think that with the Marlins winning the World Series in 1997 and 2003 that there would be great wall murals of the teams.

You can barely even find a team photo.

The food inside the building is decent-and you should really try the chicken fingers and French fries. I buy some as soon as I enter the Stadium each time I have been there.

There are rows upon rows of parking stalls outside the stadium that have grass wedged between each stall-it is kind of a parking free for all.

The atmosphere is more like a football game—with people tossing footballs even more then they throw baseballs in between the cars and the grass before and after the game.

It is a weird feeling to see so many people in line for baseball tickets yet once you are in the park they get lost in the sections.

The Marlins must do half of their attendance each game by walk-up. This must be frustrating for the staff as they can not be properly equipped with all of the amenities based on the fluctuations in attendance.

After the games, it takes hours for the parking lot to clear as well as people make it their hangout for the night. Traffic around the Stadium is still bad despite low attendance. Being just off the turnpike, and near some other main highways, there are just too many cars on the road in this Florida city.

I took my seat in the blistering heat and quickly devoured my food. The fans quickly witnessed Derek Lowe start to deal a gem for the Braves and the Marlins were down 9-0 in the bottom of the ninth. Talk about an empty stadium. I, of course, could not leave the atrocious game until the last out was recorded. At least I got to see Luis Gonzalez blast a three-run homer. Now he has always been a player I liked. The Marlins scored their token 4 runs and finally I could leave the park with a Brave win!

The drive from Sun Life Stadium back to St. Petersburg was given some relief with the blowout game taking some of the traffic out early to the highways. I was tired, but had my streak back to even games per days, while looking forward to continue on to Pittsburgh the next day.

Game#16 Day#16
PNC Park
Pittsburgh, PA
July.24/2008

I had a tough time sleeping since my flight to Baltimore was scheduled for 6:00 AM. I had driven from Fort Lauderdale all the way back to Tampa Bay, and then showered, got dressed and left for the airport. I would sleep on the plane this day. The day was not going to be fun to start. I was flying into Baltimore as part of my original schedule in order to drive to Pittsburgh. There was a reason why I had put this flexibility into plane rides.

Since I knew there was a re-scheduling risk I could drive into Pittsburgh from Baltimore in this very event. It was about a 5 hour drive, so I would arrive with a couple of hours to spare at PNC Park.

I arrived at the airport, and was waiting for my Air Tran Airways early morning flight when I caught some good luck. The airline was looking for volunteers to give up their seat—in order to give the ticket to others. This was my opportunity to wing some magic. I informed the desk agent that my intended city was Pittsburgh—and that I would gladly give up my seat if I could catch another flight to Pittsburgh—and avoid that 5 hour drive.

Not only was I granted that wish, but I was credited with 2 round trip flights from the airline. Air Tran is simple the best airline in America!

I was in Pittsburgh by 11:00 AM local time. I was able to cancel my Baltimore car rental and pick up a free rental with my Thrifty Free days at the Pit-airport. Again, the Pit airport is one of the select few in America that have a car transportation building right at the airport. With my new found time I was able to check in early to a Best Western just 3 miles from the park. I had lots of catching up to do on the internet and such. While I was online, I saw that I was requested to do another interview with Dan Russell's Sports Talk Show back at home in Vancouver. This was perfect since I had a lot more time to spare anyways.

I had listened to Dan Russell since I was 9 years old. He started a talk show in the early eighties in Vancouver and I was one of his first listeners. It is a credit to Dan's professionalism that he actually gave me a direct line—in order to call him so we could do the interview. I was not even nervous at all like I was with other interviews I had done so far. I felt I knew Dan because of listening to him on the radio for 23 years.

Doing the radio interviews helped stem the tide when it came to family and friends-as I knew they would hear me on the air back home. Making the doubleheader the previous day had been a huge accomplishment. Being able to have some down time before heading to the Pittsburgh game was essential to recovering up for the weekend. I thanked Dan for another great interview and was on my way to PNC Park. I avoided the garage where my previous car rental had been keyed this time.

The game was pretty bland at 9-1 for the Pirates, but during the night I met the Salter's from Detroit.

Joe Salter and his three boys Anthony, Jacob and Robert were at the game-and were introduced to me by one of the coolest ushers of all time at PNC. It was fun talking to these guys while watching the game. I handed them a business card to take, and agreed to keep in touch with them about the record through the social networks online. It was such a neat experience talking to all of the people I met on this trip—because baseball was important to all of them like it was to me. Little did I know that I would meet up with the Salter's again in the future.

Game#17 Day#17
Kauffman Stadium
Kansas City, MO
July.25/2008

I arrived in the airport at Kansas City-and went right to the Continental Airlines agent. I had two flights left on the itinerary, and I was not going to need the last flight on the Sunday now anyways because I booked a flight out of San Francisco the next night—in order to fly into New York.

So there I was. My flight after this game was out of St. Louis due to some more flexibility issues. It was scheduled for 6:00 AM—and was to fly into Oakland. I was simply trying to trade 2 flights in for a Kansas City flight into Oakland. The value of the flights I was going to trade in was so much higher than the fare that was to be paid from KC to Oakland.

Like so many times in the streak, Continental Airlines could not have been more-rude so yes I had to drive to St. Louis still. I would be okay though for cash as I had arranged a one way rental already lined up with the 24 hour rule.

Kauffman Stadium was under complete renovation when I entered the park and all I could think about was why? Really they should have been shooting for a new ballpark. The parking lot goes on for days, and is in the middle of both Kauffman and Arrowhead Stadium. It is truly a parking nightmare to remember where you park your car as it doesn't seem to have any flow.

It was T-shirt night when I arrived, and it was the most horrible blue t-shirt I have ever received. I needed to walk around the park a little more to feel better about the experience. I will tell you about the renovated aspect of this park right now, (2009 version) otherwise I will not have anything nice to say.

The new park had a much greater feel when I came back the next year. When I saw the statue of George Brett in Right Center-I snapped a few photographs with it. Also the party zone atmosphere they have in that general area in right field is great for watching the game, and there is plenty more room to walk around now. The kids also have a place to play baseball, and run-around past the water fountains.

When I walked into the lower concourse, I was happy to see all of the Kansas City Royals of the 80's in their Hall of Fame: Dan Quisenberry, George Brett, Bret Saberhagen, Willie Wilson, Hal Macrae and Frank White. I hated that team because they came back against the Toronto Blue Jays in the 1985 ALCS when trailing 3-1, but I understand the mystique behind the World Champion team as they rallied from down 3-1 to the St. Louis Cardinals in the 85 World Series too. I think at some point, while playing baseball growing up, that all of my friends tried throwing like the Quiz did!

I spent more of my time looking at their Hall of Fame then watching the team play on the field.

When you are driving in from I-70-you can ask see the field very clearly. Once inside the stadium you can watch the flow of traffic on the highway. So when it was rush hour, and I was watching batting practice I bet some of the people in traffic gridlock were doing the same thing as I was.

Obviously they have the biggest scoreboard in the Majors which I definitely liked for evidence. Also the grass field in center field is also awesome with the back drop of retired numbers of George Brett#5, Frank White #20 and Dick Howser#10.

The definite highlight is the Waterfalls in The Right to Right Center Field. It is a remarkable sight to see these falls during night games especially.

Overall the changes have made the park a viable place to play, but if you are comparing it to the other new parks, it is in the lower rankings. It is still an upgrade from before though.

The fans loved to sing country songs any chance they can, so certainly the most applause came when country boy Billy Butler came up to bat.

As for the game itself, I actually saw the Royals hit 3 homeruns in a game but they lost to the Tampa Bay Rays 5-3.

This time I was to driving East on I-70 towards St. Louis airport. These long road trips just to take early morning flights had been taxing. By the time I walked into the airport in St. Louis I was gassed.

Game#18 Day#18
McAfee Coliseum
Oakland, CA
July.26/2008

The airport in St. Louis had stressed me out this time. A lot of the flights I had flown so far had been pretty smooth. Here in lies a problem with certain airports when you take early morning flights. This is prone to these following airports especially: St. Louis, Philadelphia, Lu Guardia, Minnesota and Ronald Reagan Airport. Since the TSA doesn't open in most spots until 4:30 AM, (this is also the case for printing off boarding passes from you airline at the airports—yes even without luggage to check there are lines for just using the self serve kiosks)-you have to make sure you are near the area when it opens up. Print your boarding passes if at all possible before arriving at the airports.

Well I got burned in St. Louis by being very casual. While I didn't mind the reason for half of the passengers that day—because they were military soldiers flying about I was still astounded at the amount of civilians in the security lineup. I had taken 10 minutes to do a couple of internet sessions at the pay kiosks to check on some email accounts.

So what looked initially like no wait for security-turned into almost 45 minutes and I just hit the general boarding time when I reached my Continental Flight at 5:45 AM local time.

I awoke at Oakland's International Airport at 10:00 AM sporting a migraine headache. Sometimes when you start sleeping a lot on planes you miss giving your ears a chance to pop by chewing gum. I was so groggy when I walked to the shuttle bus and onto Transportation center.

I slammed back a Red Bull-and knew it was only going to be a temporary fix. I was happy his day because my doubleheader attempt only involved driving over the Bay Bridge from Oakland to San Francisco. I had been to San Francisco/Oakland to start this road odyssey 28 days ago. It was my warm-up trip before the real streaking started. I had practiced driving around the area during the last visit.

I was even more fired up when I saw my rental car upgrade for the day. Budget Rental gave me a slightly used 2008 White Convertible Mustang to drive. Are you kidding me? This put a spring in my step. I actually turned on my camera's video to record me getting into the car! I felt like whipping around Oakland before the game-but thought it would be best to get to the park early and get a situational parking spot that would suit my exit strategy.

It was hot this day in Oakland. Having treated my self to a McDonald's burger, a tradition for me at Oakland, I could really tell that my body had been putting on those pounds. It was a pound a day so far. It was a good thing I would be working that off with those newspapers upon returning home.

It was quite easy on this streak. You are sitting in ball parks, airports, airplanes, hotels. Eating whatever is available to you in every domain you are in. That day it was starting to get to me.

Oakland's parking lot is a rip-off. I always chose to pay their fee though because the neighborhood is a little sketchy at night. Today I had no choice either. It is really hard to remember where you parked in this lot. As I was making my way to the view of the numerous tailgating parties I could see the smoke fly off the grills in the area. I videotaped that as well. My day was going to get weird.

I had no clean clothes other then two Yankee T-shirts in my luggage so I had a Mickey Mantle Yankees shirt on. I was receiving some flak from the locals. I gave it back a little by saying, "What are you so angry at me for Mickey Mantle was playing for the Yankees even before you guys had a team here in Oakland. Besides I like Jack Cust off your team anyway."

Some of the guys bought my statement and some didn't. I continued into the park.

My worst decision might have been to look for a payphone around the concourse in the bleachers section. The visuals were unbelievable. The area was all dark and grungy to which no one had cleaned in weeks. Remarkably there were silver tables that featured condiment stains-and were shoved in all sorts of patterns with folding chairs along this dark concourse.

There were cracks in the uneven cement that reminded me of Shea Stadium once again. The washroom facilities were dirty and actually had toilet paper stuck in the ceiling tiles. I knew I was walking around the worst stadium in the Major Leagues.

Forget blaming all of the fans on the park itself. I can understand it is hard to get a new ball park in the works but at least maintain the one you have by basic sanitation codes!

The scoreboard is small and you can hardly see anything from how far you are away from it anywhere you are in the park. The top deck is unoccupied and covered up with ugly green tarps.

The Right Field bleachers have a little banquet style room that I have taken salvation from the crowd on nights where the temperature was chilly.

I should have sat in the top deck behind home plate like my 1st visit ever. At least from there you can see a good view of the field, and the incredible amounts of grass in the outfield foul lines.

I also could not walk around the concourse with out a few guys trying to pick a fight by intentionally running into me each time. Really! I was ready to throw down but I had to remember the streak. Losing a world record because I threw a few punches was not worth it, so I went to my seat finally.

I cheered in silence as Josh Hamilton blasted a homerun like none I have ever seen live before. I was so happy yet again when the Rangers put another 8 runs to their lead in the 9th inning and the final result was Rangers blitzing the A's 14-6-in a game that lasted 3 hours.

I ran out of the grungy stadium, through the bird-pooped parking lots—with countless debris of beer bottles and barbeque trash towards my car. It was 4:00 PM-and I had 2 hours to arrive at AT&T Park.

Game#19 Day#18
AT&T Park
San Francisco, CA
July.26/2008

It should have been so much easier then taking one hour and thirty minutes in crazy traffic to cross the Bay Bridge. I was actually forced to run fast from the parking lot—to the Park—in order to get to the game in time. I would never drive over the Bridge if given the chance again. I would always take the other route of I-92 (San Mateo Bridge) to merge with I-101 N San Fran.

It is truly a two different sides of the spectrum kind of experience when you go from the worst ball park in the majors (McAfee) to the best stadium in AT&T Park. What is not to like about this beautiful park? I will list 10 reasons why it is awesome viewing wise.

1. The Gigantic Baseball Glove right beside the Coke Neon Sign (that illuminates at night)—both are about the most iconic visuals as you will see in baseball.
2. You have a great view of the Bay Bridge.
3. The ocean view from anywhere in the Park is also outstanding.
4. The Clock on top of the scoreboard is awesome.
5. From Right Center Field bleachers you can see Palm Trees that separate the park from The Pier Boats and ocean living.
6. There is a walkway bridge-deck on the outside of the park.
7. People are always doing something at sea, whether it is kayakers, or people with yachts parked nearby, it is its own little community. You can even take yacht rides prior to the game.
8. Across from the right field bleachers there is a statue of Willie McCovey.
9. The Port Authority of San Francisco is right behind that statue.
10. On the third level deck you can see the Pier's lights around the Bay Bridge. Take a look at all of the wall murals on the third level to see historic players.

10 Reasons why AT&T is the best ball park:

1. The food is the best. There are 70 different kinds of sandwiches you can eat, ribs, calamari, steak…
2. You can pay $10 and spend your time in the bleachers walking the observation deck. This is the greatest value ticket in the majors.
3. In the concourse they constructed different sets of food menus per section—with your own enclosed off tables to enjoy the game on the multiple big screens in your area. You can't walk anywhere without seeing the game in action somewhere.
4. There is not an inch of the building or surrounding area that wasn't thought of to include all sorts of visuals. They even have marbled 3 feet baseballs lined from the Bridge Deck to the parking lot. They have retired players numbers in crooks and cranny's of the red-brick walls, and there was sidewalks made and donated for by families-that were made up from premium bricks.

5. There is not a bad picture to be had from anywhere in the park.
6. The park's climate is perfect to watch baseball games. It is not too hot ever and not too cold. Any season is fine to watch a game
7. The baseball glove and Coke sign are the best 1-2 punch for a picture, you add the Bay Bridge with lights at night, perfect.
8. Where else can you buy a Safeway deli sandwich in the majors?
9. You can get there by taking a historic trolley. One of the best ways to arrive at the ballpark ever.
10. The view of the Ocean from anywhere is incredible. The Red Brick

Just seems to bring out the ocean blue even more.

I was completely in awe of the park when I first witnessed a game in 2005 at AT&T. The crowd is about the most energetic I have seen. Especially in the bleachers-those guys hang on every pitch. I have actually seen them cheer innings being kept alive by beating out a double play. The crowd does bug the other team more then any other park I have seen too.

I buy the $10-300 section seats-and then walk around the right center field wall and watch the game standing. There is just something about watching the ocean while watching the game. The concession stands directly behind the scoreboard are my favorite ones of the park.

I have eaten rib sandwiches, chicken sandwiches, mushroom burgers, steak sandwiches. People with me have eaten Calamari, Chinese Food, Cajun food and Salmon. It truly is a smorgasbord of food to digest. After eating 3-4 items of these said items, I usually polish off a couple of cokes from the ice-cold vending machines directly under the giant glove. It is a little thing, but to have these machines available for cold drinks when that is all you want—it sure beats standing in line.

This particular night, I did go to my section on the third-deck and walked the concourse. The pictures I took were unbelievable at sunset. Even when I did sit down—I took another 20 pictures of the park from my seat. The field's grass is dark green and actually looks like field turf it is so bright and well manicured. The park looks brand new and still shines.

The extra room in right field is only highlighted by the dark brown dirt and red brick walls. The all time homerun leaders is proudly posted in right field with Barry Bonds leading with 762 homers, Aaron with 755, Ruth with 714 and other great legend the say hey kid! Willie Mays holding down 4th spot with 660 Bombs.

Directly near the right field foul pole they chart the splash hits. I have seen a few splash hits at AT&T and it is electric—my only disappointment was I never got to see Barry Bonds play live at AT&T Park because he was injured when I was in town previously.

Painfully speaking, because of where I was watching this contest, I needed another quick game. They game started at 6:05 PM-but my flight from SFO Airport was at 11:15 PM. If the game hit extra innings I might have been in trouble. Originally this was set as game#29 of the first streak and game#30 would have been in Boston the next day. It would have been a Sunday Night Baseball game so the 8:00 PM start time would have come in handy with flying into JFK overnight.

My worries quickly subsided when Arizona's Brandon Webb—and the Giants phenom Tim Lincecum started off in a pitcher's duel. They were still some anxious moments that led to a near 3 hour game, with the D'Backs winning 5-3. When the final out was recorded I ran over the 3rd Street Bridge—and ran to my Mustang rental parked on the Terry Francois St. side of the parking lot.

I was beating the general traffic, but kept all the way by the streets closest to the ocean because the 101 S was highly congested with traffic from the ballpark crowd.

I weaved in and out of side streets and went over another bridge. At one point, I was sure I was lost and thought I was near an army base. Time seemed like it was escaping me. I kept driving. If I could ever get back to the 101 highway I was home free. Somehow I managed to wind up back on that very highway and I never knew how I got there. Had I taken the other way I might have very well missed my flight. I got to say it was incredible driving around near dusk in that Mustang. It was smooth!

I felt like James Bond driving through those residential areas just off of Hunter's Point. I made it to the Transportation Center, then through the heavy security lineup in great time.

I was flying with Virgin America for the fourth time in my trip-on a red-eye flight to New York. This new airline was fantastic, the all night flights from West Coast cities to New York were ideal when non-stop. The seats are spacious—and fees of $160 for a one way ticket to New York were a great deal! I had made my double header, and was headed back East with a shot at the World Record.

Game#20 Day#19
Citizens Bank Park
Philadelphia, PA
July.27/2008

I landed at JFK at 7:30 AM—and proceeded to take the subway all the way from the airport to New York Penn Station. I had to re-do another Phillies game. I rode the subway for one hour and then bought an Amtrak ticket to Philadelphia. It was a nice thing I had done this exact trip with my brother Trent before when we came back from Yankee Stadium in 2006. He had taught me the ropes. I caught up on my sports by reading the New York Post and the New York Daily news. The sports coverage from those papers is simply fantastic and I always jump at the chance to read them in New York.

By the time I arrived at Philly's train station it was all too easy. I used Amtrak baggage service yet again and took a cab to 'CBP' for $20.

Outside the stadium, on that cloudy day, was newly inducted Hall Of Famer 'Goose Goosage' signing autographs and posing for pictures. To me when I was a kid, nothing was better then Goose Gossage coming into pitch a game I was watching on TV. The trade mark moustache. This day Goose was wearing an 'Auto Trader T-shirt' and was just setting up a booth. I took my place in line. I only had to wait a few minutes.

I told him about the streak, and what I was doing, I told him that while I cheered for the 1984 Detroit Tigers in the World Series, that I loved watching him strike those guys out. I told him that Thurman Munson was my dad's favorite player all time and that is what made me a Yankees fan. The guy could not have been cooler.

The Goose told me that he appreciated Thurman Munson maybe more then any other catcher he has ever thrown to. He asked if I wanted an upgrade ticket to the game, but I told him I wanted to pay my way through the whole streak and thanked him very much for the autograph, the picture and the conversation.

This really made my day. Mr. Gossage said he knew I would break the record because I was a good kid—that made my day. I only wish my dad was with me to have met Goose Gossage!

I would see my dad tomorrow because he was flying into Philadelphia Airport just as I was flying out to Pittsburgh before driving to Cleveland.

I had snoozed through an inning when I was awoken by rain flooding the park. It was my third trip all time to 'CBP'-and I was in line for another rain delay. I did not need this as I wanted to visit my brother and his family for a few hours after the game. It was not to be as I waited through a 2 hour rain delay. If you are going to be in any park for a big rain delay it might as well be CBP-at least I ate another two cheese steaks, and this time bought extra pop and water. I remembered this from the last rain delay that the stadium runs out of food and drinks after a certain amount of time.

If the 2 hour rain delay wasn't enough, the Phillies had taken a 12-5 into the 8th inning when Atlanta put up a 5 run inning that was at least 40 minutes. I could not stomach any extra innings on this night. CBP was torture enough the last time 3 weeks prior, with the 3 and a half hour rain delay. Brad Lidge promptly walked the 1st batter he saw in the ninth and I started pacing.

Luckily for me he recorded the next 3 outs. My brother Trent picked me up from the park 30 minutes later. So I arrived at the park at 10:45 AM for 1:35 PM game-and did not leave until after 8 PM. I had to return to the Amtrak Station pick up my luggage and then do laundry when I returned to my brother's house in Sicklerville New Jersey. I went to bed at midnight.

Game#21 Day#20
Progressive Field
Cleveland, OH
July.28/2008

Seeing my dad at the Philly airport brought my spirits up immensely. Now that family was joining me for the trip things were going to get easier for a few days. I wouldn't see them for actual games until 2 days later in Boston, but I could sense it. My dad hugged me, and told me he was so proud of me for this streak chase thus far, and that my brothers and he would take care of me through the duration of the time they were there with me.

I thought back to how I used to watch baseball every weekend during the summer when I was a young kid.

I lived at the ballpark. My dad would wake me up at 7:00 AM on Saturday mornings-and take me with him to the yard. I watched his men's league tournaments for Fast Pitch. My other brothers would come to the park later—but I always left at the crack of dawn with my dad.

It was also a way to make a living as a kid. I would be the team bat-boy, I worked on the Field Crew between games, and during the games if I wasn't doing that, my friend Rob Nelson and I would spend the day retrieving foul balls for 25 cents a crack. We were the masters at this art. Rob took the 1st base side and I took the 3rd base side. We were faster then the other kids and made a fortune. By the time my brothers showed up near noon—I had spent half the day at the park and earned more money then most kids got for their weekly allowance.

My dad was the coolest father at the ballpark too, he would hand the concession workers a hundred dollars-telling them to let his 4 boys all eat and drink whatever they wanted-whenever they wanted it. He would have us all pointed out to the concession cashiers-and we were golden for the weekend. Other kids were jealous of this treatment.

Our dad's baseball team was all I knew growing up before teen years. It was the community life at its finest. It was definitely the most fun I had as kid. Even after the baseball games were over, there would be team parties on the Saturday nights. If the team had been eliminated from the tournament-then the parties would just last longer.

My dad's team would hardly ever get eliminated on the 1st day though. Most of the time they would be winning the tournaments until after the Saturday night team parties.

By the time I reached my teen years, my dad and mom split-and dad moved to Calgary-before settling back in Vancouver again the year I graduated. I always remembered those ball yard days with him. Baseball was our best time together.

Through my teen years, my dad helped me with my baseball career to the point I almost made it to a University scholarship at Liberty University in Lynchburg, VA before knee injuries from football cost me that chance to continue playing.

At age 19 I was still able to umpire another full season after my baseball retirement—and had the good luck to work several games with my dad as an umpiring team. Again we were having fun at the ballpark together.

My dad was instrumental—in the community I grew up—in paying kids to be umpires back in the early 80's as they developed a concession stand in or to pay for the expenses of the Minor League Association—and of course that meant the umpires were paid out with some of the money raised.

For years he was the umpire in chief and taught kids how learn the rules of the baseball. Umpiring baseball only helped me grow a deeper appreciation for the game.

It was years since we had been to the baseball park until I took him to Safeco Field for Fathers day in 2006. We got to see Jamie Moyer strike out Barry Bonds two times, and I actually bought my dad his ticket-and bought him breakfast.

In 2007, we did the day trip to Seattle from Vancouver B.C Canada on my birthday. During the drive down, I had told my dad that I was going to visit the rest of my stadiums in 2008—and that I wanted him to come with me to some baseball games. We both agreed it was a good idea.

After catching up with dad for a minute, I saw my brother Clint for the first time in 3 years. Again it would be a short visit this day, but the promise of these guys joining me for the trip in a couple of days invigorated my energy. My dad also handed me a couple of crisp bills to soften the financial worry a little. While the first part of the trip I hadn't had to worry so much, the extra flights, missed games where money was still lost-had finally taken its toll on my budget. It was much needed and appreciated.

I had purchased the plane ticket at the all-star break. I was able to secure a great $90 flight from Philadelphia to Pittsburgh. Even more impressive was my car rental from Pittsburgh-that was to be returned to Akron Ohio Airport- where the one-way car rental was 'free' between airports-and the rental rate was under $50. The few hour drive was a nice one in.

After stopping for my latest McDonalds lunch, I was at Cleveland's downtown core paying $7 for a great parking spot-a half mile from the park.

I had seen the Yankees play at Progressive the year before. My impressions of the park were decent. I liked the interactive things you can do like throwing baseball at the radar guns and hit baseballs.

The park is very similar to US. Cellular Field-with a giant scoreboard in left, a big drop in the centerfield background-where each bleachers sections end.

The grass is checkered style and has a nice light green color to it. The only problems I had were how late they opened the gates. The gates were opened at 5:45 PM for a 7:05 PM game-and I don't think that was a one time occurrence either. There are several nice wall murals from the great teams of yester year.

While the concession stands are decent with food, there was not much space to eat your dinner at tables anywhere. The park is also tough to find good areas for standing while watching the game on the concourse.

Outside the park is adequately situated to the streets of downtown. It is actually quite accessible once you are able to navigate through the exit turnoffs. Walking around is not really conducive from any spot in the park either but maybe the right field lower deck section. The section's all kind of end in the lower sections.

There are several ticket gates of entrances though—so maybe that is how they can open the gates so late.

The game was quick enough with Kenny Rogers pitching for the Tigers, and even though he lost the game to the Indians-he worked quick-in a 5-0 loss. I had an easy drive to Akron-where I stayed in a nice Best Western. The next day I was flying to Atlanta for a game before flying into FLL for the night.

It was a weird plane stop over from Akron-that flew into Atlanta at 4:30 PM-and I had a 7 hour layover in order to fly to Fort Lauderdale at 11:30 PM.

That is why it was such a cheap-fare. If I missed the flight to FLL-I was carrying those free flight vouchers from Air Tran now anyway.

Originally, that morning flight from Atlanta to Boston was $200—while if I flew out of 'FLL' with Jet-Blue the next day I was able to save over $135. Plus the trip into Boston-from Fort Lauderdale-would arrive a few hours earlier to meet up with my brothers and dad. Sure it was risky to do this with the extra inning factor, but with limited cash it had to be this.

Game#22 Day#21
Turner Field
Atlanta, GA
July.29/2008

My plan did almost back fire. That is until Albert Pujols turned into a one-man wrecking crew at Turner Field. In the 6th inning with his team losing 2-1, he hit a homerun to centerfield that nearly left the stadium. The crowd buzzed with awe. In the eighth he doubled, then flashed some speed by stealing 3rd -before scoring on the next play. The Cards added 5 more runs in the 9th-and I got out of the park from the center field exit in no time.

Having been in the city earlier in the month I knew the way to the airport and was there at 10:30 PM. Since I already had 2 bags checked-I was good for security clearance and made it to my gate by 10:55 PM.

Atlanta's airport is gigantic, and you must always use the tram to get anywhere as it could be 4-6 miles from your gate once you go through security.

When I made it to the Best Western in Fort Lauderdale-it was 1:00 AM.

Game#23 Day#22
Fenway Park
Boston, MA
July.30/2008

Never trust the hotel staff ever when they are given instructions for a wake up call-and always have several back up plans! I told the guy at the Best Western 4 times not to miss out on this call as I had a 7:45 AM flight from Fort Lauderdale to Boston. At 6:23 AM, I heard my phone ring because it was set from the day before still. I had packed everything for a quick exit already and left the hotel.

As I was in the elevator, a couple had received my wake-up call even though I had reminded the hotel clerk several times of my hotel room number!

In the car, I knew at the second I was 5 minutes into my drive, that I had left my camera battery charger in the hotel room. I called the front desk from my cell phone and they had assured me that they would take care of this and they had found the battery-(Later after the streak-I would have trouble with them-they actually asked for a pre-arranged Fed-Ex package sent on my behalf-in order to send my camera charger to my brother-within the United States as they would not send it tom me in Canada. When I finally received the Fed Ex package in September it was a cell phone charger that was not even mine.) Thanks for the help fellas!!

So I had this added stress now for my drive in. I drove to the car rental return, and was fortunate the Fort Lauderdale Airport was so close to the rental center. I walked into a 30 minute security wait-and barely made my flight! I was mad throughout the flight. The camera/flip video was $300 in cost. At least at that time, I was sure I was going to get the charger back, so was able to overcome my anger. Had I known about not receiving the charger back ever I would have had a harder time burying the problem.

I still had my other digital cameras, and the camera/video player was fully charged for the last week of the trip so maybe I would get by.

I arrived at Boston International Airport at the same time my younger brother Ken had. Together, we waited for my Dad, my brother Trent and my brother Clint. Ken had flown in all the way from Calgary, while my other three family members had driven from Philadelphia, stopped off at Yankee Stadium for a baseball game that night before making to Bean-town on this day.

"You look like crap." Ken said as we were waiting around the arrivals level pickup traffic. It was already muggy outside.

"You would be too if you were on the road for a month already and had seen 30 games in 30 days." I replied. I felt lousy because I never ate at Turner Field-and ate vending food in Fort Lauderdale for dinner the previous night, only to top it off by missing out on breakfast in the morning before the flight.

"We will get some pasta in you." Ken punched me in the gut, "man you got big."

"A pound per day broseph!" I knew I was bigger as large shirts had become extra large. I had eaten everything in sight for weeks now. Sure there was some walking involved—and running for different methods of transport but there was only so much I could do.

"Yeah, I will probably put on a pound a day in Boston, New York, St. Louis and Chicago." Ken was sporting a goatee which was in better shape then my beard. He was in a Polo-shirt and khaki shorts while I had on my British Flag shorts on, the same black TPX baseball hat-(neutral to all home parks and bought on e-bay before the streak had started)-and a beige rugby shirt.

"That must be them." We saw a tan Grand Cherokee, I had advised my brother Trent-(who was an astute traveler himself)-on the best rates we could get from car rentals on the trip—and he had rented this Jeep for us.

I had booked the one airfare we would all take together—in flying from Philadelphia to St. Louis—a few days way back on a Super Saver fare 3 months before the streak started. Of course I had also pre-purchased these baseball tickets for the 'Booth Boy Summit of 2008' back then too.

Talking about a tough deal, we were going to the 4 hardest stadiums to buy tickets for. I had scouted out great deals for all of us to pay $200 Canadian-($180 U.S) each in order to get bleacher tickets at Fenway, view level seats in Old Yankee Stadium-(the last year of Yankees Stadiums existence)-right field view seats at Busch-and awesome Field View Level seats in Chicago.

The talk had been great that spring when I put the trip together. It was hard to pin everyone to a set of days that worked out for everyone's schedule. Then my world record attempt further complicated things. For a few days after that, the schedule looked bleakest for us all to be together.

That is when I came up with these 4 days in a row. Now we were here. This schedule would work for us all.

Trent booked us into Hilton's double rooms in each city, my dad was the (clubhouse leader)-in buying meals, Kenny and Clint kicked in with some extra's parking expenses and paid their share of the hotels, while I took car of the one-way SUV rental from St. Louis to Chicago.

"Look at these stragglers." My dad laughed, the Cherokee soon featured a ½ ton of Booth Boys in the car.

Over Panini, spaghetti, clam chowder, and oysters at a Boston restaurant on Commonwealth Ave, we caught up on our lives. It was the first time we had been on vacation all together since Puerto Vallarta in 1995.

I was happy and tired but driven to make it to the game with my brothers. I could take a little mental breather for a few days. Just not driving was totally fine with me today. Not fighting with traffic would help me relax.

The Hilton Hotel was less than a mile away from Fenway Park! What a great hotel it was.

Out of all my family, only Trent and I had seen Fenway before.

"This place is awesome," were the first words out of my Dad's mouth. He was wearing a new Boston Red Sox ball cap, with his red shirt and black shorts. "This was a good idea all around. His face lit up.

I had fun watching my brother's expression as we walked in passing the Statue of 'Ted Williams' and stopped for pictures

"I can't believe how tiny the park looks." This came from Clint

"The food smells good and I can smell the hot dogs and I am ready for beer, Kenny said.

We saw the pennants beyond the grandstand-and were watching all of the people maneuvering through the tiny concourse.

"RF Grandstand-34 section, this is us." Trent said.

We had a great view of the Green Monster—and the seats are probably the best area to sit for value and game viewing. I have sat in the grandstand (Field Level) on three other occasions-and did not like the pole beams intruding on sightlines-and with the seats smaller in stature, the vendors do pose a problem coming up and down the aisles.

With 5 grown men—the bleachers were the best option.

"This park is incredible," said Clint, "and we get to watch Mark Teixeira's debut for the Angels."

It was trade deadline time time-and we had seen some of the trades come down before this day come down, and more were to come down in the next 24 hours. Little did we know that the game we were watching was Manny Ramirez's last game as a Boston Red Sox baseball player.

"Don't you forget Vladdy either," I reminded Clint who was on board even before with the stadium visits for the trip—and was ecstatic when he heard we would see Vladmir Guerrero play in two nights consecutively.

The Angels were in 1st place with a 66-40 vs. the Red Sox-who were fighting out the AL East with the Rays at a 60-46 record, the pitching matchup was Joe Saunders (13-5) vs. Josh Beckett (9-7).

"I can't believe that you guys are here." I almost broke down in tears right there because it was perfect. My dad and brothers had walked into my record pursuit. Whether or not the record fell I would have the next few days with these guys and I knew it was going to be an epic trip.

My dad and I walked the concourse at Fenway midway through the game and I talked his ear off about my first trip to Fenway, and about the surrounding area. It was great. Even as a Yankee fan—you have to appreciate the history of Fenway. We watched with sheer delight as the night was sunny for the whole game. I still got to see the Red Sox lose 9-2 to the Angels.

We found a tavern across the street from Fenway after the game and played pool, and talked about baseball afterwards as we were heavily anticipating the next day. It was there where my dad told me that my brothers and he had received a citation for drinking in the Yankees Parking lot the day before!

To hear this news I laughed hard.

We hit the pillows hard at the Hilton-and were ready for the Yankees Stadium next!

Game#24 Day#23
Yankee Stadium
The Bronx, NY
July.31/2008

After a great drive through the states of Massacheutsses, Connecticut and New York we headed to the Yankees Parking lot to drop off the Cherokee before taking the subway to Times Square.

We ate burgers and fries at 'ESPN-New York' —and watched several different player transactions on trade deadline day.

Manny Ramirez went to the Los Angeles Dodgers.

The Yankees picked up Xavier Nady and Pudge Rodriguez.

Boston picked up Jason Bay.

After lunch, it was a great day walking the streets of New York with my family. Soon they would encounter what I had been fighting with the whole time during the streak. We all had drank way too much beer and water to be on the subway for 20 minutes from Times Square to Yankees Stadium—and since it was only 6:10 PM for a 7:05 PM game, I thought it would be a good idea for us to get off at the next sub station to use a washroom—and then catch the next train 5-10 minutes later.

Unfortunately we got off at the 153rd St exit, which is a rough neighborhood and also did not have a public toilet. I explained Yankee Stadium was only a few miles and that we should walk-but that was clearly a bad idea on my part. We walked briskly back to the train station and promptly missed the next train.

It was now 6:34 PM, and despite arriving in New York at 2:00 PM, I had to worry about making it to the game on time. My brothers had just entered my world, and it did not help that all of us still had to go to the bathroom!

It was a tough 10 minutes until the next train as we all said our pieces to each other. It was bound to happen during the trip at some point, we are all still brother's after all-separated by a mere 46 months from 1st born to last born, with me being 3rd male out of 4.

I was used to routine turning into circus acts with some of my traveling to the stadiums so far, now these guys were aware of how best laid plans could change so fast and go awry.

When we finally arrived in front of Yankee Stadium, I decided because my brother Ken had a camera, he should come with me and we ran into the Stadium while the other guys went to the car to pick up items for inside the park.

We made it into the park at 6:56 PM and to our seats at 7:02 PM. My brothers came up to the seats with my dad after the anthem started.

Ken was the last brother to see Yankee Stadium-and it brought back memories of us watching the Yankees play some awesome games vs. the Toronto Blue Jays on the TV.

Ken's favorite player was Steve Sax back then-and my favorite player was Don Mattingly. We cheered all year for them to beat the Jays out but they didn't win the pennant in 89'—because the Jays did.

Mattingly never really recovered after his back problems and Steve Sax eventually was traded to the Sox so Ken and I cheered for the Blue Jays more because the Yanks were not as good back then-and the Jays always made the playoffs.

I loved Dave Winfield as a player with the 80's Yankees almost as much as Mattingly—so when he went to the Jays in their World Series run of 92-I cheered. Ken and I cheered Paul Molitor the next year for the '93 run.

I was happy when the Yanks won in 1996-but it was a bittersweet celebration for me because it was a year after Don Mattingly retired. The same could be said in 2009-when the Yankees won their 27th World Series-a year after Mattingly left with the Yankees with Joe Torre, in order to become bench coach in Los Angeles.

I love the Yanks. Derek Jeter personifies baseball. I saw a play in my first game at Yankee Stadium in which his team was up by 4 runs. Jeter was between 3rd and home, when Jason Giambi scorched one to the shortstop. Bobby Abreu had been on 1st. With a drawn in infield, the shortstop-(I think it was Mark Grudzielanek on KC) had Jeter caught cold. I watched as Jeter waved Abreu to third, and also yelled for Giambi to run to second. He stayed in the run-down until the men were at 2nd and 3rd before he was tagged out. Jorge Posada hit a 2 run single as the next batter.

If Jeter gives up, there are men at 1st and 2nd only-and not two men in scoring position which was the case. Jeter is always thinking.

W e watched as the bleachers yelled role call.

My dad had come up to his seat, "I love this ritual. My dad was referring to the right field bleachers calling out each ballplayer in the field until an acknowledgement was made by each of them tipping their hat in the direction of the bleachers in right.

"These are good seats even for being in the second deck," said Clint. His favorite player Vlad Guerrero completely booted one in the field only to have my brother say, "he will hit a homer to make up for it", which Vladdy did the same inning. Clint then explained that Vladimir always tries to leg out doubles on long singles because he still thinks he was 25—which Vladimir did the next time he was at the plate. Clint was super ecstatic when Vladimir threw his helmet after failing to make it.

Just like the previous night, and in his next batting at-bat, Vladdy then swung at a ball in the dirt right into a double play at the second basemen. The previous night in Boston, the ball had hit the fence in right field for a double.

. My brother Trent and I had gone to that Jeter game in May of 2006 together and we made it onto the 'ESPN' high light reel when A-rod smashed two homeruns into our section.

My dad and I watched our first Yankees game together sometime in the mid-80's (when he was home sick for a rare occurrence in his life)-in which the Yankees beat the Jays 22-5 and Mattingly went something like 4-5 with a few doubles, a homer, and I think Rickey Henderson stole about 7 bases.

My dad loved Yankee Stadium even before he visited it-in having been a Thurman Munson fan early in his adult life.

My brother Trent had taken both my dad-(and our Grand Father Lou Booth)-to a Boston Red Sox at Yankees game the previous year at Yankee Stadium-representing 3 generations of Booths at one game. My 82 year old grandfather had the time of his life because he had never been to any ballpark in the USA before.

For this trip I bought everyone a Yankees hat and t-shirt. While we would have great fun at the rest of the parks throughout the trip too, I had the most fun at our day in Yankee Stadium and in New York.

Yankee Stadium was full of history and nostalgia from the time you walked in. The bleachers had their own private entrance-with their own bathrooms and concessions-that were secluded from the other part of the stadium, but contained the most energetic and fun fans in the place.

The concourse of the main building was quite narrow and there was little concession space, but the place carried incredible ambience. The vendors were prominent in every aisle charging 9.50 for a beer-and being the loudest vendors in the majors.

There is no park in the majors that is more represented with t-shirts and team Jerseys then Yankee Stadium was or the new park is. Almost as fun as the game itself was staying after the game and taking pictures of the historic field in the background with the sweet tunes of Frank Sinatra's 'New York, New York, playing on an infinite loop after the game.

Having all 5 of us there for a game in the last season was wicked. All of us can say we made it to the old Yankee Stadium in the final season! It is my hope that all of us can make it to the new Yankee Stadium for a trip sometime together. Thanks guys-for that awesome day in New York!!

Oh yeah, the Angels won the game 12-6-but we got to see 5 homeruns hit.

After the game, I was called on my cell phone in the car. I was interviewed back home on CKNW 980 AM Radio in Vancouver. It was a call that lasted 15 minutes-and it was awesome to be sharing the experiences that I had with my brothers and dad as we made our way back to New Jersey.

Game#25 Day#24
Busch Stadium
St. Louis, MO
Aug.01/2008

I never thought anything was going to equal the previous day. We had arrived back at my brother's house to spend a quality morning with my nieces and nephew—and Trent's wife Kristy before returning to the road. It was a quick trip from Philadelphia to St. Louis. It was going to cost us a fortune to all take the shuttle into the Hilton at $17 each-so I got us on the next transportation shuttle bus, and then negotiated a deal with Budget to give me an extra few hours head start on the 24 hour airport rule—so I would not have to return after the St. Louis game to pick up the Mini-SUV, which had been the original plan.

Budget was awesome to let me have this deal early. I am a Fast Break member with them-and have/had spent a lot of money with them. We got a Mitsubishi SUV. My brothers thought it was a little small, but for a $65.00 rental that started out in St. Louis and ended up the next day in Minnesota-it was a great deal.

Yes we had a five hour drive from St. Louis to Chicago tomorrow, but we were all tough guys. I once again told them-"welcome to my world."

That day in St. Louis was myopic. My brother Trent knew a guy at head office St. Louis, and that gentlemen made a few calls and arranged for my dad and I too receive 'Field Passes'-and to be interviewed by Fox-Sports Midwest. I was almost in disbelief of that option, but it was now going to happen later that day.

This experience was even better because none of us had been to new Busch Stadium-so all of us were there for the first time. Overall it was my 29th stadium so I only had "The Ballpark In Arlington" for stadiums left to complete my active 30.

Much like Coors, Safeco and AT&T Park, the red-brick around the whole Stadium at Busch Stadium is top-notch. The back-drop of the arch makes any picture immaculate. The scoreboard in center field with the red-birds, Budweiser sign-and all of the retired uniform numbers let you know this club is rich in team history. The five decks all feature read seating which make the stadium extremely bright.

My dad and I were summoned by the Fox Sports News Sports Anchor, and it was show time. The announcer was a cool guy-and he asked me about the streak and where I was in the contest. Then he asked my dad a few questions. We were talking to an audience in the millions-as our pictures of the trip thus far-were being showed on TV to all of the viewing audience.

My dad told the announcer that "We are very proud of Doug as he has done this trip and included us in his journey, and that Busch Stadium ranks right up there with all of the rest of the parks."

I echoed those sentiments when it was my time to talk to the camera. I was surprised I was not nervous. I had kind of been interviewed a lot over the last 6 weeks-so this was almost to be expected for me now.

To be on field at Busch Stadium with my dad was one of my top 5 memories all time with him. We have some great pictures to prove we were there that close on the field. At was at this point that all of the hard work, sacrifices, spent money, planning, studying had paid off because my brothers and my dad were going to have these memories forever. I told the Fox guy that on the camera. The guy from Fox wished me the best-and then I waved to Albert Pujols even though he did not see me that well, he waved back. Not because he knew me or anything, but because he was cool. Man that guy is big!

I was about 20 feet from him-I wanted to thank him for saving my bacon that night in Atlanta, instead I told that story to Fox too. Busch Stadium is such an awesome park-and their staff was truly amazing to us Booth Boys.

What a game we saw, we saw as Ryan Ludwick crack 2 homers into Big Mac Land in Left Field, and Pat Burrell cracked a homerun that almost hit us in the standing room area we were standing in.

Had we known how awesome our seats really were-we would have sat there the whole game-we did sneak in the last few innings. None of us wanted to leave the ball park. We were only a few hundred feet from the Hilton where we were staying.

We made the trip out of the park and we headed to Mike Shannon's for steaks and drinks.

My brothers and dad partied as I told them I would drive all the way to Chicago the next morning. It was a noon start for those guys-and I was going to drop them off at 10 in the morning or so before I made another 6 hours drive to Minnesota. At least I knew the way to Minnesota-as I had done the drive in my cross country trip with the Cavalier in 2007.

We probably didn't even need the hotel room that night. I felt bad about having to wake these guys up early and after a few hours sleep only. The whole St. Louis to Chicago trip in consecutive trips always carried that time of ballgame. It was really 4 games in 3 ½ days.

While those guys all slept, I was in the business center re-arranging the rest of my journey. I had Minnesota the next night, and then a doubleheader matchup on Sunday that would put me at 28 games in 26 days. I then had Toronto on the 4th of August-before the Chicago White Sox was the trip finale on the 5th. My flights had been pre-bought for me to fly out of Texas on 5th because I knew I could always use my mom's flight pass from Dallas Texas to Toronto on the 4th.

She had already informed me that-should I make the double header-which I would have no problem flying into Toronto on her pass on the 4th-and then flying on her pass to Chicago on the 5th.

Again my ticket with American Airlines was flying from Dallas to Toronto on the 5th and from Toronto to Chicago on the 6th. This meant I would use my original flight if I missed the doubleheader of HOU-TEX.

Game#26 Day#25
The Metrodome
Minneapolis, MN
Aug.02/2008

I was anxious to get the day started-so I kind of rushed my family to get out of St. Louis. The previous night I had actually bumped into Jayson Werth of the Phillies in the lobby of the Hilton. I just told him that he was an awesome player-and that he looked like "EDGE" from wrestling, he said everyone always tells him that. It was a neat experience. I never got a chance to tell him what I was doing but told him I had seen him play 3 times already that month so he got the picture I was a big baseball fan. It was like 3:30 AM in the morning too-so I didn't really want to disturb him.

It was a very somber and quiet drive to Chicago from St. Louis. While I was focused on what I needed to do driving next-the air was filled with sadness as this was the day that we would be separated. My brothers and dad would go to Wrigley Field all together-and I would chase history by attending another game at the 'Metrodome.' Believe me, I wanted to hang out with these guys in Chicago-but we all knew I was so close to history. I had to move on with the streak. I had told the guys what I did in not chasing the Cleveland-New York long shot double header and they told me they would have supported my try if I had gone for it.

It would have backfired on me as the Cleveland game went 3 hours and 14 minutes-meaning I would have had only 75 minutes to catch the plane ride to Cleveland-in which the plane was delayed anyway-and I would have never made it to Yankee Stadium in 30 minutes from 'LGA'- during high rush hour anyway-my 2009 streak attempt would later teach me that.

At 10:30 AM in the morning we all posed for a picture in front of the Hilton at O'Hare Airport-and then I was on my way after hugging my dad and brother's. I was visibly upset for 45 minutes afterwards. It was a lot of emotion to deal with leaving my brothers and dad in Chicago.

It was great to have my family join me on the trip for a spell. I was only okay once the game at Wrigley came on the satellite radio. I, all of a sudden, had lots of energy. That Mitsubishi SUV was a great drive. I knew my course of action. I made up so much time heading into Minnesota-and I made it to the airport at 4:00 PM. I had 2 hours before 1st pitch. I explained to the Budget guy that I was in trouble with my luggage-and asked if I could leave it at the Budget window as I was coming back after the game. I showed him my ticket for the next morning-and told him I was not staying at a hotel because I needed to save money anyway.

The Budget agent agreed to let me keep my bags there. I actually mailed him Twins tickets later that month to say thanks.

Amongst 40,000 plus fans, I saw the Indians and Paul Byrd win 5-1. If there was a game I was not totally into it was this one. But now I was anticipating a big day to see the Astros doing the day and Rangers during the night. 1 of course made game #27 in 26 days at Houston before going through that thundershower at the 'IAH' airport to halt the breaking of the record.

I had some more drama when I tried to check in for my 5th of August flight to Toronto-because American Airlines had cancelled my whole flight schedule to Toronto from Dallas and then onward to Chicago. I had called my step-mother Nancy by then to have her book my flight. I attended my 30th stadium in Arlington Texas before hitting The Rogers Center and Us Cellular Field to -potentially have tied the World Record that Guinness currently said was the record.

It was an incredible journey that took 41 days and 41 games. I was a new man after it. I even made a game in Seattle for first pitch on my way home. I was so broke at the end of the trip I was lucky Seattle's concession stand accepted Canadian currency-and paid me back in American cash-otherwise I would have ran out of United States money.

In Toronto I had cashed in all of my Air Miles Voucher for future tickets-and had bought a set of 6 tickets to the game I was attending in hopes I could sell some for money in case I needed it like a scalper.

Well, I sold the tickets for $70- and that money rescued me at the end of the trip. I took a bus back to Canada in the morning-and followed that with a cab ride home.

I had made 51 plane trips (if you include the layovers)-had seen 41 games in 41 days in 30 different parks-visited 38 states-and racked up 40,000 miles in the Air! I had also driven 10,000 miles on the road. I spent 17,000 Canadian Dollars/or 15,600 US dollars for whatever currency you have.

I had resourced every inch of my being in order to make it to the end of my journey. My journey included 15 different radio interviews-8 different news paper articles, and I had taken over 1,000 pictures to chronicle the chase.

I made it home on Aug.08/2008-and worked for 3 weeks straight before I had a half day off before working 308 days in a row.

Dan Russell (of CKNW 980 AM Sports Talk Vancouver) interviewed me for a full hour over the Labor Day Weekend of '2008'-when he came back from holidays. It was fun reminiscing with him about the trip that was. Right after the interview, I found out my record-tying quest was definitely not the record at all as Josh Robbins had set the record for 30-26. For 2-3 weeks I was miserable. It ate at me. If you took out the All-Star Break-I actually had seen 30 games in 26 days. Or even the day I went to see my mom- I could have had gone and re-done a game n Cleveland that day. I was consumed. I worked hard and began to recover in my finances from the trip.

Right around the World Series time-they had begun to post the new schedule for 2009. I took a look at it for a couple of days and knew there was a possibility. No matter what happened I would plan on making it back out to the United States for another chance at the record in 2009. This time I would not have the all-star break as a penalty

I was determined-and would not take a day off between Aug.30/2008 and July.05/2009. I was armed with too much knowledge not to attempt this feat again. Whether I liked it or not-it was still going to cost a lot of money this time. The good news was that I had 4 round-trip plane fares in my back pocket thanks to frequent flyer miles and Air Tran Airways plane vouchers. I would have 13-15 free car rentals. I would stay at Best Western's all over the place with Air Miles collected between fall of 2008-and spring of 2009.

Much like 2008, I did not know whether I was going to have enough money until spring. At the end of April 2009 I knew I had enough.

My trip would be from July.22-Aug.14/2009 for a 30-24 attempt. When the Yankees and Oakland were rained out in an April series-and the make up game was changed to July.23 at night-I now had a 30-23 attempt-because I was in Toronto for a day game anyway-and had done the research for that such attempt amongst many other doubleheader scenarios that I researched.

I was lucky with this 2009 schedule, that all of my plane trip doubleheaders were within bus distance of Toronto. In April of 2009 the physical toll of working everyday almost made me lose the trip, but I rallied after that Yankees re-schedule. If you counted the 41 days straight of the record chase-I had not had a full day off in over 500 days. I flew to Las Vegas to rest before starting this madness all over!

STREAK ATTEMPT 3
JULY.22-AUG.13/2009

30 GAMES IN 23 DAYS

"THE STREAK WAS ALMOST OVER BEFORE IT BEGAN"

(Courtesy of www.ballparkchasers.com blog updates)

July.16/2009 DCB Says:

"So, I am sitting in my car at work when I decided to check on my Visa balance for the upcoming trip, (any ballpark chaser dreads the '$200" minimum buy in at the car rentals so it is good to plan ahead), when I realized my Visa Card was gone. Also someone decided to buy a bunch of gas on it.

The bottom line was I started to panic since it was my only credit card. I start the streak in 6 days, but I am starting in Vegas tomorrow.

Luckily my card issuing company is going to send it to a hostel for me on Monday. In my travels, I found hostels to be the nicest staff of any hotel/boarding place. I especially recommend www. hihostels.com. Their locations in Chicago, Los Angeles and Boston are really close to the ballparks and convenient.

I will have my new card in time for the trip and thank you' the USA' for offering rental cars, with debit cards at airports, as that is a lifesaver.

My point is to always have a back-up plan. I start for '30-23' on the 22nd of July, with a Pittsburgh and Detroit doubleheader attempt, follow my other blogs for a detailed schedule. Updates will be posted in here almost daily. I hope to see ya out at the yard!

There will be write-up blogs that are actually going to be time of updates written by fellow ballpark chaser Ken Lee in here at www.ballparkchasers.com while I pursue the World Record. I will add a little bit too each day's (**DCB Says :)** recap in order to summarize the events that took place, so thanks again for the help again Ken."

JULY. 2009

July.21-Kenneth Lee's Blog:

I have been emailing back and forth with Chuck for a while now and he asked me if I would keep everyone up-to-date about his World Record attempt of seeing a game (complete games) at all 30 Major League Baseball Ballparks in 23 days. He starts his record attempt tomorrow, July 22nd, in Pittsburgh and he will be calling me daily to let me know how it is going so I can keep everyone apprised of where he is and how things are going. He is in Kansas City tonight for a game, but it's not going to count for his record attempt unless things go badly and he has to go back and make the trip retroactive to this game. Hopefully that won't happen though.

This should be fun. As soon as he calls me I will be posting things right here!!

Good Luck Chuck- and HAVE FUN! :)

July.22-Kenneth Lee's blog:

3:40 PM (PST) - Just talked to Chuck and he let me know that due to a bad car service, combined with a ton of school buses picking up kids on field trips at the game at PNC, he missed his flight from Pittsburgh to Detroit, so it's now a 30 in 24 attempt! He knew going in that this would probably be the toughest doubleheader of the trip (of the 7 of them he will be doing), so far it looks like he was right.

So now what? Well, he will be catching a Greyhound bus to Toronto in about 2 hours, which will get him in up there around 9am and with a 12:37 PM, game tomorrow afternoon, he should have plenty of time to make it for the Indians vs. Blue Jays game at the Rogers Centre as the bus station is only about 1/2 mile from the park. As for the game in Detroit, it gets pushed back to the last game of the Quest, August 14th vs. the Royals, where he will be coming in via Boston.

Btw, the game Chuck caught in Pittsburgh was exciting. I had been keeping an eye on it and when I noticed it was 7-7 going into the bottom of the 9th I texted him about it and as I went to look and see what was going on, I noticed Brandon Moss hit a 3-1 pitch to deep CF for a game-winning HR and just then my phone beeped with a message "Game Over". He had been standing by the gate, ready to go, watching the end of the game... little did he know that the game wouldn't be the problem, it would be the traffic. I guess that's why he has back-up plans... on to Toronto! :)

P.S.-the game he missed in Detroit was the Tigers vs. Mariners, with "King" Felix Hernandez on the hill for the M's... BUMMER!

DCB Says:

"This doubleheader attempt was a wild one. I needed a faster game then the three hours it lasted. Worse was the sedan service sent a new driver out to pick me up-and he did not know where the other guy had agreed to meet me. Despite that, I still would have loved to not lose 45 minutes before we even left the area. I probably would have made the Flight to Detroit where I would have landed at 6:28 PM. I would have had 37 minutes to first pitch in Detroit-for approximately a 28 minute drive-but it would have been rush hour traffic.

Anyways, I still have a sweetheart double header-schedule. Despite not making this 2 games in one day I still have, Toronto-New York, Cubs-Brewers, Cincinnati-Chicago White Sox, Mets-Phillies, Indians-Royals and Angels-Dodgers. For Four of the seven Double header's I have afternoon flights involved in order to arrive at the second game, (Pittsburgh, Toronto, Cincinnati and Cleveland)-all of these I have a contingency plan of a Greyhound Bus onto Toronto-in order to fly out of the next morning.

Toronto would be home base in case of a miss-which will be my course of action in case I miss the tomorrow's flight to New York City after the Jays matinee game.

My step-mom Nancy is a retired airline executive-and as a family member-I am able to fly anywhere with a travel ticket. I have an itinerary for flights off to the next city on the scheduled day from Toronto all in my briefcase-in order to go ahead with booking in case of a missed flight.

My game the next day was in Toronto anyway. Thank goodness there are three doubleheader attempts by ground transportation in New York-Philly, Chicago-Milwaukee and L.A-L.A

If I had made the Detroit game-I was scheduled to travel to Toronto via Greyhound Bus anyway. I exchanged my refundable ticket-and actually received $9.00 back in the process. It didn't make up for the $85 sedan ride I had to pre-pay for in Detroit-and a failure to make the $185 plane ticket.

One last note on that flight to Detroit, I actually had a flight to Indianapolis, IN-with a stop-over in Detroit on a NWA flight. The airline was going to charge me $520 for the non-stop flight-but by searching for possible destinations where Detroit was a 'lay-over' I came across the Pittsburgh-Detroit-Indianapolis flight-where I could just walk-off during the layover. It was a sneaky way to save

$335. I am glad I did that because that would have really been brutal to have been out $605-instead of $270.

You learn to the let-go of the money in the Pursuit."

"This game today makes it 1 game in 1 day."

July.23-Kenneth Lee's Blog:

The only update I got is that he has made both games, was expecting a call but it was really late after the Yankees game. I had been keeping an eye on the game in the Bronx last night leading up to game time because it was raining. Ironically I had told him Wednesday that I missed my game there cause of rain and I was worried I might have jinxed him. I did get a text message last night at 7:39 PM (PST) that read "I am so lucky game didn't start until 9:40 PM, arrived at 7:45 PM with a flight delay". Since they got that game in, a 6-3 Yankees win (their 7th in a row); sometimes a little rain can be a good thing. It's on to Chicago for the Red vs. Cubs at 1:20 PM, (Harang vs. Wells) and then to Milwaukee for Braves vs. Brewers at 7:05 PM (Vazquez vs. Parra) on Friday.

DCB Says:

"After that sedan debacle yesterday, I am sure to grill every other sedan driver on my travel plan—to ensure we were always on the same page from that point forward. Poor sedan service guy in Toronto fielded 3 calls from me-to navigate the proper game plan-for leaving the Rogers Center. I was also lucky to have woken up 2 minutes before the Greyhound Bus left the Buffalo station en route from Pittsburgh to Toronto after falling asleep briefly. I arrived in Toronto at 9:00 AM. The good news was that I was only a half mile from the park.

Thanks to new airline regulations in 2009, there is a fee that was new to my streak attempt-this I did not have to deal with in last year's streak. Each flight I have checked baggage would have cost me $15 per flight, per bag. This caused me to think extremely creative. I had arrived in Chicago on the 20th of July to see a White Sox game for a retro-active scenario purpose. Part of this trip though was to check my baggage with Amtrak-Milwaukee Station, so that when I flew to KC-Pit-Det-Tor-in succession I would save some money and baggage claim time. I am paying $6 per day for my 2 bags at Milwaukee-and I am due to return there on the 24th for the second leg of a doubleheader attempt. I am going to retrieve my bags on the 25th morning before flying out of Milwaukee's Airport to Colorado. The items I had in the first four days of the trip were throw away clothes. I had one clean pair of clothes for this day which I am wearing, so the game plan was to hit Roots Clothing Store-and buy a new set of clothes for the next day. I had accrued Roots Air Miles Gift Certificates by doing internet searches for the trip anyway.

After arming my self with a new set of clothes today, I ate a gourmet hot dog and fries from Union Station-where Street vendors surround the area.

The Rogers Center, while it was the first stadium with a retractable roof, has slipped in the rankings due to the other ballparks catching up. The park has a hotel within the building still, and The Hard Rock Café is still a great place to watch batting practice from. The upper deck tickets make it feel like you are forever from the ball, but the stadium is not that bad.

The scoreboard replay monitor is amongst the best in baseball. The ambience is not bad considering there are not many fans-but you will really want to go when awesome teams play like the Yankees-Red Sox or Tigers are in town.

Kerry Wood shut the door down in the 9th inning on the Jays for an Indians 5-4 win-in a game that lasted 2 hours and a half. It was 3:15 PM now and I had a 5:05 PM flight-that arrived in New York City at 6:25 PM. I was picked up correctly this time-and the sedan driver got me out of the traffic chaos-once again I had to visit the Jays on Community Youth Day just like Pittsburgh had been the day before, I am sick of those Big Yellow Buses I can tell you that.

I was at the airport at 3:40 PM-and at the International Terminal—one problem, my cell phone dropped out of pocket into the limo backseat. I raced to the payphone and used my calling card number-and dialed the sedan's driver from memory, (probably a good thing I called him four times that day) and the guy came right back. That 10 minutes would have cost me if I was in normal security, however I have the Air Nexus Pass Card. I bypassed the security line-up as a secured traveler-who has already been pre-screened on a background check. Judging on the regular line I might have missed my plane.

Still reeling from nearly losing my cell phone, I left my Day-timer at the eye-dent station. I always do a quick check after security clearance-and I realized it was missing. Good news was I found it quickly, but the bad news was had to re-do the security walk through yet again. I felt like an amateur today but I still made it to the gate with plenty of time for the flight.

My plane had not left the runaway at 6:00 PM-as I watched the rain pelt the surrounding area. The pilot informed us that we would arrive at LaGuardia Airport at 7:15 PM. I heard, (through friends by phone)-that it had been raining in New York and the game forecast also did not look good. I had to try to make it to the stadium. As per Guinness Book rules-I would not enter Yankee Stadium if I missed 1st pitch but at least I would be on pace for my flight to Milwaukee the next morning.

I could not have been more pissed off at my sedan service at LaGuardia. Not only could he not speak any English-but he did not even know where Yankee Stadium was, are you freaking kidding me? By the time I made it to the area it was 8:35 PM! Since I could not talk to the guy, I did not know whether the game had been cancelled or had started. It was raining at a steady pace for the whole time I had been in New York.

I saw a couple of fans walking down River Ave as I reluctantly handed over my $70 for sedan service. I asked them if the game had been called?

I was jovial enough to run to the gate when I learned the game never had started and was in the middle of a rain delay. It donned on me that if all would have been good with the weather I would have missed the first pitch. That sedan driver would have interrupted a historic chase with his geographical ineptness. I made it into the awesome Yankee Stadium and jammed a New York Steak Sandwich-into my face as fast I could devour it for $15. Feeling lucky to have a shot at a game, I bought a new #25 Mark Teixeira Yankee T-shirt to bring good luck.

The public address announcer made an announcement over the speaker system that they would make a game decision to play or not at 9:10 PM at night. I made it to my seat and prayed. It was windy, cold and raining intermittently from slow to medium. The stadium was only half packed-and the people were anxious. There was a tribute playing to George Steinbrenner on the JumboTron. It had been most unfortunate that the 'BOSS' died right before I made it to the New Yankee Stadium. The moment of truth had come.

They decided to play!!! It was instance where a rain delay actually helped me again. It was the first hurdle to overcome. There still needed to be 4 ½ innings to make a legitimate game Oakland jumped out to a 3-0 lead on C.C Sabathia and while I was sad the Yanks were losing-I was hoping the game would make it to the 5th inning's end with a team in the lead.

The Bottom of the 4th saw Mark Teixeira, my current favorite Yankee, blast a homer-and the Bronx Bombers took a 4-3 lead to the 5th. Sabathia just got better as the night rolled on-and the Yanks staved off the A's and the weather for a 6-3 win. It was awesome to be in the stands when the faithful, chanted a one letter C, followed up with another one letter C for Sabathia. That and the Hip Hip Jorge-for Jorge Posada are classic. Highlighted this night, was also the bleacher creature's role-call which is just as loud at the new ballpark and my favorite tradition in which positions 1-9 are called with the player's last name. The fans keep chanting until the player responds with a tip of their cap in acknowledgement.

I took public transportation in the form of a subway train (and bus)-to arrive back at 'LGA' at 2:00 AM in the morning. I now have four hours from my next flight."

"These 2 games today make it 3 games in 2 days-with an improbable-international double!"

July.24-Kennneth Lee's Blog:

5:36 AM (PST) - Just got a message from Chuck, he is in Milwaukee about to pick up his rental car and head down to Chicago. Sounds like he has a good game plan on where to park to be able to get out of there fast after the game and beat the traffic on his way back to Milwaukee for the nightcap.

5:10 PM PST) - Talking to Chuck right now, he made it to Milwaukee, just 3 minutes before first pitch... had actually sent me a video clip of him there just as the first pitch was being thrown. Was a crazy one coming up from Wrigley for this one, but he made it and sounds really excited about it. Said that Miller Park is packed tonight and the crowd is really loud, which I could hear over the phone!! He's going to enjoy this game, Braves vs. Brewers, and then it's on to Coors Field in Denver for tomorrow night.

DCB Says:

"Crazy day of emotions up and down, I arrived in Milwaukee and decided I had enough time to retrieve my baggage at the Amtrak Station-to do a trial drive from the highway into Miller Park-in order to refresh my memory once again as to the best path.

I had been so lucky that I arrived in Milwaukee a few days before the streak started. Had I not took an Amtrak train into Chicago-I would have not noticed that all trains for the summer of 2009 were to be delayed 20 minutes by construction. It helped me alter my game plan for this doubleheader attempt, but made it less of a percent chance to make the Cubs-Brewers double header.

I would arrive in Chicago and pre-drive the route back to the 94 highway West-in order to be aware of what turn offs I needed. I made the decision to find a parking spot on W. Irving Park-which would mean I only need one turn From Irving onto the highway from where I was going to park. Since it was my 4th time in the area I was aware of the traffic flow out of Wrigley Field.

I am not proud of this however lord knows I paid a lot of money for Best Western hotel stays in which I stayed there for 5 hours or under, but I will take advantage of several free continental breakfasts despite the fact I am not a hotel guest en route from city to city off of the highway. To me, I also have so many early flights out of the airports I am never eligible for the continental breakfasts from the hotels I am staying at anyway-this was just an extension of my breakfasts had I took a rain check. I have enough Best Western stuff in my briefcase to look legit with hotel gift cards, and old hotel card-keys it definitely helped me play the part. What I like about The B.W's is that they also have communal internet which is perfect for me to print off boarding passes, game tickets, and check into flights early enough to achieve preferred seating.

I was not liking the amount of construction I saw in the other direction towards Milwaukee-as I drove into Chicago on Hwy 94-East. After pre-driving the route in the morning, I paid $20 to park a few miles from Wrigley on W. Irving Park. I was going to have to run when the game ended-to give myself a leg up on the traffic. I love Wrigley Field-and was so happy to be inside with 90 minutes to spare. I tried to take a picture with my Camera/Video 16 feature device. The battery power was dead. This was not good at all for my evidence. I had been charging the camera in the car so this was a mystery to me. I had my cell phone for pictures-but this was going to be a tough one. I could take a few pictures at each park with the camera for pictorial evidence, but I was going to need a lot of use with my cell phone.

I have already started sending Ken Lee a picture from each city and to document him as a witness I am phoning and texting him for records purposes. Except my Cell phone was on a low battery and I would have to conserve the use. I realized at that point the cigarette jack fuse must have been blown in the rental Pontiac G6 that I am driving. I searched hi and low for power outlets at Wrigley-to no avail. I was too tough it out.

There is no better pure baseball experience then to watch a game at Wrigley Field. How could I be upset? I would make do with what I had. The game was flowing nicely into the ninth at only 3:50 PM. It was a 2 hour 30 minute game at this point-and I was in decent shape. Then Kevin Gregg entered the fold. He loaded the bases, took forever in between pitches, and I was resorted to watch the game in the concession area-in the concourse near the exit. I had limited power in the cell phone to only videotape one of the TV's playing in the concourse. Finally Gregg got the save-and preserved the win-despite giving up 2 runs. I guess I should thank him for not letting the Reds tie the game at least. I had the gate security guard at the exit sign my log sheet-and I took off in a sprint down Sheffield Ave, past the Sheffield House Hotel in no time flat.

It was 4:20 PM when the game had ended-and the Google map directions call for a 2 hour drive to Miller Park from Wrigley which is a joke! It is a Friday night, and I drove within the speed limits, but sped up and pulled lane changing maneuvers whenever it was warranted enough to have done my best. It was going to be close, I just could not tell with the construction, and what the foreseeable path was to be. I needed this Milwaukee game-but it would not have killed me to miss it. There was a Milwaukee make up date on Aug.15, one day after the Detroit game make up, but this would mean no margin for error from that point forward. I still have two more flight doubleheader-including a hard Cincinnati-Chicago double. Doing the streak is like a flush in playing cards. You want to give yourself enough middle cards so that you can add cards on either side from the middle, like having a flexible schedule for the 2nd game of the double header missed teams.

I made it to National Ave by 6:42 PM-Miller Park lot by 6:51 PM-and was extremely upset when the lot attendant directed me to the overflow parking- which was more than a mile from the front entrance. I never ran harder-and out of breath under that tunnel up to the gate. People were calling me 'Forrest Gump." By the time I got to the security gate it was 6:58 PM. I was looking to get in by 7:03 PM, but still needed to find an employee to sign my log book-and acquire some sort of video or pictorial evidence that I was there. Enter Milwaukee staffer Rob.

Rob recognized me from the previous year-and led me through the gate-I was so happy to see the big guy I almost hugged him- instead I opted for him to sign my log-sheet and then I texted Ken Lee a picture of me at Miller Park at 7:04 PM. No sooner did I do that and hit the video recorder option on my cell phone—I was lucky enough to tape P.A announcing "Your Milwaukee Brewers." I had made this double header by the skin of my teeth. I crumbled onto a nearby staircase and sent Ken my newest video.

My cell phone died after I called Ken-but my camera got my end of the game scoreboard pictures before giving out. The game was kind of not relevant at that point. I would not have to worry about weather either as Miller has a retractable roof. It had started to rain outside. The game ended up 6-3 for the Brew Crew.

I made this doubleheader-and am confident to have enough evidence to prove it. I actually got some sleep last night and my electronics are fully charged!

"These 2 games today make it 5 games in 3 days."

July.25/July.26-Kenneth Lee's Blog:

10:44 AM (PST) - Chuck is at Minute Maid Park in Houston seeing the Mets vs. Astros (Hernandez vs. Moehler). He was excited to find a parking spot for $3, instead of the usual $18, so he treated himself to some "Gourmet" food at McDonald's... got to love life on the road! He had a great 45 minute interview with CKNW Sports talk 980 AM, a station from his hometown in Vancouver on Saturday night.

Yesterday he was in Denver for the Giants vs. Rockies (Sanchez vs. De Le Rosa), which was an 8-2 Rockies win. He did get rained on though and at one point in the 4th it looked like they were going to have to bring the tarp out, but they got through it and he got another game in.

He heads to Oklahoma tonight, staying the night in Ardmore, and then it's on to Arlington for the Tigers vs. Rangers (Galarraga vs. Hunter) at Rangers Ballpark!
He's now seen 7 games in 7 parks in 5 days!!

DCB Says:

"Colorado did not come without a hitch as I had to watch the entire game in a threat of rain. That was not upsetting as the horrible service I received at Thrifty Car Rental-Denver Airport as the Manager had refused to rent a car to me-citing my credit card was not authorizing it. It was a confusion of the new computer system confusing Canada's CA abbreviation with CA- California. This time I was able to pay the $400 cash deposit after fighting with Thrifty's Head Office. I am worried about the rest of the trip because I am in possession of 11 more free-car rental days I have amassed from renting from Thrifty Canada year round. I have never had a problem with Thrifty Canada but Thrifty America-you almost ruined a world record streak!

My interview with CKNW was a nice way to settle down after the day in Denver. I stayed at a Motel 6 right off of 49 Ave for $48. It was a mere 3 miles from Coors Field.

The next day I was so relieved when the car agent at the Houston Airport Thrifty said I was approved for the Car rental. It was essential to have a car this day as I have a game in Arlington tomorrow and have to drive there after the Minute Maid game.

The Astros were crushed 8-3 by the Mets. After the game I thought I was on easy street-just driving to the 5 hour drive to Ardmore when a multiple car pile up delayed me by another 2 hours. I am now up past midnight but will be able to sleep in this morning in the city or Ardmore, Oklahoma."

"These 2 games make it 7 games in 5 days."

July.27/July.28-Kenneth Lec's Blog:

9:15 PM (PST) - Just talked to Chuck as he is in the great state of Texas. He made the game in Arlington-a 5-2 Ranger's win vs. the Tigers, and is now on his drive back to Houston where he will catch a flight to Baltimore for Camden Yards and the Royals vs. the Orioles tomorrow night.
He sounds like he is really having fun. Last night he stayed in Oklahoma, though he was already in Texas, just so he can say that he has been to the state of Oklahoma... so he is knocking off states, as well as ballparks!!

The rain has been following him around though, first it was in the Bronx, then Denver and as he made his drive towards Arlington he was listening to the weather on XM radio and told me from the sounds of it, he honestly thought they were going to call this game before it even got started. Then the clouds parted just long enough to get the game in, with it actually starting to rain in about the 8th inning (I was watching on MLBEI and couldn't believe he was getting rained on again!).

As we were talking he said it was starting to storm pretty good-and due to the lightning we were actually losing cell service. It doesn't storm anywhere like it does down south!
He has had a few problems though, not just missing his flight in Pittsburgh due to a terrible sedan service and lots of traffic, but he has been double charged by rental car companies which have really made things hard on the bottom line as well. The way he is doing this trip he will be using several different rentals, so to be 2 times charged for even a couple of them are a nightmare. Worst part is that he is 3,000 miles from home so it's not like he can just sit down and call the bank and rental company and say "HEY!" On his time schedule finding time, or the place, to use the internet is tough as well. He told me last night that he has even taken a few moments as he drove down the road to stop at a Best Western and feed off their free internet for a few minutes to do some banking to free up credit limits before hitting the road again... clever if I do say so myself :)

Oriole Park at Camden Yards tomorrow - Royals vs. Orioles (Bannister vs. Berken) - a look at weather.com shows 86 degrees, partly cloudy only a 10% chance of rain at game time... should be no problem getting this one in.

DCB Says:

"It was the only real mistake I have made in booking tickets and plane fares in 2009. 2008 I had made way more errors. Due to changing my plane schedule at the last minute on www.cheapestticketsnow.com-I have scheduled the wrong flight day from Baltimore to St. Louis. I have known this since back in June though. I actually have found a better alternative—which made life easier for me. Since I am in Cincinnati tomorrow, I found a flight courtesy of Air Tran Airways, for $39 that landed me in Dayton, Ohio flying in from Baltimore early. Since I have my free car rental days-I will use one of them at Thrifty and only pay a $23.32 charge of arriving in Dayton, Ohio before returning the car to Cincinnati Airport the next morning. I will have to switch cars at 'CVG' because of the 24 hour time limit for the rate, but it beats my original design for Baltimore-St. Louis-Cincinnati.

I was going to fly into St. Louis-catch the Hilton Shuttle downtown for $17(despite not being a hotel guest), and watch the game at Busch before taking an all night Greyhound Bus to Cincinnati for that same $39. The next day I would have 90 minutes to make it to The Great American Ballpark once the Bus arrived. The Greyhound Bus leaves at 3:30 AM in the morning though, so at least I will miss that.

However I called the ticket agent today on a hunch. Part of that 4 trip fare I purchased while making this mistake-included 3 more trips after the 1st trip-which I am going to miss tomorrow. I am going to be in the air to Baltimore tomorrow when I will supposed to be flying out-little did I know that if you miss the 1st fare of your itinerary-that the rest of your flight itinerary is automatically cancelled. I thought I was immune to the other three plane rides because all of them were with different airlines. Apparently whatever air carrier holds the 1st leg of your multi-airline-multiple flight bookings is the airline that is the rights holder of the whole trip. If you no-show they have the authority to cancel you out entirely in the next plane trips. I had American Airlines rip me off in the 1st year by having to not —show for a flight in which they cancelled two additional plane rides. That was a result of that Houston rainstorm that forced me to stay an additional day in Arlington

This set me off today and I spent half of the day arguing with Continental Airlines. In the end, I was charged $150 for changing my flights. Fortunately for me, the flights I am exchanging this for are cheap because of flying out of just Phoenix and Minnesota. It is still amazing to me how the airlines put the charges on you. Suddenly I am not disappointed in my self for using that layover-walk-off maneuver. Again I had to let the money go.

The game in Arlington went for the home squad 5-2. I was happy there were clouds-and that it had stopped raining-to make it tolerable to watch a game all the way outdoors at 'The Ball Park in Arlington.' It is always hard to take picture evidence of Texas's scoreboard because there are many places where you can't view it in the grandstands.

The Ballpark In Arlington has one of the fairest parking modules on the outside. The closer you are to the stadium the more the parking goes up. It is more like $1 increments rather then $5 or $10 though. The Park is very spacious and big. The area past the center field is massive, with the white grandstands ranging all the way up to the corporate offices. The bullpens along the right field fences are amongst the best sightlines in baseball. The concourse is gigantic-and there are poor sightlines for standing room only viewers. I always get energized when I hear the 'Natural" theme song when a home run is hit. I also never get tired of 'The Stars at night song.' The heat is unbearable at times but you have plenty of indoor facilities to avoid the heat-and get into the air conditioning buildings for a couple of minutes of refuge.

I made it back to Houston's Airport despite a scary gas station fill in the outer city limits-and caught the early flight to Baltimore.

When I arrived in Baltimore I could not believe how hard it was raining! For three hours (while I am in a Marriot in Linthicum, MD) I watched in disbelief, I was sure this game was not to be played tonight. I was going to make plans to switch my Aug.12 game of Atlanta to Baltimore, and then move Baltimore to Aug.15. I know my schedule so well I have a contingency plans for most of the trip. My Aug.12 flight was placed well from Minneapolis. It starts Minnesota and stops off in New Jersey for a layover and continues onto Atlanta. With it only being A.M hour's when I land in Jersey-I can take a train to any Eastern city in time for game time. Each date had a depth chart similar to what you see in sports.

At 4 PM-it was still threatening rain-but you could see it slowly dissipating. I took a cab to the game-promptly ate a barbeque rib sandwich with coleslaw and French fries, and it was totally outstanding. I have resisted eating much ball park food up to this point out of affordability and credit issues, but now that I have been paid my monthly salary from work-I have credit to spend again. I have started a string of spending at every concession stand for the next three weeks-with McaFee Coliseum being the only park I plan to miss.

What a brutal game-(that did not need extra innings-the Royals won the game 1-0.) Going back to the hotel tonight-I had no idea where I was and decided to take the light rail service all the way to the airport-that way I could print off my morning boarding pass to Dayton as the hotel's printer was out of ink. Also because of this idea came another-to take the free shuttle back to the hotel which was a better thought then trying to find the hotel in the area where I am not too familiar with. I always tip every shuttle bus driver for the airports and hotels. These workers have a tough job and deserve a couple of bucks."

"These 2 games make it 9 games in 7 days."

July.29-Kennneth Lee's Blog:

9:40 AM (PST) - Just got a message from Chuck, he is on I-70 heading towards Indy on his way to St. Louis after having flown into Dayton. No surprise to him, as things have gone, he is getting rained on! That rain seems to follow him wherever he goes! A look at weather.com says 78 degrees with a 10% chance of rain at game time, then again it said that in Baltimore also and there were t-storms right up till game time! (Side note: the irony of this rain for him is that here in Western Washington and up in Vancouver, his home town, it's been freakin' hot lately! It was 104 here in Olympia yesterday!)

So, Dodgers vs. the Cardinals tonight at Busch Stadium (Kershaw vs. Pineiro) then it's an all night drive to Cincy after for the Padres vs. Reds (Stauffer vs. Cueto) before hopping a flight bound for Milwaukee, which has a stop in Chicago where he will walk off the plane and use a sedan service to get to U.S. Cellular in time for the Yankees vs. White Sox (Pettite vs. Colon) game. He mentioned how, since he will have time, he is going map out the drive from Great American Ball Park to airport and drive it a few times, just to make sure he has it down and knows alt routes if needed.

When he makes the doubleheader tomorrow, that means the worst he could do is tie the record set by Josh Robbins at 30/26 barring any PPD's!

DCB Says:

"I was happy my credit card has worked at a Thrifty two times in a row! The Airport Thrifty Car Rental was off site-and I was worried about not renting a car-because I would have to take the shuttle back to the airport and rent a car from someone else-only to pay brutal fees for last second rentals and an even higher one way drop off fees. It was a tense few seconds at the rental counter.

Once I got the Hyundai Accent (thanks Thrifty-these cars are horrible on gas)
I was able to hook up my satellite radio-and listen to baseball chat for the drive to St. Louis. The one benefit of driving more than 300 miles in your trip is you can take the car back on empty to exercise that re-fuel option!

There is nothing like a 15 inning game to end the night either!

"This game today makes it 10 games in 8 days."

July.30-Kenneth Lee's Blog:

12:20 PM (PST) - Rain, Rain go away! And stay the heck away! Got a message from Chuck and about 1 hour into the game today at Great American Ballpark, Padres vs. Reds (Stauffer vs. Cueto), it started raining cats & dogs! He said he was actually very surprised that they didn't call the game, but they got through it as it cleared up in the 8th inning. That game is just now in the bottom of the 9th with a score of 7-1 Padres, with the park almost cleared out, which works great for Chuck with less traffic to deal with plus he has a great parking spot for a quick getaway. His flight from Cincy to Chicago is at 5:54 PM (EST), so he should have plenty of time to make that flight as the game should be over any minute now.

12:34 PM (PST) - Game is over in Cincy, 7-4 Padres, after the Reds put 3 on the board in the bottom of the 9th... too little, too late... and he is off on his way to the airport, bound for Chicago and the Yankees vs. White Sox (Pettite vs. Colon).

Last night he was in St. Louis at Busch Stadium and saw a 15 inning, 4 hour and 53 minute, marathon that ended when Pujols singled in the winning run off Jeff Weaver (former Cardinal no less). Needless to say, on the drive to Cincy this morning he was using all of the tricks he could think of to stay awake.

5:20 PM (PST) - Chuck's flight actually made it to O'Hare on the north side of Chicago about 20 minutes early, however they didn't have a gate ready so there they sat! Once he deplaned, grabbed a cab and told the driver he needed to get to U.S. Cellular before game time, the cabbie laughed. He finally got close to the park, thanks to some great driving by someone that obviously knows the streets of Chicago well, and got out of the cab at 35th street and start his run in (with duffel bag and briefcase in hand) towards the gate. As he was running, he could hear the National Anthem being performed.

After a quick deal with a guy at the gate to let him in to a section he shouldn't have been in, he got in to get his picture at 7:09 PM, just 2 minutes before the scheduled 1st pitch!! However, as he saw the field he saw it covered by a tarp still and found out the game has been delayed about 20 minutes, so he was good to go! What is it with all this rain lately??

In the morning it's back to O'Hare for a flight to San Francisco, then it a short drive to Oakland for the game tomorrow night and San Fran on Saturday with a flight to Miami looming on Sunday.

DCB Says:

"I made it to the Cincinnati airport in no time flat after the game. Driving the route before hand was the way to go. It was a tense few minutes in Chicago. The Cincy-Chicago doubleheader is unique in that you actually use negative minutes when you factor in the time change from Eastern to Central for the plane ride. If it wasn't for O'Hare being so slow-I would have had no problem at all. Chicago is the hardest airport to fly in and out of because of the wind and plane traffic. While I would not make it a habit of flying out of 'CVG' due to high plane fares, the security line-ups are minimal when you need to race to a gate fast!

"These 2 games today make it 12 games in 9 days."

July.31-Kenneth Lee's Blog:

Interesting morning for Chuck, as he sat on the plane, on the tarmac in Chicago at O'Hare for 2 1/2 hours waiting to take off for SFO! Because of that he barely had time to make it to the Oakland airport to pick up his girlfriend and get to the ballpark by 5:30 PM (PST). Had he opted for a little more rest and taken the 12:00 PM (CST) flight out of Chicago, he would have missed this game because of the delays! "Always take the first available flight!" he says, which makes perfect sense, especially after this.

7:06 PM (PST) - He was looking for blue skies, especially no rain, and he found it in Oakland on the first night of Ricky Henderson weekend. Kind of cool to be there when they salute one of the newest Hall of Fame members.

Oakland Coliseum - "Whatta dump!" Parking cost $17, which was twice the price of his ticket! The Blue Jays are in town to play the A's (Richmond vs. Braden), so he even got to hear the Canadian National Anthem tonight.

Tomorrow he just has to cross the Bay Bridge into San Francisco for the Phillies vs. Giants (Blanton vs. Lincecum). He missed seeing Cliff Lee's Phillies debut by 1 game, but he does get to see the wonder kid, 11-3 Tim Lincecum.

Sunday he hops a non-stop flight to Miami for the Marlins vs. Cubs game at 5:05 PM (EST) (Dempster vs. Nolasco).

DCB Says:

"It was another day-and yet another flight-delay in Chicago. Really, I am now surprised when there is not a flight delay from there. Just another observation-"can we get some new carpets at 'LAX'-this airport rates as one of the worst for cleanliness!

"This game today makes it 13 games in 10 days. "

August.1-Kenneth Lee's Blog:

5:00 PM (PST) - Chuck has made his way across the bay to AT&T Park...

8:54 PM (PST) - "AT&T Park is the best ball park anywhere, especially with that scenery. I must have taken 70 picture of the park tonight" is what Chuck told me tonight on the phone, with some really happy Giants fans yelling in the background. He didn't get to spend much time there as this was the fastest game so far on his trip. The game, a 2-0 Giants win in 2 hours and 14 minutes, saw Lincecum get his 12th victory by only giving up 7 hits in 8 innings and striking out 8! He was part of a crowd of 42,694, which included about 300 dogs in the bleachers taking part in the "Dog Days presented by Milk-Bone and Kibbles 'n Bits". They even had a pregame doggie costume competition. That must have been a sight to see!

Tomorrow he jumps on a plane bound for Miami for the Cubs vs. Marlins game (Dempster vs. Nolasco), where hopefully he will be able to meet up with Bob DeVries, who is also on a Quest to see all 30 this summer and Land Shark Stadium is #26 for him. He then heads for Tampa via Greyhound, for the Royals vs. Rays and a great pitching match-up of Greinke vs. Kazmir at Tropicana Field.

DCB Says:

"This game today makes it 14 games in 11 days."

August.2-Kenneth Lee's Blog:

4:22 PM (PST) - Got a call from Chuck in the bottom of the 9th, with the game tied at 1-1. As we talked about the ballpark, he told me that Jake Fox jacked a shot to put the Cubs up 2-1 and we figured this game was over. We kept talking about his upcoming schedule, with a 1:30 AM greyhound ride to Tampa, then it's off to Washington DC for Nationals Park, with 3 doubleheaders in 4 days looming in the not so far off future. As we talked it hit us both that Land Shark stadium is the 1/2 way point for him, he has now officially seen full games in 15 parks in 12 days!!

Shortly after we got off the phone I saw where Gregg gave up back-to-back jacks to Ross (his 2nd of the game) and Uggla to win it in the bottom of the 9th! Whatta finish! On to Tampa!

DCB Says:

"This game today makes it 15 games in 12 days."

August.3-Kenneth Lee's Blog:

9:00 AM (PST) - Chuck is at Tropicana Field for the Royals vs. Rays game. Although he almost did not make it……

DCB Says:

"Like I have said a few different times before, a trip such as this magnitude can send you off on roller coasters of emotions. Sunday night at 9:00 PM EST I was driving back to the rental car outlet in Miami when a circus of events transpired that almost made me miss the nooner at the 'TROP' on Monday. 1st off my car rental did not have an interior light which made it hard to navigate the directions back to Miami Intl' airport. Some of you also may know that the car rental outlets for Miami Airport are located in the suburbs.
Well, it took me an hour plus to arrive back to the car rental center. I was on the shuttle back to the airport to take a cab to the Greyhound Station-when I realized I left my sunglasses clip to my prescription glasses in the rental car!

I went back to the car rental place-but they were gone when the vehicle was re- rented. You have to move on when stuff like this happens. Stuff is lost during a record chase, plane trips are eaten, advances in payments to car service and hotel deposits still come off your credit card. So I took a cab to the Greyhound station, but the cab driver did not understand English-and took me to the bloody bus service main station for repairing and servicing and NOT THE actual bus depot! I was going to miss my bus-and have to go rent a car from the airport. I had a contingency car rental in the event of a late game-but at a 65 dollar cost plus gas.
If you book with www.expedia.com-you can actually make reservations without even using a credit card, but just by using an email address-just don't put your frequent flyer choice rewards preference in the column in case you decide to tank it! Most cities I have alternative car rental plans that were just contingency rentals in case, I have always planned to tank them but they are good to have in case of need.

The supervisor at the bus service center then told me that I was in 'luck' because the driver of my 2nd connection bus from Ft. Lauderdale to Orlando was in the back lot picking up a new bus to take. They bent the rules and allowed me on board without screening my luggage. The driver could not have been cooler because he was a fellow 'Yankees Fan'. I made my trip to Tampa Bay-and then realized that I needed the ST. Petersburg bus terminal and not just the Tampa Bay terminal.

This meant I would now arrive at 11:30 AM in downtown St. Pete for the 12:08 PM game in downtown St. Petersburg. Thank god it was only a five minute walk, but I had luggage.

Again, Greyhound came to the rescue and allowed me to leave my luggage until after the game. I made it to the game at 11:45 AM. This just shows me once again some of the easiest travel plans can be disrupted.

I will now sleep for 12 hours-before I fly to Baltimore for noon tomorrow and then drive to Nationals Park to take in a Nat's game. After the game, I will drive to New Jersey-where my brother lives-to stay until the morning hits. It is a NY Mets/Philly double header on the 5th of August, and after the game I will get another quick snooze before driving back to Baltimore for an early morning flight to Cleveland on the 6th.

I will be using the subway to and from Progressive Field for quick transport. That game in Cleveland on the 6th is at 12:10 PM-and I have a flight at 5:07 PM to Kansas City, so let's hope for a fast Indians game! It is a 26 minute subway ride to the airport from the park. I will arrive in KC at 6:12 PM-where a sedan driver will pick me up and drive to Kauffman Stadium. On Friday I have a game in San Diego-and then it is the doable doubleheader of LAA at 1:10 PM, and LAD AT 7:15 PM on SAT, what a nice doubleheader to have in the same city for a change. I will need 2 out of the three doubleheaders to break the record with a 30-25 finish, (Provided all other games are played on time and I make it there on the one off days) If I make all 3 it will conclude the 30-24 streak. Even if I collect only the LA double header I will tie the record.

I have 3 games in a row after that are in domes or retractable roofs in, (SEA/ARI and Minnesota) as these were strategically planned as well. Having domes for stadiums are better to have later in the streak because the later you are in the streak-you are not as flexible with re-scheduling games due to inclement weather. The other dome stadiums-Miller Park, The Rogers Center, Minute Maid and Tropicana Field were either only 'suitable' games based on geography (Houston was before Texas-and Tropicana was after Land Shark Stadium or part of doubleheader).

The streak is then followed up with Atlanta on the 12th, Boston on the 13h and the last game scheduled currently is the 14th in Detroit. I like my chances."

DCB Says:

"This game today makes it 16 games in 13 days."

August.4-Kenneth Lee's Blog:

1:53 PM (PST) - Chuck has made it to our nations capital. Got a quick text saying he got in at 1 PM (EST) and had time to check out the town a bit, go see the White House, and then head Nationals Park. I told him he better have a "Chili Half-Smoke" for me at Ben's Chili Bowl. It's "Free T-Shirt Tuesday" and he got a free t-shirt for the 4th time on this trip... got to love free clothes! :) Tonight's game is Marlins vs. Nationals (Johnson vs. Martin).

7:45 PM (PST) - Just got a really excited voice mail from Chuck. He said that the game he was at Nationals Park was awesome and between that and the 25K+ that was there the overall experience was great and that he's going to have to move National's Park up on his overall list now.
He is currently driving towards NJ, where he will meet up with his brother for a doubleheader tomorrow...

It is Citi Field for the Cardinals vs. Mets (Lohse vs. Niese) in the morning (the last of the current parks he needs to see to have seen them all) and then a train ride to Philly puts him at Citizens Bank Park for the nightcap of the Rockies vs. Phillies (Del La Rosa vs. Happ). After the doubleheader he drives back to Baltimore to drop off the rental car before hoping a 6:59 AM flight to Cleveland for an afternoon game, Twins vs. Indians (Blackburn vs. Carmona), then its a quick ride to the airport for a flight to MCI in Kansas City where he will have less 53 minutes to make it to Kaufman Stadium for the nightcap of the Mariners vs. Royals (Vargas vs. Chen).
The Cleveland/Kansas City doubleheader is the one I personally felt will be his toughest. When he nails it, he's got this thing in the bag baring any PPD's!

DCB Says:

"Due to a stupid construction detour on the Beltway, I lost my course for over an hour on the side streets of the Maryland State Limits trying to had back to the Beltway Highway. You always have to carry a U.S Road Map with you at all times-and not depend solely on online direction websites!

"This game today makes it 17 games in 14 days."

August.5-Kenneth Lee's Blog:

11:02 AM (PST) - Chuck has made it to Citi Field in Queens for the Cardinals vs. Mets game... he has now seen all 30 current MLB Ballparks! CONGRATS CHUCK!

1:50 PM (PST) - Chuck just called from the Amtrak Station on his way to Philly, having got there in time, he should be in to Philly at 5:55 PM (EST), which gives him 1 hour and 10 minutes to make the 25 minute drive with his brother to Citizens Bank Park. As for Citi Field, he felt it was ok... most certainly an improvement over Shea Stadium, but in his opinion a step down from Yankee Stadium. He still ranks it in the top 10, but not as high as AT&T or Busch Stadium. The game he saw was kind of a bummer, as the Mets were going away 9-0! It took 1 hour and 15 minutes for the first 2 innings alone! But it sped up after that and he got out of there in plenty of time as we know.
Worst off, he is now fighting a pretty nasty cold, or so it sounds like on the phone, and he did say that he is sick... and with a couple more doubleheaders coming up too... UGH!

3:44 PM (PST) - He has made it to Citizens Bank Park with plenty of time to spare... stay away from the Crab Fries man, they ain't worth it! :)

6:51 PM (PST) - The Phillies won 7-0 (Happ tossed 8 innings of 4 hit ball and even had a double that had the crowd going crazy!), which gave Chuck 2 home team shutouts today! Not only that, the home team has won the last 8 straight games he said. He loved the Phillie Phanatic and says that he is one of, if not the best, mascots in the majors... I totally agree, even though I am partial to the Mariner Moose lol :) As for food, he had a cheese steak and called it, "The single best ball park food." Other places might offer a better selection, but the Philly Cheese steak is the best single item anywhere. I didn't get to ask him, but I am assuming he is referring to the "Campos" cheese steaks there in center field. Ironically, I saw Campos on "Road Tasted" with Paula Dean's boys today, and man they did look awesome!!
He's headed back to Baltimore for a flight to Cleveland tomorrow, then on to KC and yet another doubleheader.

DCB Says:

"The Philly game was the most important game as flexibility was concerned. The only thing I could have done is re-do the Philly game on the 7th[th] and pay top dollar to fly out to LAX on early Saturday the 8th's date. I would have to move Seattle to the 15th at end of the streak-and pay a lot of money to fix that situation up with all penalties financially.
Even the Kansas City miss will not kill me-as I could retroactive the streak to the 21st of July and make a 30-25 record count. The Philly game was a record clincher if I can make the easy Dodgers/ Angels doubleheader."

"These 2 games today make it 19 games in 15 days."

August.6-Kenneth Lee's Blog:

8:55 AM (PST) - Chuck has made it to Progressive Field aka "The Field Formerly Known As Jacobs". He'll be seeing the Twins take on the Indians (Blackburn vs. Carmona).

4:42 AM (PST) - Kansas City, Kansas City here he comes... Chuck is in KC and getting ready to see the Mariners vs. Royals (Vargas vs. Chen). We had a great chat about the game in Cleveland, a 2-1 Indians win, in 2 hours and 37 minutes, where Kerry Wood shut down the Twins in the 9th for his 15th Save. After the game he had to sprint darn near a full mile to get to the subway station in time, he barely made it, to ride the train out to the airport for his flight to Kansas City.

In KC, he had no problems making it to the park and after sending me his pix, he called and we chatted about things, ball park food and his upcoming schedule. Tomorrow he flies to San Diego for the Mets vs. Padres game (Perez vs. Correia), then it's a bus ride to Los Angeles for a doubleheader that includes Dodger & Angel Stadiums.

DCB Says:

"Doing that Progressive to the airport via light rail station terminal practice run served me well as I nailed the timing of it coming out of the Indians game. Kerry Wood is my favorite all time closer now! He is a perfect 3-3 in the last two years of saves that I have needed in the afternoon of a day-night doubleheader. The Mariners being pulverized 8-2 did not even wreck the night.

Massive props to limo driver Timothy Cates in KC-by far the best sedan service of all time. He was waiting for me in front of 'MCI' with a name placard, had a water waiting for me, and had a pre-arranged deal with a parking lot attendant in order to have me closest he could (legally) to the park by driving. Awesome work Tim!

"These 2 games today make it 21 games in 16 days."

August.7-Kenneth Lee's Blog:

10:12 PM (PST) - Chuck is on the West Coast....he had a pretty uneventful day today. His morning flight to San Diego went as planned, he checked into a hostel which is 1 block from the ballpark and got to the game early. I got my call in **about** the 8th inning with the Mets leading 2-1. Chuck said it was actually a pretty boring game, figured the crowd had a lot to do with that... even if they were celebrating Rickey Henderson's HOF Induction there in San Diego this weekend (the 2nd time on his trip he got to take in a celebration for Rickey, the last time was in Oakland a few days ago).

He also told me that this is the 4th straight year he has caught a game at Petco Park and it's kind of lost its magic. He said he honestly thought that it might have something to do with the caliber of team on the field as well, but either way, Petco has dropped some in his rankings!

Tomorrow he heads to Los Angeles for a battle of the top 2 teams in the AL West in the afternoon game at Angel Stadium, Rangers vs. Angels (Millwood vs. Weaver). Then he heads across town for the night cap at Dodger Stadium for the Braves vs. Dodgers (Kawakami vs. Kershaw).

As I am typing this, his game in San Diego just ended... whatta finish! The Padres came back to tie in 2-2 in the bottom of the 9th with no outs. Then they loaded the bases, which included an intentional walk, and Everth Cabrera took a 3-2 pitch, the 10th of his at-bat, and jacked it for a game-winning grand slam!! Don't get much better than that and keeps his streak of home teams winning alive for another game!!

DCB Says:

"This game today makes it 22 games in 17 days."

August.8-Kenneth Lee's Blog:

7:52 AM (PST) - A few interesting stats: With San Diego's walk-off win last night, Chuck has now seen 3 walk-off wins on his trip. The other 2 were in Pittsburgh (his 1st game of the trip) when Brandon Moss hit an HR to win 8-7 and in Florida where Cody Ross and Dan Uggla went back-to-back for the tie and then the win. The Padres win also continues his streak of home team wins to 11 straight now with an overall home team record of 16-6.

8:16 AM (PST) - Chuck will be on CKNW 980AM in Vancouver at 10:40 PM (PST) TONIGHT!!! He will be live from the parking lot of Dodger Stadium.

11:31 AM (PST) - In La La Land... Chuck has made it to the land of Halos- Angel Stadium of Anaheim. Should be a great game, Millwood vs. Weaver... national TV at that! :)

4:30 PM (PST) - Got a call from Chuck around 4 PM, he was on I-5 headed to Dodger Stadium after a quick game at Angel Stadium. He told me he got a tip on some free parking that was close to the interstate and only about 1/2 mile walk to the park. He gave it a shot and it worked out great! As it is, he had just over 3 hours till the night game and I told him he had plenty of time to go to Disneyland if he wanted lol :) He didn't want to take the chance with the LA freeways… I don't blame him!! :)

This was the last doubleheader of his trip! He nailed it! Tomorrow it's Seattle for the Rays vs. Mariners (Kazmir vs. Rowland-Smith). I was hoping to join him for the game, but will be unable to do so, sadly. However, I will be here to update everyone :)

11:05 PM (PST) - Just listened to Chuck's interview on CKNW via www.cknw.com. If you missed it, he was on his cell phone still at the Dodger game because it was a long one as it went into extra frames. He was live on the air as he told us that the Braves won it, and broke his streak of 12 home team wins by beating the Dodgers. It was a really good interview.

DCB Says:

"These 2 games today make it 24 games in 18 days."

August.9-Kenneth Lee's Blog:

12:43 PM (PST) - "Home Sweet Home"… Chuck is in Seattle at Safeco Field and ready for game # 25 of his trip, the Tampa Bay Rays vs. Seattle Mariners (Kazmir vs. Rowland-Smith). The end and World Record is in his sights now with Arizona, Minnesota, Atlanta, Boston and Detroit left on the schedule in the next 5 days.

2:17 PM (PST) - Got a great call from Chuck just a few minutes ago... he's at Safeco and was justifiably excited about getting parking a few blocks from The Safe for $7 to go along with his $7 bleacher seat and his amazing Garlic "Rally" Fries! We talked about the Mariners and how Ichiro always has a great game when he is there.

But let's back up a bit... last night at the Dodger game, he finished his interview with CKNW and ended up falling asleep in his car in the Dodger Stadium parking lot.

Much to his surprise nobody came by to wake him up and tell him to move along. Luckily he woke up in time to get to John Wayne Airport at 6:20 AM for his 8 AM flight. He made it but never anticipated the full hour it would take to get through security!! He made his flight, which was slightly delayed, and he got to Seattle, a bit late, but with his buddy waiting at the Denny's across from Sea-Tac airport with a meal ready for him, he had a bite to eat and headed for the ballpark.

After the game tonight he heads home for a bit and with some clean clothes he will head to Phoenix tomorrow for a game at Chase Field, Mets vs. D'Backs (Pelfrey vs. Davis). Minneapolis and the Metrodome await him on Tuesday...

DCB Says:

"This game today makes it 25 games in 19 days."

August.10-Kenneth Lee's Blog:

6:37 PM (PST) - He's made it to the desert! He was scheduled to make it to Chase Field in Phoenix a couple hours before game time, but thanks to flight delays (yet again!) and being thankful he wasn't picking up a rental car (cause it would have taken too long), he arrived at the park via cab with only 10 minutes to spare! Had he needed to get a rental car, he would have been toast!

Thankfully he had done his homework and knew it would be better to just cab it... being prepared and knowing the lay of the land pays off yet again!

Tonight's game is the Mets vs. D'Backs (Pelfrey vs. Davis). He has certainly been getting his fill of the Mets as this is his 4th or 5th time seeing them on his trip.

Chase Field is ballpark # 26 in 20 days! Tomorrow marks the 3 week mark of the trip and he will be at the Metrodome for the Royals vs. Twins (Davies vs. Blackburn).

DCB Says:

"Unfortunately this date was always a risky proposition as I needed to be back in Canada between Aug.7th and Aug.11. I needed to cash my work pay-cheque in person, and it was another strategically placed time frame where I ran out of clothes. A week or so back my girlfriend had met me in the BAY area with a duffel bag full of clean clothes and she was able to check it because I flew her down to Oakland with Southwest Airlines-the only airline that does not charge for baggage.

Clothes considerations ran rampant throughout the trip:

July.17-20 I was in Las Vegas, Atlanta, Milwaukee and Chicago, I checked two bags at Amtrak baggage service July.19-(1 dirty-1 clean.)

July.21-July.24-I had three sets of disposable clothes as to enter the Rogers Center with my briefcase-with a change of clothes for the next day only. The clothing I wore on the 20-21-22 was thrown out. The clothes I wore on the 23rd had been washed at the hostel in Chicago on the 20th.

July.24-I was able to do laundry at the hotel in Milwaukee-I now had 6 days worth of clean clothes.

July.25-July.29-I had a car each day-and did not have any doubleheader attempts so I was able to have clothes in cars when they were not in hotels.

July.30-I have one clean set of clothes-and had the other dirty day of clothes is in my briefcase. I even threw out a vacation bag with 4 days worth of clothes before my flight to Chicago.

July.31-My girlfriend showed up with a nice sized Duffel bag with 4 days worth of clothes. I had no double headers again until the 5th. I gave her 2 days worth of laundry to take home.

Aug.6th-I washed all of my 5 sets of clothes at my brothers and only took 2 days worth of clothes-(1 on me and 1 in briefcase.)

Aug.07-I took 2 loads at 2 separate times to have clothes for the 8th and 9th clean.

Aug.10-I will fly to Arizona with only one extra set of clothes that I am able to have clean when I go home to Canada for one night on the 9th.

Aug.11-I will wash my aug.10 clothes in Phoenix.

Aug.12- I will do another load of laundry in Atlanta. I will buy another day's worth of clothes from EWR Airport.

Aug.13-I will do a load of laundry in Williamsport PA. I am driving the rest of the way and make it back to New Jersey or another hotel to do the 2 sets of clothes I will have with me."

"This game today makes it 26 games in 20 days."

August.11-Kenneth Lee's Blog:

6:38 PM (PST) - Chuck's World Record attempt has him in the Twin Cities tonight for a game at the Metrodome, Royals vs. Twins (Davis vs. Blackburn), where he will be seeing the Royals for the 4th time in 3 weeks (plus he will see them in Detroit on Friday to complete the trip).

He had an easy flight in, finally. He took the light rail from the airport to the game, and will take it back as well. He was able to get a cheap seat for the game, $10, out in the home run porch. He's got an early flight out in the morning headed to Atlanta for the Nationals vs. Braves (Stammen vs. Lowe) game.

Speaking of the light rail (public transportation), he told me that he has found so far that for less than $10 R/T you can take public transport to and from the parks in Minneapolis, Cleveland, Arizona, San Diego, Baltimore, Oakland, Pittsburgh and for both parks in both New York and Chicago. Got to appreciate that, much cheaper than getting a rental car, and more than likely faster as well…. plus no fee for parking at the game!

On his trip so far the home teams are 19-7. With a quick look at the Twins game right now, it's the top of the 4th, and the Royals are up 9-1… Twins got a long ways to go if they are going to give Chuck another home team victory.

DCB SAYS:

"This game today makes it 27 games in 21 days."

August.12-Kenneth Lee's Blog:

3:37 PM (PST) - Chuck made it to Atlanta just after 3 PM (EST). After having issues, yet again, with trying to get a rental car from Thrifty (some problem about his credit card being used too much, too many times, with the difference between CA meaning Canada and CA meaning California… whatta hassle), he grabbed a cab and headed into town. With a quick stop at the nearest Best Western to use their internet for free, he made it to Turner Field for tonight's game, Nationals vs. Braves (Stammen vs. Lowe). He got his tickets when he got to the park and was able to pull 2 upper deck seats, behind home, for $11! Day of game tickets can be an awesome way to go…

After talking to him for a while I got to thinking about a few things, so I asked some questions. There are things that he has to deal with that most of us, meant American citizens, and wouldn't have to deal with on a trip like this, such as: When booking cars or hotels online as a Canadian citizen you have to deal with the exchange rate. So if you book something in advance, the price you pay when you use that reservation may be more than when you booked it… talk about a pain in the wallet! This is why he has booked as much as he could on Priceline and prepaid for it, the problem with that is if your schedule changes, you're out. But if everything goes smooth, your set and you don't have to worry about the exchange rate.

Another issue is that after tomorrows game in Boston, Tigers vs. Red Sox (Verlander vs. Bucholtz), and he has to drive to Detroit. It's not the fact he has to drive, as it's the way he has to drive. Most of us would just go the quickest route, which takes you from Boston to Detroit, via Buffalo and into Canada. No big deal, right? However, as a Canadian citizen, he can not drive a U.S. rental car into Canada. So he has to take a different route that, according to my mapping software, adds just over 2 hours of drive time!! It really makes you think about how hard this trip would be for anyone to do, yet when you add to that the fact that there are things that he simply can not do, it makes it that much more difficult as well as much more impressive!

DCB Says:

"The whole Thrifty-crap cost me an additional $125 last night because I had a free rental day. Instead of driving around comfortably to my hotel in the city outskirt-you left me at the Car Rental Facility-3 miles from Atlanta's airport! I called a cab at my own expense and made the guy an offer. I did not need transportation hassles. I had an early flight to Boston today so I gave him $125 for-Four cab-rides-over 12 hours-that included transportation to and from Turner Field.

Robert, the cabbie from Atlanta, you saved my bacon yesterday day pal! He waited outside the exit of Turner Field for me after the game-and I made it to the hotel in no time.

I learned too many times never to take anything for granted while traveling. I can only imagine now that had I not made the right decision to fly back to Seattle for that Aug.09 game-and risk that 5:42 PM Phoenix land on day of game-in order to line my pockets with some extra cash for the last few games of the trip-1 would have been in Atlanta yesterday without money to spare. I would have been risking public transit. Once again, thanks a lot Thrifty! You can bet I wrote your customer survey up very negatively back to you when you sent it me your satisfaction survey! You will make novel history for the worst car rental place in America!

"This game today makes it 28 games in 22 days."

August.13-Kenneth Lee's Blog:

10:49 AM (PST) - A Yankee fan in Beantown... Chuck has made it to Boston Tigers vs. Red Sox! It is going to feature-(Verlander vs. Bucholtz). This was originally scheduled to be game # 30 in 23 days, but is now # 29 in 23 days. He had been worried about the weather and so far so good. He is under cover in case it starts raining, sitting in the right field grandstands.
He got to see an interesting pregame ceremony as today is "Tickets for Troops" day and they saluted the military with over 1,000 tickets being donated to members of the armed forces by both regular fans and season ticket holders. I got to watch the ceremony on TV here at home and it was quite touching, including having the father of a local soldier that was killed in Afghanistan throw out the first pitch.

After the game he has to get outta town right away and head to Detroit for # 30 in 24 days. He had a decent drive ahead of him, just over 850 miles or so to do in about 25 hours or less. The World Record is in reach now... as long as the rain holds off in Boston!

2:00 PM (PST) - The rain held off, thankfully, and the game is over, # 29 is in the bag and Chuck is on his way to Detroit for # 30 and the World Record. He was able to get his rental car, a Toyota Yaris, without any issues this time and will be making a stop tonight in Williamsburg, PA, home of the Little League World Series, which puts him right about 440 miles outside of Detroit.

Next up: Game #30 - Comerica Park, Royals vs. Tigers (Greinke vs. Washburn)... history will be made!!

9:45 PM (PST) - I just got a call from Chuck and he is in Wilkes-Barre, PA, about 70 miles from Williamsport. He called to let me know that he will be on CKNW Sports Talk Radio at 10:10 PM (PST). So in just a few minutes you can go to www.cknw.com and listen to Chuck... maybe even call in and ask a question!!

DCB Says:

"That Boston game still scared the crap out of me because I had no recourse of action if the game was called today. Boston was not playing at home again for a while. It was always a hard game to get out of the way in Beantown. I liked this particular option because I was done the game at 4:30 PM-and if I needed to drive anywhere left in the streak I could have. I could have even made it to Milwaukee if I had to make up that game by car. I had pre-purchased a car for a four day rental in Boston-as that was where I would end this streak either way(fail or succeed) and I can take a flight back to Vancouver from Boston on the 17th.

I was in touch with the guys at CKNW back home while I was driving last night but I was not sure if I was going to find a good enough phone line to be interviewed for the spot at the right time. I found a gas station that had a payphone with decent reception.

It was good to hear from Dan Russell last night, as he had been on vacation for the first few interviews this summer but his fill in host Stu Walters has done a great job setting up every interview I had ever had with 980 AM Sports Talk Vancouver for the last 2 summers. I informed Dan that I thought it was poetic justice that I was staying in Williamsport PA for the night-during the time the Little League World Series is being played-before driving to Detroit today. After I finished on the radio I made it to the Best Western here in Williamsport for one of my 5 hour stays.

"This game today makes it 29 games in 23 days."

August.14-Kenneth Lee's Blog;

12:18 PM (PST) - The day is finally here... today Chuck Booth will make history as he becomes the fastest person to see a home game at all 30 Major League Ball Parks. I can only imagine how he is feeling as the game draws near...
I did get a call from him a few minutes ago. He let me know he was about 25 miles outside of Detroit and would be meeting up with some friends there to hang out before time and then head to the game together.
Funny story is that this family, the Salter's', met Chuck at a game last year when he made this attempt. They had read an article about him in the Detroit Free Press last year and then saw him at a game and introduced themselves. They have been big supports of his on both of his attempts. What's really interesting is that they were all supposed to get together for game # 2 on Day # 1 of the trip, but after missing his plane in Pittsburgh bound for Detroit, he reluctantly had to tell them he wouldn't

be there. Now, because of that, the Salter's family gets to be with Chuck as he attends game # 30, at Park # 30 on Day # 24!! You really got to love how things all work out like that.

Game time is 7:05 PM (EST) at Comerica Park, Royals vs. Tigers (Greinke vs. Washburn). As soon as I get confirmation he is at the game, I will post it!!

3:11 PM (PST) - With just under an hour to go until game time, I have confirmation that Chuck is at the ball park with the Salter's...

6:27 PM (PST) - CONGRATS CHUCK BOOTH!! You are the World Record Holder!! With a walk-off HR by Brandon Inge in the bottom of the 9th, the game has ended in Detroit and thus Chuck has officially seen 30 games in 30 MLB parks in 24 days!!

Just got a call from Chuck, he is celebrating! What a way to end your World Record breaking trip with your 4th walk-off if the trip! He and 35,000+ Tiger fans got to see an awesome 2 hour and 20 minute game that ended 1-0 thanks to Brandon Inge.

DCB SAYS;

"Thank you to the Salter's for enjoying this record breaking last game with me. Ken summed it all up there. Fireworks in a 1-0 walk off homer for the home team to end the streak-is priceless!! This game makes a historic 30 games in 24 days-and officially makes me the World Record Holder!!

This game today makes 30 games in 24 days-which sets a new world record by 2 days-and beats my 2008 best attempt by 5 days.

DCB FINAL WORDS OF THE WORLD RECORD 2009 TRIP:

"While this 2009 record trip did not have as much fan fare or publicity-it was fun to enjoy the baseball games for what they were. I chose to write about the 2008 more because it was way more entertaining-and carried much more drama! Plus the additional family members that were part of 2008 made for a better story.

It was also pure luck that on two double headers, (being saved by rain delays) in my favor to help attain the record. I also had the knowledge of being to each of the stadium before hand-so I was well prepared.

I have applied to the folks at "Guinness for my 30 games in 24 days submission"-I was tentatively accepted—provided I give them some more documented evidence on the Milwaukee and Chicago doubleheader. I have since re-submitted the claim-and will know if I am the Guinness Book of World Record Holder very soon-for now I will be happy enough being the 'World Record Holder.'

If I can steal a line from the movie 'Rudy' that always resonated with e in all of the stadium chasing- "In this world you have nothing to prove to anybody but yourself."

My family and friends thought I was crazy in trying a second attempt-but I knew I could break the record in my heart. Even if I would have failed what an incredible experience to have done this journey 2 years in a row. Having only gone to 11 games throughout the whole year in 2010 I recognize how lucky I am to have done what I did in the summers of 2008&2009.

My advice to you is to chase your dream and don't let other dissuade you from them-they are your dreams and not theirs! Another saying I came up with during the chases is-persistence is not only an option it is the only option!

Of course I always have quoted the great Vince Lombardi—"The Quality of One's life is in direct proportion to their commitment to Excellence." Yes I wrote this exact quote in another book it always applies to life

Thanks and happy baseball park chasing!! **DCB**

BALLPARK RANKINGS:

<u>NOTE FROM CHUCK BOOTH REGARDING BALL PARK RANKINGS:</u>

For the purpose of this book, I comprised a ranking of all 30 current Major League ballparks based on a number of columns, from Stadium Experience, to food, to tickets, to parking and accessibility, staffing, affordability and value. I came up with these ideas by polling 10 *Ballpark Chasers* that had been to all 30 current ballparks-and the polling came back with this ranking scheme. It was not my initial intention to post these in the book- but felt the merit of the book would have suffered if I did not share these results. <u>Ballparkchasers.com</u> has **nothing** to do with these rankings as they provide the write-ups and guides on how to experience each ballpark with no bias whatsoever given to any given any specific ballpark. It is ballparkchasers.com opinion that everyone should experience each park for themselves and make their own decisions of rankings later.

The ballparks are put in the chaser section based on the rankings I have come up with-along with counting all the votes from other *Ballpark Chasers*. Here are the top 30 ballparks: they will appear in order as they stand here in the section that you are reading below.

BALLPARK RANKINGS 1-30

1. **AT&T PARK-SAN FRANCISCO, CA**
2. **FENWAY PARK-BOSTON, MA**
3. **WRIGLEY FIELD-CHICAGO, IL**
4. **PNC PARK-PITTSBURGH, PA**
5. **COMERICA PARK-DETROIT, MI**
6. **SAFECO FIELD-SEATTLE, WA**
7. **BUSCH STADIUM-ST. LOUIS, MO**
8. **CITI FIELD-FLUSHING MEADOWS, NY**
9. **COORS FIELD-DENVER, CO**
10. **NEW YANKEE STADIUM-THE BRONX, NY**
11. **MILLER PARK-MILWAUKEE, WI**
12. **ORIOLE PARK AT CAMDEN YARDS-BALTIMORE, MD**
13. **CITIZENS BANK BALLPARK-PHILADELPHIA, PA**
14. **TARGET FIELD-MINNEAPOLIS, MN**
15. **THE BALLPARK IN ARLINGTON-ARLINGTON, TX**
16. **DODGER STADIUM-LOS ANGELES, CA**
17. **MINUTE MAID PARK-HOUSTON, TX**
18. **GREAT AMERICAN BALLPARK-CINCINNATI, OH**
19. **US CELLULAR FIELD-CHICAGO, IL**
20. **PETCO PARK-SAN DIEGO, CA**
21. **NATIONALS PARK-WASHINGTON, D.C**
22. **TURNER FIELD-ATLANTA, GA**
23. **CHASE FIELD-PHOENIX, AZ**
24. **PROGRESSIVE FIELD-CLEVELAND, OH**
25. **ANGELS STADIUM-LOS ANGELES, CA**
26. **ROGERS CENTER-TORONTO, ONT, CA**
27. **KAUFFMAN STADIUM-KANSAS CITY, MO**
28. **TROPICANA FIELD-TAMPA BAY, FLA**
29. **SUN LIFE STADIUM-MIAMI, FLA**
30. **MCAFEE COLISEUM-OAKLAND. CA**

CHUCK DOUGLAS BOOTH SAYS:

"The old Yankee Stadium would have ranked in the top 3 but it is no longer active so it is excluded. Also, Shea Stadium-(had it been included) would have ranked in the bottom four ballparks. The 'Metrodome would have been in the bottom 5 or 6 parks of rankings A lot of people would say that the old parks of Fenway and Wrigley should be number one-to which for stadium experience alone they would be 1 and 2. However, there are other categories to factor. Simply put, those parks are just too expensive compared to the top park in San Francisco. The reason San Francisco was so high is because they finished in the top 3 in every category. The park is immaculate! They have the best food, they offer affordable tickets, the park is easily accessible, their staff is amongst the best in baseball-and to top it off the fan atmosphere is incredible (along with being in one of the best cities of America). While the ballparks ranked in the bottom 10 are in that position, there is never a bad day when you are at one of these parks. Each ballpark has their own identity-and it was incredible to have *chased* all of these parks two years in a row-in under a month! I did most of the first columns of: **TRANSPORTATION: and INTANGIBLES:** based on my travels from each cities airport and ballpark. I have put forth some additional items into the 'Chaser Guides' (that were not there before)-based on my experiences. Unless it is outlined in the guide itself, most of the information comes from all of the members at www.ballparkchasers.com. If you have purchased and e-book-just click anything under linked in reference to hotels or sights if you are on the internet-and it will take you right to that website.

Look for the 'DCB SAYS'— for my personal write ups.

Ballparkchasers.com-was created by Craig B. Landgren with the vision of connecting baseball fans around the world, especially those with the life goal of visiting all the 30 Major League Ballparks. Since going live, Ballpark Chasers has doubled each year in total members and quickly has become the Internet's largest collection of amateur ballpark images. Whether it is learning how to score tickets, acquire a game plan before embarking on your ballpark travels or creating an online scrapbook to capture your baseball vacations, Ballparkchasers.com is the *Mecca* for ballpark enthusiasts-and we hope you join our community soon. There is always room for more members at www.ballparkchasers. com and it is free to sign up!

The Chaser Guides are a compilation of all the suggestions, tips etc. passed on by the founder of Ballparkchasers.com along-with the members within his website. Craig's vision is to make each park visit a little easier and with a world of wisdom and knowledge. We hope you find the information useful and enlightening.

BALLPARK CHASER GUIDES:

1. AT&T PARK

SAN FRANCISCO, CALIFORNIA
HOME OF THE SAN FRANCISCO GIANTS

TRANSPORTATION:

The skinny on San Francisco Int'l Airport-(SFO) is: When bidding on flights to San Francisco--do it from www.kayak.com--make sure you click the icon that says nearby airports. Oakland is only a 40 minute drive away from the ballpark and 'SFO' is slightly faster at 20 minutes. Always figure out the best price. You may even find that flying into either 'SFO' or 'OAK' is cheaper flying in-and cheaper flying out of the other airport. You must consider the one-way car rental option as an expense. If you are flying from the 'Pac Coast'-there will be many non-stop flights that are offered for good rates. If possible, try and fly with 'Virgin America or 'Alaska' as they are the best airlines on the West Coast. If you are flying anywhere else pick the cheapest flight. Keep in mind that Oakland is on the list of 'Southwest Airlines' favorite cities, and have reduced fares. This is the key because they are the only airline to offer free luggage checked. 'SFO' is one of the more expensive places to rent your car from--the car rental facility is also located a 'tram' ride away from the main terminal in the 'transportation center.' The best option here is to bid on your car on with www.priceline.com. First find out what the average daily rate for the given day you want and bid 50% of that column—the strategy here is too low ball the offer and gradually increase it until it is accepted. If your bid is accepted then Priceline takes full payment from you right there on the spot--if it is declined they make you alter your class of car to re-bid within 24 hours. Don't be discouraged to wait the 24 hours--bidding in anger is not the answer. If you are staying in the downtown area you do not need a car mostly everything is accessible for a small cab $15-20 cab ride. If you do have a car you are going to pay a parking fee at hotels and this can be quite pricey. The ballpark charges a lot for parking as well--note here if you are going to visit the Fisherman's Wharf take advantage of their $10-15 daily rates that gives you till midnight to take your car out of their lot. When you are at the Wharf it is about a $10-15 cab ride to the park and the same to return. This will eliminate traffic. There are any cab-stands outside Pier 39. You will pay $40 for parking between AT&T Park and the wharf anyway. Most car rental agencies offer a gas deal if you drive less than 75 miles--you don't have to refuel at the return and they give you the best gallon rate-if you are just going to Oakland and back it is nice or within S.F. There is however a toll for going over the Bay Bridge-coming in from Oakland-and traffic is very difficult from 12pm-6pm. The 'Golden Gate Bridge' also carries a toll so carry lots of small bills! If you decide not to take a car then the 'Light Rail Tram'- is located on the bottom deck of the 'Transportation Building' and hits many of the main streets of San Francisco.' The Light Rail service lasts long in to the night--however return trams to the SFO airport are less frequent. The price is $8-11. The Northbound Tram goes all the way to right outside the 'McAfee Coliseum' even. If your hotel is in the downtown/Chinatown you are a few miles within AT&T Park. Note*****Do not try to walk to the Fisherman's Wharf from downtown sector unless you wish to walk about 3 miles of hills. Pay the $10-15 cab ride as the cabbies know the street better than you do (lots of 10 miles mph speed limits).

WHERE TO STAY?

The following lodging is within 1.5 miles of AT&T Park.

Unlimited budget

Harbor Court Hotel
Courtyard by Marriott- San Francisco Downtown Hotel
The Palace Hotel

Moderate budget

Best Western Carriage Inn
Beresford Hotel
Hotel Mark Twain

DCB SPECIAL:

Powell Hotel -this is for those people that can afford a 3 star hotel at a reasonable rate. I stayed there for 2 nights with my girlfriend and it was perfect--they offer lots of packages with built in tickets already. The hotel is a 20 minute walk from AT&T-and is closely situated to the trolleys for a historic ride or two.

Chaser Budget Traveler

Bay Bridge Inn
Super 8 Union Square
Best Western SFO Airport- Is a more moderate rate and convenient towards the airport for future travels.

******Extreme Ballpark Chaser Special--Especially for those dedicated travelers that are looking to save money. Check out www.hihostels.com . San Francisco has 3 of these hostels. These hostels run for about $37-$40 and have continental breakfasts in some cases--ideal for that singular traveler. I have stayed at HI Hostel's in San Diego, Los Angeles, Boston and Chicago and they are lifesavers as most of them have a communal student center to which there is a decent price on internet searching and vending is always good. Lots of these hostels have built in deals with restaurants and entertainment facilities to save a few dollars in that city as well.

WHERE TO EAT?

The Acme Chophouse is the place to go before a Giants game. Attached to AT&T Park, the Acme is home of the best organic, naturally raised meats without those yucky hormones and antibiotics. We recommend making an online reservation if eating here before or after the game. To get a real feel of

San Francisco, try the Paragon Restaurant (only 1 block from AT&T Park). Locals hit up the Paragon for drinks and a meal before each Giants game. It wouldn't hurt to make reservation there as well. If you don't want to worry about booking a reservation, check out the 21st Amendment Brewery just 2 blocks from AT&T Park. This fun brewery has your token bar food with a great selection of homemade brews!

Once inside AT&T Park, you don't have to look long for a good concession stand. Some of our top favorites include: "Say Hey! Willie Mays Sausages", other places include: Crazy Crab'z, Gilroy Garlic Fries and Fresh Catch. To make it easy, get the Ballpark Chasers Meal: a crab cake sandwich from Crazy Crab'z, garlic fries from Gilroy's and a beverage of your choice.

DCB SAYS:

Simply put, AT&T Park has the best selection and quality in all of 'MLB.' Last visit I ate parts of a mushroom burger-rib sandwich-chicken burger and garlic fries. There is also a Safeway in the bottom deck of the right center field area. They have full deli sandwiches for purchase. Another note here is that there are 'Coke' vending machines underneath the kids play area--and adjacent to the big green 'Coke Neon Sign' and big baseball glove. They sell for $3-because how many of us hate waiting in line for just a pop? The best food stands are directly behind the scoreboard to the right. There is also pizza, fish and steak to eat in this little food court, the food is also just amazing.

INTANGIBLES AT PARK:

The reason this park rated the highest of all ballparks is its location to the ocean in every direction. You have McCovey's Cove directly behind the red brick wall in right that leads to the waters of "The Port Authority OF San Francisco'. Across the waters there is a statue of Willie Mays on the other end. You also have iconic pictures to be had of the 'Bay Bridge' and the several piers nearby. Do yourself a favor and up go to the 3rd deck-and walk it pillar to post to take some great pictures of all of these aforementioned places. The Giants also have great wall murals of past greats up there on the 3rd deck.

WHERE TO BUY TICKETS?

As the Giants look to follow up there World Series victory, tickets to AT&T Park become more difficult to purchase. The 2010 season had the park 90% full on average, which ranks in the top 5 of Major League Baseball. We recommend any seat along the 3rd base side to get a wonderful view of the McCovey Cove and the San Francisco Bay. Otherwise, you can't walk 10 feet without running into a scalper trying to unload tickets around AT&T Park.

Alternatively to get the full effect of this park without breaking the bank you should just buy the cheapest ticket possible and walk around the whole game viewing it from different vantage points. If you are 1 or 2 people I suggest www.stubhub.com for e-tickets to purchase. This is an easy to make a purchase. 'StubHub' only charges about $10 for sending out e-tickets and lots of season ticket holders use the site in S.F.

Always bring a coat-especially at night . There is intermittent fog for a lot of the games whether it is day or night.

WHERE TO PARK?

The area around AT&T Park offers <u>several parks lots</u> including: Parking Lot A, D and Pier 48. Look for additional parking north of the stadium between Embarcadero and Bryant (Pier 30 & 32).

Ballpark Chasers Tip: avoid the busy San Francisco traffic by getting a hotel close enough to the stadium to walk. Otherwise, use the Muni Metro, Cal Train, bus, ferry or even one of those cool San Francisco cable cars to get the game!

WHEN TO GO?

The San Francisco Bay area has mild temperatures year round, with average temperatures not breaking into to the 70s until September. I know, <u>we didn't believe it</u> either! Even in the summer we suggest bringing a jacket for a night game. Ballpark Chasers recommends the months of August and September to travel to AT&T Park for the fog will clear and the sun will come out.

WHAT ELSE TO SEE?

Spend a morning or afternoon down by the Fisherman's Wharf. Look for Pier 33 and hop on a ferry boat for one of San Francisco's greatest landmarks, the Alcatraz. The round trip ride lasts about 2 ½ hours and is the most fun when touring at night. This former jail was once home to the most famous mobster of all time, Al Capone and the notorious criminal Machine Gun Kelly.
If you really want to go all out and see everything at once, try a <u>San Francisco helicopter tour!</u>
Are you a movie buff or just want to see more of the city of San Francisco? If so, don't pass up the chance to take a <u>San Francisco Movie Tour</u>. This 3 hour tour bus begins at the Fisherman's Wharf and takes you all across town to see the actual film locations from over 100 movies filmed around the bay area!
If you would rather have a relaxing day without the hustle and bustle of the city, go to the <u>Golden Gate National Recreational Area</u>. This national park is the largest urban national park in the world and is home to over 74,000 acres of land and water. The recreational area is the perfect place to take pictures of the San Francisco Bay and Golden State Bridge.
If you like those little tourist attractions and have some extended time in S.F don't forget also to check out the 'Coit Tower' and the 'Crookedest Street.'

BALLPARK CHASER'S VACATION?

The California area leaves it available for you to combine a trip to AT&T Park along with a few other stadiums around the Bay area. Ballpark Chasers recommends adding 1 or more of the 4 stadiums below to your trip to AT&T Park.

1.) <u>Oakland Coliseum</u>- 16 miles/30 minutes
2.) <u>Dodger Stadium</u> – 381 miles/6 hours
3.) <u>Angel Stadium</u>- 409 miles/6.5 hours
4.) <u>Petco Park</u>- 503 miles/8 hours

*You can visit both Oakland Coliseum and AT&T in the same day.

2. FENWAY PARK

BOSTON, MASSACHUSETTS
HOME OF THE BOSTON REDSOX

TRANSPORTATION:

'Boston International-Logan Airport-'BOS' is a short distance of 6 miles from Fenway Park, but once again you must give yourself plenty of time to make it to the park in gridlock traffic. The car rental facilities are a good shuttle bus distance of a few miles from the airport. The I-90 Highway includes a toll and a tunnel--this is a faster way but you must focus on taking your right exit (Exit 25) as there is no immediate U-turn and you will be fined another toll by the 'Massachusetts's Toll Agency' if you do one. We have heard of $13 administration fees billed from car rental agencies to process these late tolls—in addition to the fine as well-this is almost as bad as the toll operators in Illinois! Of course if you drive along the East Coast you have become numb to all the tolls anyways. If you are only going to be in Boston for a short time you might think about taking a cab everywhere as it is way cheaper than paying multiple parking fees.

WHERE TO STAY?

For two travelers or more we suggest the 'Best Western Adams Inn' because of its location towards all public transport and free shuttle service to Logan Airport. It is located right off the 'Neponset River' for about $125 a night it is well worth it in Boston.
For that singular traveler, there is yet another hostel right on Hemenway St. about a block from the ballpark offered through www.hihostels.com . The price goes for about $50 a night and you must book well in advance to ensure of a bed. Really, this is a great way to be right near the ballpark for a decent price.

WHERE TO PARK?

Ballpark Chasers suggest taking the "T" to Fenway Park if you are staying at a hotel that is not within walking distance. Subway access is conveniently located all over the downtown Boston area and is much cheaper than parking. All subway lines will connect to the Green Line which you then take to the Kenmore stop. From there, just follow the heard of crazy Bostonians. If driving to the ballpark, we highly recommend arriving early to ensure a parking spot that fits your budget. Prices range from $6 to over $50 for walking distances between 2 and 20 minutes.

Note****Remember the address 808 Commonwealth Ave 'just past the turnoff to Hwy 2 North on Commonwealth.' This is a special Parkade reserved for University Students so the charge is only $10 and the place is under a mile walk from the ballpark. Everyone is able to park there during baseball games.

WHERE TO EAT?

Just across the street from Fenway Park is Boston's world renowned sports bar, Cask'n Flagon. Since 1973, the Cask'n Flagon has been serving food and drinks for all of Red Sox Nation. Ballpark Chasers love this restaurant for their great food, service and overall atmosphere. With over 60 high definition televisions, it makes a perfect place to hang out before or after the game. Just one piece of advice – leave your Yankees gear at the door! Another sports bar close to the stadium is Beer Works, Boston's oldest and largest restaurant and brewery. For you microbrew lovers, Beer Works is the place to go. From their Bunker Hill Blueberry Ale to their Gold Medal winner Red October, Beer Works Brewery offers a variety like no-other. In addition, they have over 9o food items that include several on the lighter side. Who are we kidding? Go with the Fenway Burger and Fiery Fries! For those looking to avoid the sports bar scene and have a quieter meal, we recommend the Audubon Circle Restaurant. The Audubon is a casual restaurant serving a wide range of food, including many vegetarian items. Keep in mind that the last time we visited there was only one television, so be prepared to go elsewhere if you need your SportsCenter. Our last recommendation is Canestaro, located on Peterborough, just a few blocks from Fenway Park. Canestaro's serves some of the best Italian food we have sampled in all of North America. We hear they have a great menu other than just pizza, but honestly the pizza is so good we can't bear to try anything else. With so many great restaurants and bars outside of Fenway Park, Ballpark Chasers recommend eating before entering the stadium. With that being said, there are still a few good options within the park. Although it's hard to miss, look for Yawkey Way, an extension of the Fenway Park concourse that offers pre-game live music, entertainment and amazing Italian sausages. Some of our favorite ballpark items include a bowl of Legal Seafood's Clam Chowder, Fenway Franks and the Panini sandwich. For a snack, head to the Big Concourse to try Fenway Park's famous Kettle Corn – the local fans swear by it! Another place chaser's swear by is to eat at 'Bertucci's Pizza Oven Ristorante' right on Commonwealth Street' about a half block from the ballpark. Bertucci's serves oven deep dish pizza better than any place in America East of Chicago.

INTANGIBLES:

Ballpark Chasers Fun Fact: there is a lone, red-seat surrounded by a sea of green in the Right Field section of Fenway Park. This seat marks the longest home run ever hit inside Fenway, some 502 feet away! The shot came from Ted Williams' bat on June 9, 1946. Good luck trying to get this ticket in Section 42, Row 37, Seat 21.

Fenway Park and Wrigley are the oldest ballparks in country so make sure you take this into consideration. While they are gorgeous with sights and views, give yourself the heads up that moving around the park takes time. Be prepared especially if you are traveling with people that have limited movement.

WHERE TO BUY TICKETS?

Fenway Park is the oldest ballpark in all of Major League Baseball and arguably holds the greatest and most loyal fans. Many times the Red Sox will travel to other stadiums and bring as many fans as the home town team; hence they are referred to as "Red Sox Nation". Sellouts don't sometimes occur, they always occur- since May of 2003 to be exact! Fenway Park was on average 100.9% full during the 2010 season! What does this all mean? Buy your tickets before going to the game or else bring plenty of cash to fork over to scalpers. Don't delay!

WHEN TO GO?

The Boston area has fairly mild summers with light rain and humidity. To increase your chance for a warm summer day, Ballpark Chasers recommend late June, July and/or August. We also suggest avoiding the months of April and May as wide temperature swings are very common with averages rarely exceeding 70 degrees.

WHAT ELSE TO SEE?

Since "Beantown" can be an expensive place to visit, we thought we would suggest a few local attractions to see on a limited budget. For just $6, you can get a true feel for New England's rich sports history at The Sports Museum. Located at the TD Bank North Garden (home of the Boston Celtics and Bruins), The Sports Museum is nearly a half-mile filled with historical memorabilia and exhibits. Some of our favorites include: Ted Williams' locker, the infamous baseball that struck Tony Conigliaro, Nancy Kerrigan's skates and Larry Bird's shoes! Do you want to go to a place in Boston where everyone knows your name? Well, look no further than a little pub called "Cheers". Okay, so they will not actually know your name when you walk in the door. Norm will not be at the corner seat and Sam will not be behind the bar reminiscing about his former playing days with the Red Sox. However, it's a pretty fun stop to see where one of the most successful television shows in history was inspired. Stop in for a quick drink and finish in their gift shop for a Cheers souvenir. Don't leave Boston without seeing their historical landmarks by foot. The Freedom Trail is a 2.5 mile long self-guided walking tour through the city that is marked with a red-brick line to make it easy to follow. Because the Freedom Trail is not a circular loop, we advise starting your walk at the Boston Commons (don't forget to pick up a map here too). Famous stops along the way include: Paul Revere's house, America's first public school, the location of the battle at Bunker Hill and the Boston Massacre.

BALLPARK CHASERS VACATION?

Fenway Park is one stop in the "Northeast 3", which includes seeing Yankee Stadium and Citi Field. By far, this is the most popular of all Ballpark Chasers vacations. If possible, extend your trip by another day to visit Cooperstown, home of the Baseball Hall of Fame. Cooperstown, New York is just over a 4 hour drive from Boston and New York and provides a once in a lifetime

3. WRIGLEY FIELD

CHICAGO, ILLINOIS
HOME OF THE CHICAGO CUBS

TRANSPORTATION:

'O'Hare Airport'- 'ORD' is definitely the better option to fly in for a Cubs game. Otherwise, if you are driving from east or west sooner or later you will connect through the 90 and 94 highways. ORD is one of the bigger airports in America with lots of restaurants and amenities within. They built the airport knowing full well that many of the travelers would be experiencing delays from the 'windy city'. This city is a ballpark chasers nightmare for flying in and out of. ORD is a strong hub airport for the airlines America, United Airlines and US Airways. Your cheaper flights like most airports are always going to be early. Because of the close proximity to Milwaukee, you are better off to fly to and from 'MKE' for cheaper fares—especially if you are combining Chicago with Milwaukee in a baseball trip. Using 'Amtrak Trains' is a phenomenal way to travel between Milwaukee and Chicago--for $22 for a one-way ticket, the train only takes 75 minutes between cities and they run every few hours. Sometimes there are also cheaper flights when flying into Chicago's other main airport 'MDW'.
If you are not going anywhere but to baseball games we do not recommend driving a car. Not only is it very expensive with multiple tolls (in every direction) and insane parking fees, but the traffic is some of the most intense in the nation. The subway/buses system however, might just be the best in America. Visit www.transitchicago.com for all your subway information
When coming in from ORD— they have a subway terminal in the bottom floor of the airport. The blue line will take you all the way into town. Particularly if you are going to 'Wrigley Field' you will still need to take another bus to the game. The easiest solution is to take the blue subway until you can connect to the 'Red Line Howard' train until you arrive at the Addison stop. Subway rides go for a mere $2.50 per trip.

If you are travelling by car, there is a quick shuttle from ORD to the car rental facilities. Weekdays are quite pricey at about $70-100 per day. Even with a Priceline bid you will still pay upwards of $50 per day. Weekend days are not bad. We highly recommend 'Budget Rental Car' at ORD, the 'Fast break Members' receive top-notch service at this facility and it is well worth the time saving and hassle to rent with them. Drive on the 90 highway to the game until you come upon the exit of W. Irving Park and take that street until you hit N. Sheffield. There are nice parking lots out there for $10-20 and it is only a mile walk away from Wrigley. Travel the same way coming in from 94 East. Under no circumstance is it good to drive anywhere near 'Wrigley Ville' before or after the game.

WHERE TO STAY?

Unlimited budget– all 4 are within 1.5 miles of Wrigley Field

Majestic Hotel
Willows Hotel
Best Western – Hawthorne Terrace

City Suites

Moderate budget

Days Inn- Chicago 1.5 miles from Wrigley Field

Chaser budget traveler

Old Chicago Inn

Ballpark Chasers Tip: be careful when reserving a motel in downtown Chicago. There are several "bargain motels" close to Wrigley; however, they are not ballpark chaser recommended.

DCB SPECIALS:

—Chicago Hostel at '25 E. Congress Parkway.' www.hihostels.com for that singular traveler the rate is only $37 per night for a bed and you receive a free continental breakfast. This location is right in downtown Chicago and about a mile away from historical 'Grant Park'-where President Obama made his acceptance speech. This particular hostel is perfect for either a game at Wrigley or US Cellular Field. One block from the hostel is 'State Station' which connects you to the 'Red Line 95th/Dan Ryan Expressway' towards' US Cellular Field' for 15 minutes—and the 'Howard Train'—which takes about 20 minutes to Wrigley. This hostel is also a short walk from Chicago Union Station—where you can travel via 'Amtrak Train' recommended by Ballpark Chasers unless you see them above. Also recommend is staying at the 'Sheffield House Hotel' www.sheffieldhousehotel.com This affordable hotel is located about a mile from the park and you can stay there for under a hundred dollars for a normal room and only slightly more for king-sized beds. Keep in mind with most Chicago lodging; be prepared to pay for parking.

WHERE TO PARK?

Wrigley Field is one stadium that you do not want to drive to. The Chicago Cubs and Ballpark Chasers everywhere recommend finding public transportation to and from the game. If possible, hop on the CTA Red-Line, one of Chicago's many train lines. The Red Line train provides direct access to Wrigley Field via the access station at Addison. Otherwise, the Purple, Blue and Yellow Line trains connects to the Red Line. Talk to your hotel front desk for the closest option.

It is unruly to pay the parking fees close to the ballgame at $30-40 per game—if you are willing to walk 2-3 miles you can find decent prices for parking that are about half of that fee. Remember the parking lots near W. Irving Park.

WHERE TO EAT?

There is a battle happening in Chicago's north-side other than the one at Wrigley Field. The 'WrigleyVille' restaurant owners are fighting for your attention before and after every Cubs home game. No other ballpark in the country can compete with the sports bars that you will find outside of Wrigley Field. After extensive hands-on research (including pain staking food sampling and bar hopping), Ballpark Chasers have narrowed down the top 4 sports bars in WrigleyVille.

The Cubby Bear, Murphy's Bleachers, Harry Caray's Tavern and Sluggers World Class Sports Bar are all unique in their own way. The Cubby Bear offers size (over 30,000 sq. ft), Chicago sports memorabilia and over 70 satellite televisions broadcasting tons of sports throughout the day! Murphy's Bleachers gives you more of an authentic Wrigley Field experience, located directly across the street from the entrance to the bleacher section. Harry Caray's Tavern gives you a taste of Chicago Cubs history. Sluggers is the entertainment spot, offering a second floor filled with batting cages, trampoline basketball, virtual driving games, air hockey, electronic basketball, and football, ski and golf simulators! In addition to those activities, Sluggers is also home of the dueling piano bar. With so many awesome restaurants and bars around WrigleyVille, why bother eating inside the park? Besides the Chicago Dogs and sausages, the 4-pound pretzel (Northside Twist), Italian sandwiches and Buffalo Dogs, there isn't much worth purchasing inside Wrigley Field. Do yourself a favor and pick from one of the four restaurants featured and let us know your favorite!

Ballpark Chasers Tip: if you want to find a seat at one of these WrigleyVille sports bars on game days, make sure to arrive 3 hours before the first pitch. Otherwise, head over to the original Billy Goat Tavern (about 5 miles from Wrigley Field). The Michigan Ave. location is home to the original bar of William Sianis and his infamous Billy goat. Stop by to learn about the curse of the Billy goat that still haunts the Cubs to this day.

INTANGIBLES:

Much like 'Fenway Park' there is a buzz around the park that creates an electric atmosphere to watch a game. Make sure you plan to stick around after the game for a while as exiting this old ballpark can take some time. For those people with limited movement or who are traveling with people who have limited movement-please take this into consideration. Don't forget to sing 'Go Cubs Go' after the Cubbies win the game.

WHERE TO BUY TICKETS?

On average, Wrigley Field was 92% full during every game of the 2010 season! Needless to say, we recommend purchasing Cubs tickets from your favorite online dealer or through the Cubs website once you reserve plane tickets. Otherwise, you can always count on scalpers all over WrigleyVille.

Ballpark Chasers Tip: "standing room only" tickets mean that you will be standing to watch the game and there is a good chance that you will not have a full field view. Don't let scalpers fool you into thinking that you will be able to find a seat to sit-in.

WHEN TO GO?

The Chicago area is known for its extreme climates and seasons. During the baseball season, you can expect temperatures gradually increasing through the summer months with the peak coming in July and

August. Thunderstorms are quite common in the summer. June typically gets the most rainfall, so don't forget to pack a light jacket.

WHAT ELSE TO SEE?

The windy city offers so much to do and see that the toughest part is deciding. From the world renowned Art Institute of Chicago to the Magnificent Mile, tourists can easy spend an entire week here. One stop not to miss is Millennium Park, located roughly 6 miles from Wrigley Field. The newly opened 24 acre park is home of amazing and truly unique art, music and architecture. Don't leave without checking out the Crown Fountain, a 50 ft. tower that projects facial images with an opening that shoots water out of the image's mouth! Another attraction at Millennium Park is the Cloud Gate sculpture. Imagine a gigantic 66 ft. long upside-down jelly bean that looks like mercury and has a mirror-like finish which reflects the viewer's image back in weird shapes. Sounds pretty cool, huh?

Another quick, fun and inexpensive destination in the Chicago area is the Sears Tower, North America's tallest building (110 stories tall). On a clear day, the view from the sky deck allows you to see over 40-50 miles out, including Michigan, Indiana and Wisconsin! Try and time it so you can catch a sunset by arriving at the sky deck about 30 minutes before the sun sets.

DOUBLEHEADER ATTEMPTS:

Chicago has a lot of double header attempts as the Cubs play so many day games. Those Saturday 12 pm games especially lend themselves too many chances to see two games in one day.

CHI WHITE SOX—there is only a 30 minute subway trip between parks or about an hour in traffic to drive.

MILWAUKEE BREWERS—'Ballpark Chaser Special'—during weekdays there is a train that leaves 'Chicago Union Station' at 5:08 PM and arrives in Milwaukee about 6:45 PM. This is where the flight to Milwaukee ties in perfectly. You could take an early morning Amtrak train into Chicago and then take the 'Red Line Howard' to Wrigley. After the game take the 'Red Line D. Ryan Exp' back to the station in order to board the returning train back to Milwaukee. All you have to do is park at the Milwaukee Airport (Amtrak Station) in the morning and then drive the 10-15 minutes into town upon a night return. Then take Highway 94 East before turning onto 'National Ave'—all the way to 'Miller Park'. With many games ending by 4:00 pm in Chicago you routinely can make this trip work. In driving you are capable as well but it is a lot tighter and massive traffic still may stop you.

4. PNC PARK

PITTSBURGH, PENNSYLVANIA
HOME OF THE PITTSBURGH PIRATES

TRANSPORTATION:

PIT AIRPORT, (PIT)-'DCB SAYS:

"In all of my travels I was never as pleased as my trip to Pittsburgh through their airport. While it is a far distance from the actual city, it is one of the top airports to fly in and out of. First off, they have the most convenient car rental facilities in America as they are a small walk from the arrivals level. If you are a preferred member at any of the rental companies it will take you 5 minutes to get out of the airport once you arrive. Not only that, but as cities go Pittsburgh car rentals are extremely cheap whether it is the weekend or not. You are looking at about $35 per day and in the mid $250's for the week.

PIT Airport is a hub for the airlines—Delta, US Airways and Southwest but also have strong flight considerations from Midwest and Air Tran Airways. In fact, these little airlines often have the cheaper fares and include non-stops to other cities.

Now if you are on limited time to get to downtown the 28x Airport/Pittsburgh Downtown will take you all the way to and from the airport for just a few dollars. You can exit at Liberty St and 6th Ave and walk over the Roberto Clemente Bridge to the game.

If you are driving in from the 376 or 279 highways make sure you give yourself ample time as the town is very beautiful because of the bridges but is traffic gridlock. Keep in mind the 'Fort Pitt' tunnel is the only main choice for travelers to go north and it is quite busy during the pm hours.

WHERE TO STAY?

Unlimited Budget - all options are within walking distance to PNC Park

Spring Hill Suites by Marriott- North Shore
Renaissance Pittsburgh Hotel
Omni World Penn Hotel

Moderate Budget – all options are within walking distance to PNC Park

The Priory Hotel
Hampton Inn & Suites
Double Tree Hotel & Suites – Pittsburgh

Chaser Budget Traveler – both options are within 2 miles of PNC Park

<u>Best Western Parkway Center</u>
<u>Days Inn</u>- Pittsburgh

DCB SPECIAL:

Best Western Parkway Center Inn- For about $100 a night you can stay 5 miles away from downtown. They also have a free shuttle to and from games at 'PNC Park' if you leave early enough. It is also close to other attractions such as: 'The Andy Warhol Museum'-'Carnegie Museum' and 'Heinz Field'.

There is also a Motel 6 about 30 miles from downtown in 'Weirton WV' on highway 22 that can be found for an unbelievable $30 a night. This is good if you plan on travelling to Detroit, Cincinnati or ST. Louis for a game after Pittsburgh.

WHERE TO PARK?

The north side of PNC Park offers several parking lots and paid garages. Parking ranges from $10-$30 on the North side of the stadium. If you are coming in from the East, West, or South side of PNC Park, Ballpark Chasers suggests parking downtown Pittsburgh and walking over the Clemente Bridge. The bridge provides a great view of the stadium as well as parking lots starting at only $5!

Ballpark Chasers Tip: look out for Station Square and let their Gateway Clipper Shuttle boat take you across the Allegheny River. Parking at Station Square is typically $6 and the round trip ticket on the Gateway Clipper is $10.

WHERE TO EAT?

As the locals say, you can't come to Pittsburgh and not stop for a sandwich at Primanti Bros. They must be doing a few things right since the first Primanti's opened as a street vendor during the Great Depression! Don't be fooled by thinking you can grab a sandwich inside PNC Park. You need to experience an actual Primanti's restaurant (the closest is on Market Pl- a 1o minute walk from PNC Park). When your sandwich comes topped with French fries and coleslaw, don't be scared, it's amazing!

Two other restaurants that are highly recommended by Ballpark Chasers are Atria's Restaurant & Tavern and Mullen's Bar & Grille. Atria's is another local favorite with 7 locations in Pennsylvania, one of them being located on the grounds of PNC Park. They have a diverse menu, offering everything from steaks and seafood to pasta and chicken dishes. Mullen's, on the other hand, is just one block away from the stadium and is a great Irish-themed sports bar with plenty of televisions to watch your favorite team. It's one of those "neighborhood" restaurants to hang out in and hear conversations about their towns beloved Steelers and not so beloved Pirates!

Once inside the park, look no further than the Hall of Fame Club Restaurant. This sports bar is located just beyond left field and offers 20 flat screen televisions, an outdoor patio and bar, an amazing menu and a great view of the field. The Hall of Fame Club is exclusively for ticket holders and will open on game days 30 minutes prior to the main gates. For a quicker option, head over to the third base side for Pops Plaza, a food court with a variety of options. Try the Ballpark Chasers meal which includes a beef gyro, freshly cut fries and a local microbrew of your choice.

The Bucs also have the most amazing pizza joint in the majors. It changes every year in name— but "Greentree Pizza' as it was last time is the closest restaurant to the Clemente Bridge (just past the left field bleachers). It is costly for a loaded pizza but if you just like Pepperoni Pizza or Cheese you can get a Large for $15. Otherwise, you can always order by the slice. Pittsburgh is also famous for loaded-ticket Tuesday nights where you get bleacher seats for $14 that already have $5 automatically loaded onto your ticket.

Note here*** You can order pizza from this restaurant even if you are not at the game—it is the best pizza in the 'Allegheny' and it is cheaper from your hotel room than at the game.

INTANGIBLES:

There are many vendors outside the game that sell hot dogs, peanuts and soda for a few dollars and you are allowed to take the items with you into the game (much like 'Coors and Safeco Field'). There is nothing like watching a game from the bleachers at PNC. They pay great homage to their heroes all throughout the park. Note is that the outfield concourse does not go all around the park. So while it has a great view of the Three Rivers, it might not get you to your seat. There is also a restaurant outside that hires bands to sing after the games.

WHERE TO BUY TICKETS?

Despite having a beautiful stadium with not one bad seat in the house, the quality of talent on the field overrides and makes PNC Park in the bottom 5 of Major League Baseball attendance. Tickets can be easily purchased online, through the Pirates box office or with your favorite ticket broker. If you choose to buy your tickets before the game, the Pirates offer a designated ticket reselling area between Heinz Field and PNC Park (at the corner of North Shore Drive and Dorsett Way). This is a great way to find tickets from fans and therefore bargains are easy to come by. Keep in mind that scalpers are required to buy and sell outside of this designated area.

WHEN TO GO?

Pittsburgh is a city that experiences four very distinct seasons. Summers tend to be warm and humid with frequent cloudy days that quickly turn into rainy days.

May is traditionally the wettest month while August and September tend to bring less rain with warm and sunny weather. PNC Park is an open-air stadium, so don't forget to bring a light rain jacket.

WHAT ELSE TO SEE?

Make sure to arrive at PNC Park early in order to check out Highmark Legacy Square, located inside of the Left-Field entrance. This interactive exhibit pays tribute to the Negro Leagues, with special attention given to the Pittsburgh Crawford's and Homestead Grays. Plan on spending between 30-45 minutes to view the life-size bronze statues, interact with the video wall, watch a short documentary and brush up on your Negro League history through a photographic timeline.

Another sports related attraction in Pittsburgh is within walking distance of PNC Park. The Western Pennsylvania Sports Museum, located within the Heinz History Museum, offers an amazing collection of historical artifacts and exhibits, all related to Pittsburgh's rich sports heritage. With more than 70 youth and adult interactive exhibits, audio/video programs and a 2-story theater, Ballpark Chasers recommends this spot for more than just fans of Pittsburgh sports.

Before leaving town make sure to take a ride up the Duquesne Incline for one of the most "romantic spots" and "most beautiful views" in the country (according to MSN and USA Weekend Magazine). Open 365 days of the year, the Duquesne Incline offers Spectacular views of the downtown skyline, PNC Park, Heinz Field and the famous three rivers of Pittsburgh. A $4 ticket will get you parking, a round trip ticket in the antique car and a self guided tour of the machinery room. Ballpark Chasers will make an afternoon out of it by staying up top for a meal at one of the many restaurants on the top of Mt. Washington.

BALLPARK CHASERS VACATION?

PNC Park is part of "*The Rust Belt*" Ballpark Chasers vacation. This trip includes seeing the Indians at Progressive Field and the Tigers at Comerica Park. Those Ballpark Chasers looking for a longer vacation also include Cincinnati to see the Reds play at Great American Ball Park. On average, the drive from PNC Park to Progressive Field takes 2 ½ hours, while Progressive Field to Comerica Park takes 3 hours. Make sure to have a comfortable car as it is nearly a 5 hour drive back to Pittsburgh from Detroit.

PNC Park can be combined with Cleveland's Progressive Field when Cleveland has those Thursday summer matinee games that start at 12:10 PM.

5. COMERICA PARK

DETROIT MICHIGAN
HOME OF THE DETROIT TIGERS

TRANSPORTATION:

Detroit Metropolitan Wayne County Airport (DTW) is 23 miles/30 minutes to Comerica Park. It is a brisk drive in traffic and can be grueling if under construction. DTW is the second largest hub for 'Delta Airlines' as well as the second biggest hub for 'Spirit Airlines.' The airport itself is near Taylor Michigan-off of highway 94-West by a few miles. Generally, it is really expensive to fly in and out of Detroit and they are better suited for earlier flights. We recommend that if you are planning a trip with multiple parks that you fly into the nearby cities of Cleveland, Cincinnati, Chicago and Milwaukee as they are less expensive. Only nearby Toronto is higher to fly in and out of. You can expect to pay high rates for rental cars as well: $50 per weekday. The rental facility is a quick shuttle away and there are several other off-site rental agencies that you may be able to achieve a better deal. Travelling to the downtown core by cab or mass transit is not considered a good idea and is expensive. Be careful in Detroit as it is a nice place but like any other big metropolitan city in America it has its bad area's.

WHERE TO STAY?

All hotels below are within walking distance to Comerica Park.

Unlimited budget

MGM Grand Detroit
Athenaeum Suites Detroit

Moderate budget

Hilton Garden Inn Detroit Downtown
Westin Book Cadillac Hotel
Courtyard by Marriott Detroit Downtown

Chaser budget traveler

Double Tree Guest Suites Detroit Downtown

Ballpark Chasers Tip: Keep in mind that there are a lot of "bargain motels" close to the stadium, but if they are not listed above, they are not recommended by Ballpark Chasers.

WHERE TO PARK?

The Tigers conveniently offer several parking lots surrounding Comerica Park. These parking spaces are open to the public and are on a first come, first serve basis. Parking ranges from $5 to $25, depending on the proximity to Comerica Park. Cabs are easy to come by as well, if you are staying at a hotel that is too far to walk. Furthermore, many restaurants and bars offer complimentary shuttles to Comerica Park for their patrons (see section: "Where to Eat").

WHERE TO EAT?

Hands down, the best sports bar in all of Detroit is Hockey Town Café. Whether or not you are a hockey fan, Hockey Town Café is not to be missed! Located just around the corner from Comerica Park, this sports bar gives you plenty to look at. Hockey Town is filled with hockey memorabilia, statues, and full size motorcycles! Menus range from salads to burgers, pizzas, sandwiches, Panini's and of course, red wings!

If you prefer a nostalgic sports bar with a taste of old Tiger Stadium, check out Nemo's. Don't worry that they are a little further away as Nemo's has a fleet of full-size school buses to hall you to the game. Make sure to get the Ballpark Chasers meal: cheeseburger, side of "world famous" chili, French fries and a beverage of your choice.

Loco's Tex-Mex Grille is our favorite spot for Mexican food. Located within walking distance of Comerica Park, Loco's has a full menu ranging from burgers to burritos. They also provide a complimentary shuttle to every Tigers game. Check out their site for their latest coupons. Ballpark Chasers usually go with the combination plate in order to sample multiple foods.

Once inside Comerica Park, you have three options for dining: Big Cat Food Court, Brushfire Grill and Beer Hall. The Big Cat Food Court is near the main entrance of Comerica Park and offers a variety of ballpark foods. For dessert, make sure to try elephant ears and the homemade donuts. Beer Hall is a great option if looking for full-service restaurant. This tavern offers a traditional sports bar cuisine with a plethora of domestic and international brews from a 70 ft. bar!

If you love pizza and have never experienced 'Little Caesars Pizza' certainly check it out. The owner of the Detroit Tigers, Mike Ilitch, is also the founder of the pizza chain.

INTANGIBLES:

Comerica Park is an outstanding venue and has the some of the most scenic pictures to take at night with the 'Fox' sign and the 'Pepsi Porch' sign. The Tigers on the scoreboard are also some of the best images to take a picture of. Being one of the oldest franchises includes the retired name of 'Ty Cobb' actually being displayed without an actual uniform number. There are many interactive things to do at the park: Whether it is pitching or batting there is plenty to keep your self occupied. Comerica has several art drawings and painting shops that are amongst the best in baseball. So not only is the Tigers history shown but so is the history all of 'MLB.'

WHERE TO BUY TICKETS?

Comerica Park dropped to 15 in Major League Baseball attendance during the 2010 season. Although tickets are usually available at the box office before the game, Ballpark Chasers recommends purchasing your tickets ahead of time through your favorite online broker or from a local scalper outside of the park.

Ballpark Chasers Tip: look for scalpers hanging out more than 500 yards from Comerica Park. Local law prevents them from going closer. Furthermore, if you are selling extra tickets (even under the face value) make sure you are far from the stadium to avoid a trip to the nearest Detroit jail.

WHEN TO GO?

Detroit has a continental climate which provides for warm and humid summers, with temperatures frequently hitting 90 degrees. June and September bring the most rainfall, while July tends to be the warmest on average. Ballpark Chasers tend to find late May and late August as the best times to travel to the Detroit area.

WHAT ELSE TO SEE?

Detroit is a city with vast history, filled with a number of great museums. If you only have time to visit one, make sure to check out the Motown Historical Museum. This museum has done a fabulous job showcasing the impact that Motown had on pop culture and how it still influences music to this very day. From the beginning of 'Hitsville USA' to the major enterprise of Motown Record Corporation, guests will see everything from the original loan granted to finance the first record to the actual "Studio A" where the greatest hits were once recorded!

Another inspiring museum to visit while in Detroit is the Museum of African American History. With over 30,000 artifacts and archival materials, make sure to leave a half-day to see it all.

If your trip to Detroit happens to fall on the first or third Saturday of the month, make sure to sign up for the Auto Heritage Walking Tour. This guided tour starts at the Model T Automotive Heritage Complex (the birthplace of the Model T) and traces the footsteps of Henry Ford and the streets of Detroit to show where the history of the automobile began.

BALLPARK CHASERS VACATION?

Comerica Park is part of "The Rust Belt" Ballpark Chasers vacation. This trip includes seeing the Indians at Progressive Field and the Pirates at PNC Park. Those Ballpark Chasers looking for a longer vacation also include Cincinnati to see the Reds play at Great American Ball Park. On average, the drive from Comerica Park to Progressive Field takes 3 hours, while Progressive Field to PNC Park to takes 2 ½ hours. Make sure to have a comfortable car as it is nearly a 5 hour drive back to Detroit from Pittsburgh.

6. SAFECO FIELD

SEATTLE, WASHINGTON
HOME OF THE SEATTLE MARINERS

TRANSPORTATION:

SEATAC AIRPORT-(SEA)/HIGHWAY 5/HIGHWAY 90

The furthest Northwest ballpark in the Majors has only a few options. Flying in to SeaTac Airport is the best option as the nearest ballpark outside of Washington State is OAK/SF which is over 13 hours driving away. Safeco Field is a good 20 minute drive from SeaTac Airport and 40 minutes if it is during the week. If you are driving from North or South on Hwy 5 be prepared for that horrific Seattle Downtown traffic. SeaTac is a primary hub for 'Alaska Airlines' and 'Horizon Air.' The best way to fly on extensive road trips that include air travel if your from the West is to fly down to California with Alaska and use 'SFO' or 'LAX' to find cheaper flights back east from the legacy airlines. Use the same instructions in reverse if flying from east to west

DRIVING IN TO THE GAME:

Despite the online maps saying to take the side roads for a quicker drive to Safeco, it is not advised for those people who do not know the area.
The Car Rental Companies are all a far distance from the airport and they each have their own shuttle buses. You must cross the jet bridge on the arrivals floor to cross first, and then take the elevator/escalator to the shuttle bus waiting area. It is a major inconvenience due to the distance away from the airport that the rental companies are not all in one central location. Be prepared to pay $50-$70 a day on the weekdays for a car rental and $70-$90 on the weekend days. Seattle ranks low on the pricing of their car rentals.

WHERE TO STAY?

Seattle can be an expensive city for hotel stays. This is made easier by the fact you are usually heading to your next destination via car or plane so the best hotel deals are all near SeaTac Airport, but here are some options downtown.

Unlimited Budget

The Fairmont Olympic Hotel

Silver Cloud Inn (across the street from Safeco)

Seattle Marriott

Moderate budget

Best Western Pioneer Square Hotel

Sheraton Seattle Hotel

Chaser budget traveler

Unfortunately, you will need to leave downtown Seattle to find quality lodging under $100 per night. Ballpark Chasers does not currently recommend any downtown hotels/motels in the chaser budget category.

Airport Accommodations:

Best Western 'International Boulevard'-suits the middle class business man looking for a quiet night to work and sleep for around a $100 night.

Red Roof Inn on International Boulevard-is similar to the Best Western in price but offers a more family orientated environment for your same $100 a night.

There are three Motel 6 motels directly near SeaTac that are moderately priced for those ballpark chasers looking to save a few dollars. You can expect to pay about $50 for the night in the Motel 6's—and the area is actually not a bad place to stay with lots of amenities and shopping nearby.

WHERE TO PARK?

Street, metered, paid lots and garage parking are available. Depending on the day of week and the Mariners record, parking can range from $5 to $40.

Ballpark Chasers Tip: Find the intersection between 1st Ave. S. and Holgate Street. Behind the Paper Zone store is an alley that has a long strip of free parking. Come early as these fill up quickly!

*****Extreme ballpark chaser tip here from **DCB**—"The closer you park to the park, the more horrific the traffic will be afterwards. The police cordon off the roads heading up to Edgar Martinez Way en route to Highway 5 in either direction from north of S. Holgate Street. If you park lower than the 'Krispy Kreme Doughnuts' on 1st Ave you can head south towards 'W Seattle Bridge Hwy' where you take a left to merge onto the highway. With the flow being blocked off north you have a great advantage to get ahead of the traffic. From S. Holgate, the more you drive to the South, the less the parking costs as well. About 4 or 5 blocks down the way, they have pay-parking for $10 maximums for those prime games like Yankees and Red Sox where they triple or quadruple the normal price of parking at the lots. If you get to the ballpark early on the non-prime game you can actually park at the Krispy Kreme/Key Bank for really cheap prices. Make sure you back in and take the alley exit to avoid delays heading out on 1st Ave."

WHERE TO EAT?

Located across the street from Safeco Field, the <u>Pyramid Alehouse</u> is the place to be before a Mariners game. Whether you want to stay for a sit down meal inside their fabulous brew house or just grab a drink in the beer garden, the Pyramid is a Ballpark Chaser favorite! Don't leave without trying the Pyramid burger and Haywire Hefeweizen. For those staying in the nearby Silver Cloud Hotel, check out their restaurant, Jimmy's on First (across the street from the Left Field gate). If you are looking for a quicker option, find the alley between Occidental and Royal Brougham Way. Dozens of vendors are found selling everything from polish sausage to kettle corn!

DCB SAYS: —"Just this past summer I tried a burger joint a few miles up north from Safeco that was featured in that prominent TV show 'Man vs. Food'. This place was called 'Red Mill Burgers.' www.redmillburgers.com Located just off of Hwy 99 and it was an incredible burger joint. Thick Onion rings came as a side dish to this double-decker bacon cheeseburger with fresh lettuce, hand chopped onions, tomatoes and the special sauce. The place literally had a half an hour wait out the door and no one minded at all once they ate."

Once inside the park, the food selection gets even better! Safeco Field is a Ballpark Chaser favorite when it comes to concessions. Make sure to get the Ballpark Chasers meal: Kidd Valley burger, world famous garlic fries, and a Red Hook beer (or a milk shake for those young chasers). It's a must to wash down those calories with a ShishkaBerry fruit on a stick. Other great options are Garlic Jim's pizza, Ivar Dog, Sushi and Sake Ichirolls or Thai Ginger. If you prefer a sit-down option, check out Safeco Field's best kept secret, the Bullpen Pub. Enjoy tradition sports bar cuisine while viewing the bullpen and watching the manually operated scoreboard in action. Just make sure to come early as seats with a view go fast!

INTANGIBLES:

Quite simply, if this was a rank based on architectural mastery and sightlines, Safeco Field would be the best in the Major Leagues. The best ticket to buy is the absolute cheapest to gain entrance to the park and then walk the concourse. With the grandstand roofs high enough not to impede with spectator sightlines, you can watch the action from anywhere in the park.

WHERE TO BUY TICKETS?

Same day tickets at the box office are not a problem when attending sporting events in the state of Washington. The only time to plan ahead for tickets is when the Red Sox and Yankees are in town. Keep in mind you can always count on scalpers to be available on all sides of the stadium.

Ballpark Chasers tip: Don't fall for a scalper's first offer. Always walk away and you can save yourself another $5 per ticket. If they ask you to make an offer, always start $10 under face value!

WHEN TO GO?

It is hit or miss in Seattle, Washington. However, Safeco Field has a retractable roof so there are no rainouts to spoil your trip! The best months to travel to Seattle are July, August and September. Bring a light rain jacket and enjoy a nice cup of coffee to go along with the summer drizzle.

WHAT ELSE TO SEE?

Pike Place Market is a short cab ride away from Safeco Field. This is a great place to come for breakfast, lunch or dinner. Fun local vendors, great people watching and of course the famous flying fishes make for an entertaining stop before the game!

Just 2.5 miles from Safeco Field, the Space Needle is a token Seattle landmark to visit year round. Adults can expect to pay $16 ($8 for children under 14) for a ride up to the viewing deck. We recommend staying for a meal to enjoy more of the Seattle skyline. The Sky City restaurant serves lunch and dinner throughout the week and brunch and dinner on the weekends. Lunch plates start at $25 and dinner plates start at $34. A short walk from the Space Needle is one of the country's most unique looking buildings. The Experience Music Project (EMP) is a must-see for anyone who has an appreciation for music. The EMP is an interactive museum that does a fabulous job representing all types of music, including the rich history of Seattle's music scene.
Our final recommendation is Bill Speidel's Underground Tour. Located about 1 mile from Safeco Field, this guided tour of Seattle's underground is one of the most unique tours in North America. Make sure to bring cash for your ticket as well as a few extra dollars to tip your guide, as they make the tour lighthearted and very entertaining.

BALLPARK CHASERS VACATION?

Unfortunately, Safeco Field is the lone Major League Baseball stadium in the Northwest. Therefore, make this trip a quick 3-day weekend getaway and see a couple of Mariner games. Or if you are flying during the weekend try to go with a cheap flight to San Francisco or Oakland which are only a few hours plane ride away.

7. BUSCH STADIUM

ST. LOUIS, MISSOURI
HOME OF THE ST.LOUIS CARDINALS

TRANSPORTATION:

Lambert St. Louis International Airport-(STL) is 14 miles/20 minute drive to Busch Stadium. 'STL' is a huge hub for 'American Airlines' and 'Delta'. It has flights nearly around the clock as its central location makes many flights possible to either east or west. The car rental facilities are 3 miles from the airport. St. Louis is not a very forgiving when it comes to daily rates for cars, you can expect to pay about $70 during the weekdays, whereas the weekend days are usually about one-third of that. Be sure to give yourself plenty of time to head downtown after securing your car rental. Many hotels offer shuttle services for $15-20. Most of the time the shuttle operators don't check if you have a reservation, so if it is just you traveling save yourself some cab fare and hop on one of these shuttles to take you downtown. Also make sure you arrive to STL within that two hours before the flight—is even worse early in the morning as the TSA doesn't open the lines up till 4:30 AM despite many flights leaving right around 6:00 am.

WHERE TO STAY?

Unlimited budget- all 3 options are within walking distance to Busch Stadium

The Westin- St. Louis
Hilton- St. Louis at the Ballpark
Omni Majestic Hotel

Moderate budget – all 3 options are within walking distance to Busch Stadium

Drury Plaza Hotel
Sheraton- St. Louis City Center
Millennium Hotel- St. Louis

Chaser budget traveler- the following lodging is within 2 miles of Busch Stadium

Holiday Inn Express- St. Louis

WHERE TO PARK?

Over the past few seasons, we have found <u>parking lots</u> and covered garages around Busch Stadium to fluctuate between $8-25. Prices depend on the day of the week and the opponent the Cardinals are facing. Ballpark Chasers recommend the west side of the stadium as it is much easier to get through traffic after the game. If you get lucky, you might find free street parking.

WHERE TO EAT?

At trip to St. Louis wouldn't be complete without stopping for a bite at <u>Ozzie's Restaurant and Sports Bar</u>. Ozzie's was founded in 1998 by "The Wizard" (Ozzie Smith) and has been voted in the top 3 sports bars in the country by ESPN's morning show, Cold Pizza. Unfortunately, it is a 30 minute drive from Busch Stadium so plan accordingly

Another local favorite and ex-Cardinal owned restaurant is just seconds from Busch Stadium. Mike Shannon's is a little pricey, but well worth it if you are a fan of fine steaks and seafood. Despite being an upscale restaurant, Mike Shannon's is fan-friendly and has no problem with your baseball attire on game days. However, if your pocket book doesn't allow a lunch or dinner at Mike's or if you simply forgot to <u>make reservations</u>, Ballpark Chasers suggest walking outside to their beer garden. "The Outfield" (which is located in the back of the restaurant), overlooks Busch Stadium and is open before and after Cardinals home games.

In keeping with the trend of famously owned restaurants, J. Bucks rounds out our recommendations of pre-game stops. Named after famous broadcasters Jack and Joe Buck, J. Bucks is another fun stop for a little piece of Cardinals history and great views of Busch Stadium. If you are traveling with those finicky eaters, this is the place to go as Buck's has just about everything you can imagine.

The opening of the new Busch Stadium in 2006 brought a broad selection of new ballpark concessions. Ballpark Chasers favorites include: Bratzel's, St. Louis Seasoned Fries, Toasted Ravioli's and Broadway BBQ. What is a Bratzel you ask? Well, it is quite possibly the best kept secret in all of Busch Stadium. The Bratzel consists of a soft pretzel wrapped around a bratwurst and can be found in section 152. Trust us, it's delicious.

INTANGIBLES-'DCB SAYS':

The Cardinals have been one of the better franchises for the last few decades. Who wouldn't want to watch Albert Pujols play baseball? The staff members at 'Busch Stadium' are amongst the best in major league baseball. I had the opportunity to be interviewed on the field before a game in my 2008 streak attempt. I was given a Temporary Media Pass and the staff offered to give my 3 brothers, dad and myself a tour of the park. Unfortunately, I did not have the time. The red brick everywhere is a lot like AT&T Park, Coors Field and Camden Yards. I personally think that color pattern is the best in baseball.

WHERE TO BUY TICKETS?

Cardinal fans are one of the most loyal in all of baseball and therefore it is no surprise that Busch Stadium is consistently in the top 5 of Major League Baseball attendance. Because of this, Ballpark Chasers recommend purchasing your tickets in advance if you want to sit in a specific section of the stadium. Otherwise, be prepared for scalpers to take advantage of you outside of the park.

WHEN TO GO?

The summer months in St. Louis are hot and humid for those not accustomed to the Midwest climate. June, July and August tend to be the warmest on average and therefore we recommend avoiding it! If your travel plans allow, try your ballpark vacation to Busch Stadium in late April or May.

WHAT ELSE TO SEE?

A perfect way to spend a few hours before the game is at the Gateway Arch in downtown St. Louis. The Arch is the largest man-made monument in the United States, standing 630 ft. tall. Other than just riding the elevator to the top, you can also check out their documentary on the making of the Arch, explore the Museum of Westward Expansion, take a one-hour sightseeing cruise, rent a bike or even splurge on a helicopter ride!

Are you on a tight Ballpark Chaser budget? Not to fret, St. Louis is filled with numerous free tourist options and it is silly not to take advantage of them! Some of our favorites include: driving old Route 66, following the footsteps of Lewis and Clark, exploring Forest Park, taste-testing at the Anheuser Busch Brewery Tour or checking out the 5000 plus animals at the St. Louis Zoo.

An attraction to look forward to is the St. Louis Ballpark Village. Projected to open in the near future, the village will be located on the grounds of old Busch Stadium and will house new restaurants, shops, entertainment and the St. Louis Cardinals Hall of Fame.

Ballpark Chasers Tip: wait for the completion of the Ballpark Village before planning your trip to Busch Stadium as the Hall of Fame is in storage until completion.

BALLPARK CHASERS VACATION?

Busch Stadium is part of the Ballpark Chasers "Midwest 3" baseball road trip. This includes seeing Kauffman Stadium, Coors Field and Busch Stadium. We recommend finding the cheapest airfare to either Denver or St. Louis and using a rental car to drive in between. The drive from Denver to Kansas City is roughly 9 hours, or about 610 miles; whereas the drive between St. Louis and Kansas City is about 240 miles or 4 hours.

8. CITI FIELD

FLUSHING MEADOWS, NEW YORK
HOME OF THE NEW YORK METS

TRANSPORTATION-(SEE YANKEES GUIDE FOR NY AIRPORTS)

Much like Yankee Stadium, the subway is the best way to arrive at Citi Field. The 7 route train may not be so scenic--marred buildings with massive graffiti, but the convenience is nice. From Times Square to the ballpark is under an hour. 'LGA' is a mere 3 miles away from the ballpark. Note--if you take a cab to the ballpark it will cost you a minimum of $35 for a cab after the night games. A lot of the driver's come from the airport and will not leave until they receive at least that amount of money. Also, it can be about as hard to hail a cab during this time frame. So make sure you have your transit game plan done beforehand. You can book sedan car services for one way trips within city limits of New York for about $49 plus tax (this is a good option if traveling in a group). Look at www. limoquote.com for the best deal. With parking at Citi Field, it can be cheaper to take sedan service. LGA is an interesting airport as it is located completely in a suburban area. The car rental facilities are all off-site and require a quick shuttle. Give yourself extra time and a full stomach--particularly for early morning flights. The security lines are long and cramped much like the gates. The airport itself takes on the most travelers per year in the US. 'LGA' is a strong hub for 'Air Tran Airlines'-one of the best airlines in America and known highly for non-stop early morning flights out of New York to: Milwaukee, Atlanta, Denver and Minnesota. You can watch a day game in these cities by catching an early morning flight out after visiting New York. JFK is good for arriving non-stop flights from the west coast cities like SF/DEN/SEA/ Las Vegas/Houston and Dallas-JFK is a hub for: 'Delta Airlines' and 'American Airlines'. The car rental facility is a tram ride away. They have a big long-term parking lot at JFK-for reasonable rates so it is a good idea to park your car at the facility if you have more games to see on the Eastern Seaboard-and eventually fly back to New York. Note--there are many charter buses that leave downtown New York for either JFK or LGA-that cost about $13.

'EWR' is about a 60 minute drive away from 'Citi Field.' EWR airport features a lot of 'Continental Airlines and 'US Airways' flights from abroad. I would not recommend EWR unless it provides a cheaper price on airfares.

Car Rental prices per day

EWR-$45-$60 Weekday and $40-$55 Weekend
JFK-$75-$100 Weekday and $55-$70 Weekend
LGA-65-$85 Weekday and $50-$65 Weekend

Public Transit

VIA 7 TRAIN

The express subway option is the best way to travel to and from Citi Field. Board or get off at The Mets/Willits Point Station and makes stops in Manhattan at Times Square, 5th Avenue and Grand Central Station. The subway stops at the same spots in reverse. If you are not on the 'Express Subway' then it will take much longer

VIA E F G R or V TRAINS:

Connections to the 7 train can be made at the 74th Street-Broadway / Roosevelt Avenue stop in Jackson Heights.

VIA N or W TRAINS:

Transfer to the 7 train at Queensboro Plaza

Long Island Railroad

Train service to Mets/Willets Point Station is also available on eastbound Port Washington Branch trains from Penn Station and westbound trains from Great Neck and Port Washington. The train ride is just 18 minutes from Penn Station to Mets/Willets Point Station. For those traveling on the LIRR from Long Island, the new ballpark is just six minutes from Woodside, 17 minutes from Great Neck and 27 minutes from Port Washington. From Long Island, customers may go directly to the stadium from Port Washington Branch stations. Customers from other branches should transfer at Woodside.

For fare and schedule information, call (718) 217-5477 (New York City) or (516) 822-5477 (Long Island).

WHERE TO STAY?

 All lodging below is within 2 miles of Citi Field

Unlimited Budget

Sheraton LaGuardia East Hotel (0.9 Mi)

Fairfield Inn by Marriott New York LaGuardia Airport (1.1 Mi)

Moderate Budget

Holiday Inn LaGuardia/Citi Field (0.3 Mi)

<u>Lexington Marco</u> LaGuardia Hotel (0.9 Mi)

<u>Clarion Hotel</u> LaGuardia East (1.7 Mi)

Chaser Budget Traveler

Due to the location of Citi Field, (within walking distance of LaGuardia International Airport), there are very few chaser budget hotels. Those motels/hostels, under $100 per night, are not Ballpark Chaser recommended.

Ballpark Chasers Tip: If you want to avoid driving in this big city, Holiday Inn LaGuardia is truly the only hotel within walking distance of Citi Field (due to highways and construction). If you don't mind the subway, also consider picking a hotel in Manhattan to get the full New York experience!

WHERE TO PARK?

All parking lots open four hours prior to the first pitch. The Mets are one of the first teams in the area to offer credit card usage in the lanes at Citi Field. In addition to credit card, cash is also accepted. Parking is $18.00 per car during the regular season and $25.00 during the post-season.

Primary Lots-There is 5 parking lots within the fence line of Citi Field that provide fan parking. B, C, D, E, and F Lots are located on the west side of Citi Field and accommodate pre-paid parking. G Lot (Official Parking Lot) is located on the south side of Citi Field and offers employee, premium, front office, player family, press and guest parking.

Ballpark Chaser Fun Fact: D Lot is the lot where most of Shea Stadiums playing field was located and there are cement and brass markers showing where the pitcher's mound, home plate and bases once rested.

PARKING

Remote Lots- There is 4 parking lots outside the fence line of Citi Field that provide general parking. Marina West, Marina East, Flushing Meadows Park and Stadium View are other options to consider if arriving late.
Mass Transit – NYC Subway
If you are staying in a hotel outside the Flushing area, this is the only way to travel to a Mets game. Don't be intimidated by the NYC subway! Leave plenty of time and confirm directions with your hotel's front desk. <u>Hopstop.com</u> is the easiest way to get the most updated directions from your hotel to Citi Field.

WHERE TO EAT?

Unfortunately, Citi Field is one of the worst ballparks for finding local restaurants and sports bars outside of the ballpark. The area around Citi Field has nothing exciting to offer for pre or post game meals. If you don't want to eat in the park, you will need to take the train since nothing is within walking distance. Not to worry as the food inside the ballpark is a whole new ballgame! Citi Field has one of the largest selections of food offerings in the major leagues and is worth saving your appetite.

Here is a rundown of the non-traditional ballpark fare offered at concession stands around Citi Field and is Ballpark Chaser approved. Shake Shack is one of New York's most popular hamburger and hot dog stands. If you can't make it to one of the Manhattan locations, don't leave Citi Field without sampling a burger. Blue Smoke features amazing barbecue pulled-pork sandwiches and Kansas City Ribs. Box Frites serves freshly-cut, Belgian-style fries with a number of fun and tasty dipping sauces. Catch of the Day, inspired by award winning seafood chef Dave Pasternack, offers lobster rolls, clam chowder, fish sandwiches, and local microbrews. Mama's of Corona serves Italian style sandwiches, salads and desserts and Cascarino's Pizza offers a taste of authentic New York style pizza. If this leaves your head spinning from too many options, just get the Ballpark Chaser meal: a Shake Shack cheeseburger, chocolate shake and a side of Box Frites.

In addition to the concession stands, Citi Field offers 5 clubs/restaurants for fans to sit down for a relaxing meal. The Delta Sky360 Club, Ebbets Club, Caesars Club, Acela Club and the Promenade Club are all exclusive to patrons who have a specific ticket. With so many fun and new concession stands, Ballpark Chasers recommends to skip these over-priced restaurants.

INTANGIBLES 'DCB SAYS':

"The park sight lines are immaculate from every seat and viewpoint in the stadium. I was really impressed with the way they created 'Citi Field' with the exception of the deep-right alley. The scoreboard is a monster--and easily viewed. The background is much more scenic then Shea Stadium. With the old park being demolished it should help even more."

WHERE TO BUY TICKETS?

Tickets to Citi Field were at one time in high demand with the Mets opening the doors to their new ballpark. However, now that the inaugural season is over, tickets are generally easy to come by. Keep in mind that the Mets are one of the teams who started tier pricing. These fluctuating ticket prices will provide a discounted ticket to value games against teams such as the Nationals and Marlins while the price goes up with Platinum games against the Yankees, Phillies, Giants and Rays.

Again there are cheap alternatives in the upper deck--season ticket holders like to sell their tickets on 'Stubhub' for about face value.

You can walk around the stadium with the lowest ticket much like Yankee Stadium and see all the park has to offer.

WHEN TO GO?

Weather is never a huge problem during the season in New York. April and the beginning of May can get cold, but not unbearable. The general consensus is to travel to New York in September and we couldn't agree more. The weather drops to the mid 70s and the evenings are still pleasant. Citi Field is cooler than most places since it sits close to Flushing Bay, which also increases wind, especially in the Promenade Level. Do yourself a favor and bring a jacket if attending a night game.

WHAT ELSE TO SEE?

It's New York City - there is something to do on just about every block! Our favorites include the Empire State Building, Metropolitan Museum of Art, Central Park, Ellis Island (Statue of Liberty), Rockefeller Center and Times Square. However, if you are looking to get off the tourist path, make sure to check out the Ground Zero Museum Workshop in Manhattan's Meatpacking district. Founded by Gary Marlon Suson, the Official Ground Zero Photographer for the Uniformed Firefighters Association, the museum is like no other you will ever visit. After spending 6 months with the recovery workers, Gary has captured some of the most moving and emotional images from the aftermath of September 11th. Gary (who is an Honorary FDNY Chief) also has on display various non-personal artifacts that were salvaged from Ground Zero including window glass, a computer keyboard, lobby marble and a wall clock frozen in time at exactly 10:02:14 (the time the South tower collapsed). Plan on a 2 hour visit that includes a self guided audio tour of the 100+ images and artifacts. And if you are lucky, Gary will be around to welcome you and talk a little baseball. Get tickets in advance (tours sell out fast) by calling ZERVE at (212) 209-3370 or visit their website at www.GroundZeroMuseum.com. Some of the museum proceeds benefit the 'FDNY Foundation' and the 'Brotherhood Foundation'. The Museum is currently work-shopping a new Off-Broadway play, "American Brother" which is ground zero-themed, so stay tuned.

DOUBLE HEADER PARTNERS:

Much of the same as New York Yankees---except for you get a running start on those night games with the Mets playing several games that start at 12:10 pm.

Yankees—you can get to 'Yankee Stadium' by either driving or subway.

Phillies—Via 'Amtrak Train' or driving.

Red Sox—via driving is definitely an option when New York Mets have those noon matinees. It is still a stretch to make it for 1st pitch with Boston's city traffic.

9. COORS FIELD

DENVER, COLORADO
HOME OF THE COLORADO ROCKIES

TRANSPORTATION:

Denver International Airport-(DEN) is 24 miles/30 minute drive to Coors Field. Unfortunately there is no real public transportation to and from the airport. With that being said, you are going to need a car or shuttle bus into town. Car rentals are amongst the cheapest in the nation at $35-40 per day during the weekdays and about 30 percent lower on the weekends. The car rental building is a 5 mile venture from 'DEN' airport. Make sure that you fill up your rental downtown before returning your car rental as there are no visible gas stations within miles of the airport. Denver International airport was voted the 'best airport for travelling' by Business Traveler's Magazine. The airport is a big hub destination for low-fare airlines 'Frontier' and 'Air Tran' along with being a strong hub for 'United and Southwest Airlines.'

WHERE TO STAY?

All are within walking distance (less than 1 mile) of Coors Field.

Unlimited budget

The Westin Tabor Center (most opposing teams stay here)
Ritz-Carlton Denver
Hyatt Regency Denver Colorado Convention Center

Moderate budget

Residence Inn by Marriott - Denver City Center
Hotel Monaco Denver

Sheraton Denver Hotel

Chaser budget traveler

Hampton Inn & Suites - Downtown Denver
Comfort Inn - Downtown Denver

WHERE TO PARK?

Street, metered, paid lots and garage parking are available around Coors Field. Parking can range from $5 to $30 on a typical day. Denver is like most Major League cities and will price gouge when big market teams come to town. Expect to pay up to $50 for close parking when the Red Sox, Cubs and Yankees are visiting.

Ballpark Chasers Tip: If seeing a game during the week, drive north of the stadium (5 blocks or more) for free street parking. Come early as these will fill up quickly when the locals get off work.

WHERE TO EAT?

Great options within walking distance from Coors Field include: Breckenridge Brewery, Old Chicago and Lodos. All three restaurants are great and unique in their own way. Go to Breckenridge Brewery for their microbrews and burgers, to Old C's for their pizza, and Lodos for the pre-game atmosphere and rooftop views of Coors Field! On the other hand, for a more formal option, check out the Chop House for amazing steaks, chops and seafood.

Inside Coors Field there is a wide assortment of food options. Hit up the Blue Moon Brewing Company (behind section 112) before the game for a meal and great microbrews! Unique Coors Field stadium foods include: Denver Cheese Steaks, Blake Street Burritos, Buffalo Hot Dogs and Brats and the Ultimate Nachos. Be sure to try the famous Ballpark Chasers meal, which consists of Rocky Mountain Oysters and a Blue Moon beer. If you are unsure what Rocky Mountain Oysters are, make sure to ask after you eat them. Finally, for those young Chasers, Buckaroos is a concession stand by section 149 featuring traditional ballpark options in child-size portions.

INTANGIBLES:

The outfield concourse is a huge area to watch the baseball game from or to take in the view of the Rocky Mountains. Watch for those vendors outside the park to bring in your own food. The security staff is very accommodating to this perk. If you park at the general parking lot there are shuttles that stop at various spots along the way as the busses move closer to Coors Field. This is an excellent option for those people with limited movement. You can also find many handsome-cab ride operators who will transport you for a nominal fee within the parking limits.

WHERE TO BUY TICKETS?

Box office tickets are typically available before each Rockies home game unless the Cubs, Red Sox or Yankees are visiting. You can always count on the $4 and $1 "Rockpile" tickets to be available 2 ½ hours prior to game time. These center field bleacher seats are a last resort and not for those wanting to pay close attention to the game. Another cheap option is the "purple seat". This upper deck row of purple seats is located exactly a mile-high above sea level. For a last minute purchase, scalpers are clearly identifiable with their "Need Tickets" signs all around Coors Field.

WHEN TO GO?

As the saying goes, "If you don't like the weather in Colorado, just wait 15 minutes". The weather here is as un-predictable as it comes! Play it safe and travel to the mile high city in the months of June, July, August or September. Remember to dress for cool evening temperatures anytime during the year and don't forget the rain gear.

WHAT ELSE TO SEE?

Just a half block west of Coors Field is one of Lodo's (lower downtowns) newest attractions. B's Ballpark Museum is a must see for any Ballpark Chaser! The creator and curator, Bruce "B" Hellerstein, houses one of the top ballpark collections in the country and has already received praises from the Smithsonian. If you are lucky, Bruce will be around for a complimentary guided tour of his current exhibits. Our favorites include the lights from Ebbets Field, pieces from the Green Monster and original seats from old Crosley and Forbes Field! Plan at least 30 minutes inside the museum before a Rockies game.

The 16th Street Mall is a short walk from Coors Field to fun shopping and dining experiences. If you have a rental car and want the true Colorado experience, take the beautiful drive (1-70 west for 35 minutes) to Idaho Springs. This quaint mountain-town has quite possibly the greatest pizza in the country.

Complete your Ballpark Chasers experience by stopping at Tommy Knocker Brewery for an appetizer and beverage of your choice and then enjoy a downtown walk through this former mining town to the world famous Beau Jo's Pizza. Make sure to save your pizza crust for the honey!

BALLPARK CHASERS VACATION?

There are no other ballparks from 'MLB' in the area for almost 1000 miles anywhere but it can surely be combined with a: STL/CHC/CWS/MIL (Central Trip) or a SEA/SF/OAK (West Trip) weekend with early morning flights if you end out west to fly home.

10. NEW YANKEE STADIUM

THE BRONX, NY
HOME OF THE NEW YORK YANKEES

TRANSPORTATION:

LGA/JFK/EWR AIRPORTS

If traveling from out of town there are many ways to end up at Yankee Stadium. Remember to bargain for best price buy using www.kayak.com and click on the nearby airports feature. Any one of these 3 airports listed above may take you to a ballgame.

LGA is the closest option for Yankees and Mets games--you are a simple bus ride and subway to the game. Traveling time is one hour through this mode of transportation from LGA. Landing in JFK is not a bad option either. Take the Air Tram to the transportation building-then proceed to the light rail-transit deck on the bottom level. The train takes a solid 1hr and 15 minutes to put you in front of Yankee Stadium.

From EWR, it is attainable to get to the park even quicker than the others because the 'Amtrak Train'. Service from 'EWR Station' will place you at NY Penn Station in about a 30 minute ride where you can transfer onto the subsequent trains in order to arrive at Yankee Stadium in under an hour

Automobile rentals in any airport are extremely expensive--especially for the short term. The only tip I can add here is that some cheap flights get you to any of the airports early and you should check the flights out of town for the cheapest flight out. Using a one-way car rental to rent from any of the 3 airports and return it to another will not cost you very much money (around $15 but it is worth it rather than fighting traffic and incurring tolls).

Car rentals can range from $55-115 per weekday or weekend. It is the cheapest to rent a car at EWR.

'DCB SAYS'—'TRANSPORTATION OBSERVATION:'

If you are arriving at Yankee Stadium from other eastern cities such as: Baltimore/Washington/Boston and Philadelphia it is the best method of transportation on the 'eastern seaboard.' If you are planning a trip to any of these cities combined with New York City's two teams-I am talking about and highly endorse traveling via 'Amtrak'. Prices range from $45-100 based on city to city-and they run all times of the day and night. You will pay that much on a drive from Baltimore to Boston in tolls on the turnpikes and highways (Baltimore to New York will cost you $30 alone). Amtrak is spacious, time-saving and the best feature is the luggage. For the singular ballpark traveler this can be a big savings ticket. You can use your tickets for any Amtrak train with the same fare as you purchased--you are not tied to a singular ride. Also, the value of the tickets may be transferred towards another fare by changing at any Amtrak ticket station. Again, in most of the stations you can check two pieces of luggage for $3 per item per day. The Train Stations will allow you to pick them up at any time during office hours. This helps those travelers without a vehicle to store their luggage during baseball games and retrieve them later before heading for a hotel or another city—ideal for doubleheader attempts.

'New York Penn' Station has this luggage service and it is invaluable. The train station is also the gateway to all transportation in New York State and New Jersey's 'Light Rail Service.'

WHERE TO STAY?

Unlimited Budget

Unfortunately, there are no 4 or 5 star hotels within 5 miles of Yankee Stadium. If you are willing to take a cab or subway to the game, check out these hotels.

Hilton Garden Inn West 35th St.
Casablanca Hotel
Sofitel Hotel New York

Moderate Budget

Econo Lodge
Days Inn Bronx Yankee Stadium
Howard Johnson Inn Yankee Stadium
Best Western Bronx Inn

Due to the location of Yankee Stadium, there are very few chaser budget hotels. Those motels/hostels, under $100 per night, are not Ballpark Chaser recommended. Sleep at your own risk!

Ballpark Chasers Tip: If you want to avoid driving in this big city, stay in Manhattan and take the subway or cab to the ballpark. This will give you hundreds of hotel/motel options as well as the full New York City experience.

WHERE TO PARK?

Ballpark Chasers strongly suggest taking public transportation to and from your trip to Yankee Stadium. The Yankee Stadium subway stop is located on East 161st Street and River Avenue. The No. 4 train (East Side) and the B and D trains (West Side) make stops at 161st Street/Yankee Stadium. Plan at least 30 minutes from Midtown Manhattan and up to one hour from lower Manhattan. If you are new to the NYC subway system, leave an extra 30 minutes early in case you have any trouble with directions. Overall, it's very easy by subway and is a lot cheaper than a cab or driving yourself. If driving is your only option, leave early, as traffic and parking can be a nightmare! Pre-purchasing your parking spot in advance to insure a space will be available is the only way to go. Expect anywhere between $19 and $40 for parking around Yankee Stadium.

Ballpark Chasers Tip: for a truly unique experience, purchase a ticket aboard the Yankee Clipper! This relaxing cruise will take you to and from the game and also serve a pre-game meal.

WHERE TO EAT?

Don't leave New York without sampling these 3 establishments: a local pizzeria (preferably famous Joe's Pizza and/or Lombardi's), a sidewalk hotdog stand, and a neighborhood deli for a fresh sub. Once you have accomplished this checklist, enjoy the thousands of local New York City restaurants.

The neighborhood surrounding Yankee Stadium is not the greatest for dining options. With that being said, Ballpark Chasers recommends trying one of the 4 main Yankee sports bars: Billy's Sports Bar and Restaurant, Yankee Tavern, The Dugout, and Stan's Sports Bar and Restaurant. It's really hard to differentiate these, as they all serve the same token bar food and expensive drinks, and get real noisy during game days. Nevertheless, it's still a lot of fun to hang with the local Yankee fans and take in the atmosphere. Our favorite for the best food, cheapest beer, most memorabilia and history is Yankee Tavern. What's yours?

Inside Yankee Stadium, food options only get better as there is a place to eat around every corner! This is a major improvement from old Yankee Stadium. There are two choices for a sit-down meal: Hard Rock Café and NYY Steak. Both restaurants are open year-round and, as expected, get very crowded on game-days. The Hard Rock offers indoor and patio setting along with 12 big screen televisions. Although the décor is a little different from other Hard Rock Café's (featuring Yankee memorabilia as well as pieces from local NY musicians and artists), the traditional menu of burgers and smokehouse items is very similar. The one place in the stadium that makes you feel like you are not at a ballpark is NYY Steak. With plates going for over $50, this upscale NYC steakhouse is not for those budget chasers.

For a quick option, Yankee Stadium concessions are abundant and rank in the top 5 of Major League Baseball. Ballpark Chasers favorites include: Brother's Jimmy, Nathan's Hot Dogs, Lobel's and Carl's Steaks. For a healthier snack, check out the Farmers Market's selection of local fruit. Don't forget the Ballpark Chasers meal: a steak sandwich from Lobel's, BBQ beans from Brother's Jimmy and a beverage of your choice from the "Beers of the World" cart.

INTANGIBLES—'DCB SAYS'
-(Full disclosure: Yes, I am a Yankees Fan!)

"Once you arrive at the ballpark area you will notice a bevy of stores that have Yankees memorabilia and jerseys. A lot of them are reasonably priced and they have all the legends from Ruth-Gehrig-Mantle and Mattingly to modern day players-Teixeira-Jeter and Rodriguez. I bought 10 Yankee T-shirts for $150. These are quality t-shirts made from 'Cooperstown Clothing'. If you are arriving via car, make sure you arrive there early to scope these places out.

Yankee Stadium allows you to wander freely around the park with just a bleacher ticket (unlike the old Yankee Stadium where it had a separate entrance). They have banners and flags that archive all the history of the franchise and they moved the monument area over to the new park as well. It looks like the old park just with new modern amenities. It is big, brash and has the pinstripe logo in every corner of the stadium. It truly is the most luxurious stadium ever much like the team it stands above the rest of the league. The only reason it did not take number one is affordability and value. It is just too much money to watch a game. Like Sinatra always said, "If you can make it in New York, you can make it anywhere."

WHERE TO BUY TICKETS?

With the combination of a new ballpark and diehard fans, tickets to a Yankee game are very hard to come by. In fact, the Yankees sold the most tickets in baseball at just over 3.7 million. Ballpark Chasers highly recommends purchasing your tickets in advance to avoid a sellout. Although scalpers are present outside Yankee Stadium, don't expect a bargain or to find a cheap seat before the game. Plan accordingly by purchasing directly through the Yankees or using your favorite online broker.
If traveling alone, you can simply pick up a bleacher ticket for $25-30 on 'Stubhub'. Pairs of tickets will be almost double face value! A strategy that has worked is to wait until a few days before and enter a bid for tickets or watch the price point come down from the sellers at Stubhub. Sometimes you can get them for under face value this way.
The good news is that the Yankees actually possess a Stubhub ticket office nearby to the stadium that you can receive day of tickets from sellers—not only that but the Stubhub/Ticketmaster ticket window is so much quicker than the general ticket window. If you can't wait for your tickets then exhaust all avenues to look for tickets. Other brokers to explore are: www.cheapesttickets.com, www.ticketsnow.com and www.ezticketsearch.com. It is really tough to buy Yankees tickets so don't beat yourself up about the price if you can't find a deal. It is New York City and everything costs lots of money.

Ballpark Chasers Tip: if you discover that your scalper sold you crappy seats or maybe the tickets you bought online were too expensive for the amount of time you will be in your seat, check out the Yankees Stadium Ticket Window (in the Grand Hall). To trade up, you just pay the difference in price. To trade down, the Yankees will issue "Bomber Bucks", better known as gift certificates that can be used at any establishment within Yankee Stadium.

WHEN TO GO?

Weather is never a huge problem during the season in New York. April and the beginning of May can get cold, but not unbearable. The general consensus is to travel to New York in September and we couldn't agree more. The weather drops to the mid 70s and the evenings are still pleasant. If seeing a night game in the Bronx, bring a light jacket or sweatshirt.

WHAT ELSE TO SEE?

It's New York City! There is something to do on just about every block. Our favorites include the Empire State Building, Metropolitan Museum of Art, Central Park, Ellis Island (Statue of Liberty), Rockefeller Center and Times Square. However, if you would rather get off the tourist path, make sure to check out the Ground Zero Museum Workshop in Manhattan's Meatpacking district. Founded by Gary Marlon Suson, the Official Ground Zero Photographer for the Uniformed Firefighters Association, the museum is like no other you will ever visit. After spending 6 months with the recovery workers, Gary has captured some of the most moving and emotional images from the aftermath of September 11th. Gary (who is an Honorary FDNY Chief) also has on display various non-personal artifacts that were salvaged from Ground Zero including window glass, a computer keyboard, lobby marble and a wall clock frozen in time at exactly 10:02:14 (the time the South tower collapsed). Plan on a 2 hour visit that includes a self guided audio tour of the 100+ images and artifacts. And if you are lucky, Gary will be around to welcome you and talk a little baseball. Get tickets in advance (tours sell out fast) by calling ZERVE at (212) 209-3370 or visit their website at www.GroundZeroMuseum.com. Some of the museum proceeds benefit the 'FDNY Foundation' and the 'Brotherhood Foundation'. The Museum is currently work-shopping a new Off-Broadway play, "American Brother" which is ground zero-themed, so stay tuned.

We also recommend following up your time at the Ground Zero Museum Workshop by visiting the World Trade Center Tribute Center. Located on the South side of the World Trade Center site, the Tribute Center offers five galleries of images, artifacts and first hand stories from that fateful Tuesday morning. Catch a guided walking tour conducted by various survivors, recovery workers, firefighters, and family members of 9/11.

BALLPARK CHASERS VACATION?

Yankee Stadium is one stop in the "Northeast 3", which includes seeing Citi Field and Fenway Park. By far, this is the most popular of all Ballpark Chasers vacations. If possible, extend your trip by another day to visit Cooperstown, home of the Baseball Hall of Fame. Cooperstown, New York is just over a 4 hour drive from Boston and New York and provides a once in a lifetime experience for all baseball fans.

DOUBLEHEADER AVAILABILITY:

METS- is a short distance from Mets 'Citi Field' and you can get there either by driving or transit.

PHILLIES-providing one of these teams plays at 1:00 PM and the other at 7pm or later. Note: because of the Yankees and Phillies being so popular, you may get that 'Sunday Night Baseball Game' from one of these parks to start at 8 pm instead of 7pm. Amtrak train is your best option to make 1st and last pitches of both ballparks.

Trips from New York Penn Station-Philadelphia's 30TH ST. Station run every 45 minutes to an hour and it only takes 100 minutes to between cities. Driving can easily take over three hours. Try and beat the crowd to the Subway Station AT E 161ST/1st, and then brave the 20 minute train back to 'NYP'. In Philly there is a cabstand outside the station to take you to the park within 20 minutes.

ORIOLES- is only another 75 minutes down south and if you don't mind arriving an inning or two late it is possible.' BWI station is a 15 minute cab ride from Camden Yards.

11. MILLER PARK

MILWAUKEE, WISCONSIN
HOME OF THE MILWAUKEE BREWERS

TRANSPORTATION:

MKE-(General Mitchell Airport) is in close proximity from Miller Park—and in terms of value may be the best airport to fly in and out of in the US. There are cheap flights from 'Air Tran Airways' and 'Midwest Airlines' to highlight this little airport. It is easily the most accessible airport in the way of security and transportation. I have used this airport countless times for early morning flights coming and going—many of which included one-way drives from other cities just to take advantage of the cheap flights out of MKE.

The car rental building is across the street from the airport. Milwaukee is known for cheap car rentals and you can easily shop for a bargain at Priceline www.priceline.com in the name your own price section. There have been bids won for $15-30 which make Milwaukee one of the cheapest ballpark cities to drive. If you arrive by 'Amtrak or Greyhound' they are more than viable options especially from Chicago—you are an easy cab ride away from the park at $15-20 near the downtown sector.

Ballpark Chaser Tip—'Amtrak' offers baggage service drop-off at the station downtown for $3 per day, a great thing to combine with a doubleheader with Chicago-of course minus the luggage. Both the 'Amtrak and Greyhound Station' are positioned in the same location—remember you can also exit at the airport station and take the free shuttle bus to the airport or to rent a car. Subsequently, you can take this train from the airport to the downtown Amtrak station for a $7.50 fee. Again this would even enable you to use the baggage service if there was a day game in Milwaukee before heading out somewhere after.

WHERE TO STAY?
 All lodging is within a 5 mile drive of Miller Park

Unlimited budget

Iron Horse Hotel
Residence Inn – Milwaukee Hotel
Intercontinental Hotel – Milwaukee
Ambassador Hotel – Milwaukee

Moderate budget

Hampton Inn and Suites – Milwaukee
Doubletree Hotel - Milwaukee City Center
Hilton – Milwaukee City Center

Chaser budget traveler

Best Western – Woods View Inn
Best Western Inn Towne Hotel

Ballpark Chasers Tip: the only hotel within walking distance to Miller Park is the Best Western (Woods View Inn). If you prefer to avoid parking fees, this hotel is the way to go!

'DCB RECOMMENDED HOTELS':

"If you are staying I highly recommend bidding on hotels at www.priceline.com. You can get a hotel room by bidding $25-30 per night. I have used this 3 times already in trips. Most likely they will wind up putting you into the 'Super 8' nearby or the 'Extended Stay America Hotel'-both are in Wauwatosa within 6 miles of the park. They both cost roughly $60 for the night by themselves. The Super 8 has a continental breakfast and a communal internet computer—the Extended Stay is a good option for chasers with young families as they offer kitchenette sets with actual dishes, pots and pans, and a full fridge. If you are staying near the airport for a quick getaway in the morning, I recommend the 'Motel 6-At the Airport'—for $45 per night. Also remember that at a Motel 6, you can check in at 12 PM and you don't need a credit card. This is very convenient for that ballpark chaser to keep their entire credit limit intact for future purchases.

WHERE TO PARK?

The Brewers conveniently offer several large parking lots surrounding Miller Park. When purchasing your game tickets online, look to pre-pay for parking as well. Otherwise, you can purchase an advanced parking pass over the phone by calling 414-902-4000. Make sure to purchase a pass 7 days in advance of the game. You can only pre-purchase in person at the Brewers box office. Advance parking ranges from $8 to $12 depending on the distance to the stadium. Same-day pricing can range from $8-$15 on weekdays, $10-$18 on weekends, and $15-$25 for Marquee parking.

Ballpark Chasers Tip: because the Brewers parking lot tends to be a nightmare after each home game, we suggest using a restaurant shuttle. Kelly's Bleachers, Long Wong's, Rounding Third, McGinn's, Steve's on Bluemound, Fiesta Garibaldi and Derry Hegarty's Pub all offer free shuttles to and from each Brewer game for their customers.

WHERE TO EAT?

With the layout of Miller Park and its centralized parking spaces surrounding the stadium, it isn't really practical to park and walk to a restaurant. However, Miller Park has one of the best and liveliest tailgating scenes in all of Major League Baseball and we highly suggest walking through the parking lot to soak up the ambiance. Don't worry about bringing your own food as Klement's Sausage Haus will take care of you. Klement's, located in the East parking lot, serves great sausages, brats and a few other menu items along with a good selection of microbrews. Make sure to check out their electronic-racing sausage game that imitates the famous outfield race that takes place before the 7th inning of every Brewer home game.

Once inside Miller Park, head over to left field to grab a bite at Friday's Front Row Sports Grill. Friday's serves your traditional American cuisine while providing a great view of the field. Other worthy ballpark options include brats, Italian sausages and Polish sausages. Come on now, you can't leave Miller Park without trying one or more of their staple ballpark sausages!

If you prefer a sit-down option with a larger menu, Ballpark Chasers recommends eating at Kelly's Bleachers or Mollica's Pub. Both local sports bars offer a free shuttle for customers to Miller Park before each home game. One of our favorite restaurants a few miles away is Miss Katie's Diner. This mom-and-pop 60's style diner serves breakfast, lunch and dinner and will make you want to go back for all three meals! We recommend trying their omelets, French toast, pancakes, chicken wings, burgers, open face turkey sandwich, patty melt, chili, meatloaf, BBQ ribs or any of their homemade soups. Did we miss anything? If so, we recommend those items too!

Although it's tough to beat Katie's ribs, we think we have found a Milwaukee restaurant that gives her good competition. Saz's, located about 2 miles from Miller Park, and has been serving "award winning ribs" and steaks for over 30 years. Saz's is so good that they even have their own line of signature sauces in grocery stores across the country!

Check out recently opened Ryan Braun's Waterfront Grill in the Third Ward neighborhood of downtown Milwaukee. Located right along the Milwaukee River, Braun's new restaurant offers indoor and outdoor dining with great views. The menu features fresh seafood in addition to steaks and chops, burgers, chicken, pastas, individual pizzas, sandwiches and hamburgers and kids fare. We haven't had a chance to try it out yet so make sure to give us your review.

INTANGIBLES—'DCB SAYS':

"'Miller Park' has the best ballpark staff in the majors! The first time I was in the park was in April of 2007 to watch a series between the Cleveland Indians and Los Angeles Angels. Milwaukee agreed to help Cleveland out because of the massive snow storms in that opening week. The entire staff showed up and pulled off accommodations for 20,000 fans in the most unusual of circumstances. I was happy to buy floor tickets for $10 each. In 3 or 4 cases I have interacted with the staff—they were the most pleasant staff when it came to the verification process of my "GUINESS BOOK OF WORLD RECORD CLAIM'. Many ushers even gave me their home phone number and were willing to write letters on my behalf as witnesses to me making the first pitch on two different occasions. I give big kudos to the Park too because not only is tailgating not banned on the grounds it is encouraged—heck they give away a free bar fridge to the best tailgate party every game. You rock Milwaukee!"

WHERE TO BUY TICKETS?

Don't call the Brewers a small market team. With the combination of a new ballpark and diehard fans, Miller Park hosted over 3 million fans during the 2009 season, ranking in the top 10 in Major League Baseball. Consequently, Ballpark Chasers recommends pre-purchasing tickets through your favorite online dealer or directly at Brewers.com. Despite the centralized parking lot and "no reselling tickets" signs around Miller Park, scalpers are still to be found if you need a last minute ticket.

Ballpark Chasers Fun Fact: upon entry, keep your eye out for a free copy of Brewers Gameday Magazine. Free copies are distributed at all gates to all fans around Miller Park!

BALLPARK CHASER SPECIAL

—Buy the tickets in Bernie's Dugout Section for $9 and then walk the concourse throughout the game. Tickets are almost always sold out but the ticket agents-outside before game time-have them and are not too expensive. If you go to your seats it is quite entertaining with Bernie having two cheerleaders help him cheer on the Brewers right from his dugout but the sightlines to the game are not as good.

WHEN TO GO?

Milwaukee is on average the second coldest metropolitan city in the country, only behind Minneapolis St. Paul. Annual average temperatures in Milwaukee are a balmy 46 degrees; July and August are the only months to break the 80 degree mark! Although Miller Park has a retractable roof and there are no rain outs, Ballpark Chasers recommend traveling to Wisconsin from late June through August.

WHAT ELSE TO SEE?

Whether or not you are a fan of motorcycles, the Harley Davidson Museum is a must see attraction while in Milwaukee. Located just 10 minutes from Miller Park, the Harley Davidson Museum celebrates the century old Milwaukee based company. Besides seeing hundreds of old and new Harleys during your audio tour, the museum also offers a "hands-on" demonstration, memorabilia, corporate archives, an in house restaurant and of course a gift shop!

If your trip to Miller Park falls over a weekend, head over to the Milwaukee River to take a brewery tour followed by a boat ride on the "Milwaukee Maiden" or the "Brew City Queen II". Customers get to choose between one of 3 local brew houses: the Lake Front Brewery, The Ale House and the Rock Bottom Brewery. The Brewery Tour and boat ride are for ages 21 and older and tickets must be pre-purchased. Ballpark Chasers recommend the Lake Front Brewery tour!

Our final stop gives you a real feel and taste of Milwaukee with a unique 19th century architectural style. Old World Third Street, just west of the Milwaukee River, is an area of downtown that offers entertainment, dining, shopping, and an up close look at Wisconsin's heritage. Whatever you do, make sure and stop at Mader's for a bite to eat and see why they have been open for over 100 years!

BALLPARK CHASERS VACATION?

Miller Park is part of the Ballpark Chasers Midwest Extravaganza! This baseball trip includes a trip to Chicago to see the White Sox at U.S. Cellular Field and the Cubs at Wrigley Field. Expect a 2 hour drive from Milwaukee to Chicago and a 20 minute drive between Wrigley Field and U.S. Cellular Field. Because the Chicago ballparks are so close together, it is possible to take in a day-night doubleheader. It is much easier for 'Milwaukee' to be the second leg of the trip with traffic and with

'Amtrak' schedule and because of the intense Cubs matinee scheduling. If you are okay with missing 20-30 minutes of a Sox or Cubs game you can watch a Milwaukee matinee day game first and catch the 5:45 pm train to arrive at Chicago Union Station at 7:14-from there you 15-20 minutes away from either team via subway.

12. ORIOLES PARK AT CAMDEN YARDS

BALTIMORE, MARYLAND
HOME OF THE BALTIMORE ORIOLES

TRANSPORTATION:

BALTIMORE/WASHINGTON INTERNATIONAL AIRPORT-(BWI) is a 10 mile drive from the ballpark; however, you have options from several different ways. If you are flying into to 'BWI', make sure you give yourself ample time to and from. BWI is a strong hub for both 'Southwest Airlines' and "Air Tran Airways.' The prices are very convenient with both carriers and many early morning non-stop flights are available for under a hundred dollars-particularly anywhere in the Eastern Seaboard or the 'State of Florida.'

If you are driving, not only is Maryland adjacent but Virginia and DC are filled with high volume on the main highways but the 'BWI Transportation Center' is a good 3-5 mile shuttle bus from the airport. Car rentals are expensive to start with at $55-80 for a weekday but may be bargained for at www.priceline.com or www.expedia.com to drop the price.

If you are coming from Washington it is the doomed highway that connects the 'Beltway traffic.' Unless you have to drive a car, public transport is a more viable option. Coming from the East states of New Jersey and Delaware will cost you about $17 in tolls once you enter the NJ Turnpike, and if you are coming from the State of West Virginia it is not as taxing in the pocketbook and the drive is easier.

It depends where you are staying but light rail from the airport all the way to downtown Baltimore is time effective at 20-25 minutes—along with being cost effective.

Another viable option is taking 'Amtrak Train' from either east or west. There are several trains that run from as south as Raleigh North Carolina all the way to Boston of the North East. In between the main ballpark cities of NYY/PHI/WSH the fares range from $45-60 per traveler or if you wish to take an 'Acela Express Train' (which acts like a business class travel of train riding) you can pay double for quicker trains that have less frequent stops.

The 'Amtrak Station' downtown is only a few miles from the ballpark and will cost you about $15 for a cab. This is ideal for that passer through chaser who might watch a day game in Baltimore before heading to Washington or New York afterwards. Much like downtown stations everywhere there is even baggage check service.

WHERE TO STAY?

All hotels below are within walking distance to Oriole Park

Unlimited budget

<u>Hampton Inn</u> Baltimore Camden Yards
<u>Hyatt Regency</u> Baltimore
<u>Residence Inn</u> Baltimore Downtown/Inner Harbor

Moderate budget

<u>Baltimore Inner Harbor Marriott</u> at Camden Yards
<u>Hilton</u> Baltimore
<u>Hampton Inn & Suites</u> Inner Harbor
<u>Springhill Suites by Marriott</u> Baltimore

Chaser budget traveler

<u>Sheraton Baltimore</u> City Center

DCB TIP FOR BALTIMORE:

"I highly recommend using Priceline for bidding on hotels nearest to the airport. You can typically get a $200 a night hotel for about $70-80. I personally stayed at the 'Marriot Residence Inn At BWI Airport'-this is located in nearby Linthicum, Maryland. There was a free shuttle bus to and from the airport. I used the free shuttle bus on the way back from the O's game after using light rail to the airport. I wasn't sure where exactly the hotel was from one of the light rail stations so this ensured I would be taken back to the hotel safely at least."

WHERE TO PARK?

Over 30,000 street metered, garage and paid lot parking spaces are available surrounding Oriole Park. The downtown/Inner Harbor area of Baltimore offers plenty of parking, ranging from $5 to $25, depending on the distance to the stadium. Expect a 5 to 20 minute walk to the stadium from these parking lots.

Ballpark Chasers Tip: be cautious of the "free street parking" signs. Not only is there usually a 2 hour limit, but game days will void any free parking.

WHERE TO EAT?

Downtown Baltimore is one of our favorite cities for pre-game food and beverages. It was difficult to narrow down all of the great sports bars and restaurants next to Oriole Park, but we have managed to recommend the top three. As of now, Pickles Pub takes the top honor for our favorite local sports bar and restaurant. Ballpark Chasers come here for the pre and postgame atmosphere and to hang with the local Oriole fans. Whatever you do, don't leave without trying your luck in a game of corn hole.
Camden Pub is just 2 blocks from Oriole Park and even closer to the Babe Ruth Museum. It's the place to go before and after an Orioles game if you want a crowd of lively sports fans, an assortment of pub food and great beers on tap. Ballpark Chasers rate this pub so high because of their sports memorabilia collection. Make sure to save room for a plate of their famous wings! For those beer connoisseurs, check out The Wharf Rat on Pratt Street. With over 15 homemade Ales to choice from, the Wharf Rat is a perfect restaurant if you are looking for more than just a quick bite. Make sure to order the Ballpark Chasers meal: cheese fries to start, Henry VIII's meatloaf for the main course and an Oliver Summer Light for your beverage.
Once inside Oriole Park at Camden Yards, you must try <u>Boog's Barbeque</u>. Don't even worry about where to find it; just follow the smell as it will lead you to their stand! Owned, operated and sometimes served by Boog Powell himself, one of Baltimore's local legends for his big bat and 4 World Series appearances. Boog's is consistently voted as one of the top ballpark foods in all of baseball and is worthy of a sample of beef, pork or turkey BBQ sandwich. Another Oriole Park favorite is the Bud Light Warehouse Bar (located on Eutaw Street). —right close to the warehouse across from the ball yard. The ballpark cooks old style burgers, ribs, hot dogs, with delightful sides of coleslaw, potato wedges or French fries—and the best baked beans ever had. These delicatessen style eats are reasonably priced at $12-15 for the lot including drink. The aroma alone from this barbeque row will draw you to the park.
Stop for a pregame meal and watch the live broadcast of the Orioles All-Access Show. With all of these choices in and around Oriole Park, be forewarned of a potential gut-bomb from over indulgence!

INTANGIBLES:

Oriole Park was one of the first "new ballparks" built in the Nineties. The unique feeling of the ballpark players of yesteryear prominently displayed resembles a once proud franchise. You can try walking around where all the homerun balls (marked all in that same area as the Barbeque pit directly adjacent to the ware house)were hit by home and away ballplayers from yesteryear.

WHERE TO BUY TICKETS?

The 2010 season ranked Oriole Park at Camden Yards in the bottom third of MLB attendance. On average, half of the stadium was empty when the Orioles took the field. Unless the talent improves on the field or the Orioles are playing the Red Sox or Yankees, tickets will be easily available last minute at the main box office. Keep in mind that the city of Baltimore allows the resale of tickets outside of Oriole Park as long as one is selling at face value or less. Ballpark Chasers love to get their tickets this way due to great bargains from season ticket holders trying to dump their seats.

Ballpark Chasers tip: Bring your best appetite for the Left Field Club Picnic Perch. These seats go for $40 ($45 on game day) and include all you can eat hot-dogs, peanuts, nachos, ice cream, soda and popcorn.

WHEN TO GO?

Baltimore's coastal climate tends to bring warm and sunny summers. On average, July and August tend to the warmest and most humid, with temperatures in the mid to upper 80s and even reaching into the 90s. Rainfall is pretty consistent month-to-month during the summer. Ballpark Chasers find May and June the most pleasant time of year to travel to Camden Yards.

WHAT ELSE TO SEE?

The perfect way to spend an afternoon before an Orioles game is to visit the Babe Ruth Birthplace Museum and the Sports Legends Museum. Both are within walking distance from one another, as well as from Oriole Park. Since 1974, the Babe Ruth Museum has been a shrine to arguably the greatest baseball player of all time. Current exhibits include the 500 Home Run Club, artifacts from the Babe's childhood and the actual room where the great George Herman Ruth was born!

The Sports Legends Museum at Camden Yards is a two-floor, 22,000 sq ft. former train station that had Abraham Lincoln pass through on several occasions. Thankfully, the building was saved and remolded throughout the years and converted into a top notch sports museum. Showcases include: the history of Orioles baseball, the 1958 World Champion Baltimore Colts football, Johnny Unitas' jersey, minor and amateur baseball in Maryland, Negro Leagues and a "locker room" for kids to try on uniforms and jerseys.

About 30 miles North of Baltimore is a small town called Aberdeen where sports fans come to pay tribute to the "Iron Man"! Aberdeen is the birthplace of Cal Ripken Jr. as well as the hometown for most of the Ripken family (Cal, Cal Sr. and Billy Ripken). The Ripken Museum is quite small so don't plan on spending more than 1 hour here. If you need something else to do, head over to Ripken Stadium to catch an Aberdeen Iron Birds game.

BALLPARK CHASERS VACATION?

Oriole Park at Camden Yards is part of the "East Coast Swing" Ballpark Chasers vacation. This trip includes seeing the Phillies at Citizens Bank Park and the Nationals at Nationals Park. We suggest finding the cheapest flight to Washington DC, Baltimore or Philadelphia and getting a rental car to drive in between. Expect up to a 1 hour drive from Baltimore to DC, a 3 hour drive between DC and Philadelphia and 2 hours from Philadelphia back to Baltimore. Keep in mind that these times reflect little traffic but that will never happen during the weekdays. The "East Coast Swing" can easily be done in three days but plan for 5 to have time at local attractions and museums.

DOUBLE HEADER PARTNERS:

WASHINGTON-if there is a day-night scenario, despite the bumper to bumper traffic, you would be able to make the two city doubleheader.

PHILADELPHIA-I highly advise that you take the train in between cities in some form to make first and last pitch.

YANKEES/METS-You have a chance to see most of the second game should you choose to do New York first then take the train to Baltimore for the second game. There is an Amtrak Train that leaves New York Penn at 4:30 is and you get to Baltimore around 7:15 pm or so, with a 15 minute cab ride.

13. CITIZENS BANK BALLPARK

PHILADELPHIA, PENNSYLVANIA
HOME OF THE PHILADELPHIA PHILLIES

TRANSPORTATION:

Philadelphia International Airport-(PHL) is only 6 miles away from the park and is about 15-20 minutes in driving. 'PHL' is a clustered airport with not enough room for the amount of passengers it sees on a daily basis. The airport is a hub for US Airways and has strong flights with Southwest as well. The flights are not cheap and it may be easier and less expensive to fly out of 'BWI' or 'EWR' instead. The car rental facilities are a quick shuttle ride and are actually not that bad considering the rest of the airport is so sideways. Parking long term at 'PHL' is also a nightmare with a long shuttle bus to the economy lots. Car rentals per day are one of the most expensive deals at about $80 for a weekday and not much less on the weekend. If you are flying to Philadelphia for a one off trip then I would bid on www.priceline.com to get your fare reduced. There is one other option—this would mean you would be in the city for more than a week and within Philadelphia City Limits at all times. Rentawreck.com gives you a weekly rental rate for about $175 for the week, but has miles restrictions of penalties over 200 miles for the week. There is also a shuttle you have to pay $25 to and from to get this deal at Mt. Laurel Shopping Center but $225 overall for the week is about half of what you would pay at the airport. With sights like the Philadelphia Zoo, 'The Liberty Bell' and the 'Rocky Balboa' steps maybe you can squeeze out a week in the city.

Ballpark Chaser Tip—Make sure you get to the airport early for the security lineups in this airport and please check out your flight itinerary if you fly with 'US Airways'. If you are flying out of the 'F Terminal' be aware that this gate is entirely separate from the airport and you will need to take a secondary shuttle that comes with big lines and takes a lot of time.

It is fantastic that Citizens Bank is so close to the airport in Philly, but it is not so convenient for lodging. Citizens Bank Park is in the same Sports Complex that features 'Lincoln Financial Field' and the 'Wachovia Center'. This can prove very bad for traffic if another one of these sporting events coincides with a baseball game. If you are coming from the south, the 'Walt Whitman Bridge' on I-76 will carry a toll of $4.00 with it. If you are coming from the Jersey Turnpike—you can avoid the tolls by driving into the city of Philadelphia. Use www.googlemaps.com to see the routes to avoid the tolls.

AMTRAK OPTION

If you are coming from Baltimore, DC or New York City, you would be well advised to use an Amtrak train. They are fast-traffic efficient and a convenient way to travel between cities. New York to Philadelphia starts from $45.00 fees for a one-way ticket. The Amtrak/Greyhound/30th station is about a fifteen minute cab-ride into the ballpark. You can even park at the station when travelling abroad and back. Again with Amtrak it helps the hardcore chaser attempt many of doubleheaders with the eastern cities close by.

WHERE TO STAY?

Unlimited budget- all 3 options are within 4 miles of Citizens Bank Park

The Rittenhouse Hotel - Philadelphia
Double Tree Hotel - Philadelphia
Sofitel Philadelphia Hotel

Moderate budget

Holiday Inn – Philadelphia Stadium (walking distance from Citizens Bank Park)
Alexander Inn

Chaser budget traveler – both options are within 5 miles of Citizens Bank Park

Days Inn – Philadelphia Brooklawn

Travelodge – Philadelphia

WHERE TO PARK?

The Philadelphia Phillies offer a number of parking lots surrounding Citizens Bank Park. Car parking is $12 and can easily be found on all sides of the stadium. If you want to avoid driving in the city of Philadelphia, catch a cab from the airport and stay at the Holiday Inn that is featured above. It is the only hotel that is within walking distance of Citizens Bank Park.

WHERE TO EAT?

Close to Citizens Bank Park and one of Philly's best kept secrets is Pastificio. Serving homemade pastas, hoagies, salads, fresh mozzarella and everything in between, Pastificio will make you want to come back a second time before leaving town!
The Reading Terminal Market is one of the most diverse places in all of Philadelphia for dining. With over 80 vendors, including 30 restaurants, you can find just about everything at this farmers market. Don't leave without sampling from the famous 4th Street Cookie Company, finding Philbert the Pig and making a donation to his piggy bank! One more thing, avoid eating the Scrapple – trust us there are two restaurants within Citizens Bank Park. First, McFadden's Restaurant and Saloon is located at the 3rd Base Gate and is the place to be before a Phillies game. Come here for an amazing cheese steak sandwich and chat it up with the locals about their 2008 dream season.

Second is Harry the K's Broadcast Bar & Grille which is located underneath the left field scoreboard. Citizens Bank Park is one of Ballpark Chasers favorite stadiums when it comes to concession stands. This park offers a smorgasbord of options to choose from. Some of our favorites include: The Schmitter, Bull's BBQ and Chickie's and Pete's Crab Fries.

If your tickets are in the 'SRO Section' you are conveniently located near numerous food courts so you must east a Philly Cheese steak at 'Tony Luke's--Quite Simply the Cheese steaks there are probably the best 'singular food' at any park in the majors.

INTANGIBLES:

The concourse is awesome for that roaming chaser who paid just to get inside the ballpark and take it all in. Citizens Bank is also one of the best for people with disabilities and/or if they are handicapped. The only problem we have encountered is during a rain delay there is not much undercover shelter so bring your raingear!

WHERE TO BUY TICKETS?

The Phillies are always competitive which means one thing when it comes to ballpark attendance: sellouts! Citizens Bank Park was on average 103.5% full during a game in 2010! Buy your tickets ahead of time through Phillies.com or your favorite online dealer. If all else fails, you can count on a sea of scalpers working the streets before the game. However, be skeptical of scalpers outside of Citizens Bank Park. Ballpark Chasers reported that not only are bogus tickets common, but also counterfeit cash is often returned with your purchase! For that singular traveler you have Stubhub www.stubhub. com that you can see for decent prices on E-tickets. Don't be afraid to buy SRO'S as thousands do it every year. These are not bad tickets because you can watch the game near 'TONY LUKE'S inside with so many other ballpark fans. The sightlines for these tickets are really good.

Ballpark Chasers Tip: a fun and social way to catch a Phillies game is buying a "Porch Package" ticket. This ticket gets you in the leftfield scoreboard area along with a $10 credit for food anywhere in Citizen Bank Park.

WHEN TO GO?

July tends to be the hottest, wettest and muggiest month in Philadelphia. Spring-like temperatures stick around through April; therefore, Ballpark Chasers find the best time to travel to Citizens Bank Park is in the months of May, June and August.

WHAT ELSE TO SEE?

A trip to Philadelphia isn't complete without soaking in some of our country's richest history. Just 3 miles from Citizens Bank Park is Independence Hall. There you can see where Benjamin Franklin, Thomas Jefferson and John Adams announced the Declaration of Independence, where the United States Constitution was drafted and where the American Flag was agreed upon! Although tickets are complimentary, you are required to <u>reserve ahead of time</u> (same day is allowed).

After you work up an appetite walking around the streets of Philadelphia, make sure you fill up by taking a <u>Philly Food Tour</u>! This delicious 2-hour tour includes seven stops to local mom-and-pop restaurants that give you the true taste of Philadelphia. Make reservations and save room for Italian hoagies, pizza, chocolate pretzels, cheesecake, tastykakes and much more authentic Philadelphia favorites!

Another fun way to spend the afternoon and see Philadelphia is at Rittenhouse Row—a premier neighborhood filled with shopping, dining, galleries and cultural venues. Come see why this is nicknamed "Restaurant Row" and don't leave without grabbing dinner at the Palm Restaurant!

BALLPARK CHASERS VACATION?

Citizens Bank Park is part of Ballpark Chasers "East Coast Swing". This trip includes seeing <u>Nationals Park</u> and <u>Oriole Park</u>. We suggest finding the cheapest flight to Washington DC, Baltimore or Philadelphia and getting a rental car to drive in between. Expect up to a 1 hour drive from DC to Baltimore, 2 hours from Baltimore to Philadelphia and a 3 hour drive between DC and Philadelphia. Keep in mind that these times reflect little traffic but that will never happen during the weekdays. The "East Coast Swing" can easily be done in three days but plan for 5 to have time at local attractions and museums.

DOUBLE HEADER PARTNERS:

Philadelphia is ideal for a doubleheader 2nd leg of a day night dip with their eastern city companion. Amtrak has service from 'New York Penn Station' with trains every 20 minutes between 3pm and 5:15 that get you to 30th station in time to hail a cab. From there expect a 20 minute cab ride to Citizens Bank Park. You have a number of trains that leave in the 4:30-5:30 range that also get you to Baltimore and Washington with a shot a game time when PHL is the 1st leg of the trip. You are better off trying BAL/WSH to PHL only on the weekend.

All of: BAL/WSH/NYM/NYY are capable of day/night doubleheaders by car if you can luck out by car in traffic however I would not suggest this as the New York traffic at rush hour is crazy---even tougher is that 'Beltway traffic'. Now if it is the weekend, you have a decent shot in driving to any of these. Don't forget if any of these teams have the special 8 PM Eastern start times for 'Sunday Night Baseball Games.'

14. TARGET FIELD

MINNEAPOLIS, MINNESOTA
HOME OF THE MINNESOTA TWINS

TRANSPORTATION:

Minneapolis St. Paul International Airport-(MSP) is 14 miles/21 minutes from Target Field. MSP is a strong hub for 'Delta Airlines' and for cheaper airlines 'Air Tran Airways' and 'Sun Country Air'. Much like Milwaukee, this airport runs a great deal of early morning flights both east and west. From 4:30 AM and onward, this airport is bustling with travelers. This is one of the finest airports in America for cleanliness and vending within the area. The transportation center is located a tram ride away. Car rentals are decently priced for the weekdays at $35-$55 and even cheaper on the weekend. One nice thing about this transportation center is that it features a security check point in the 'Lindbergh Terminal' that can save you several minutes. This feature is only available to those travelers without checked luggage.

BY CAR

Major routes into Downtown Minneapolis:
From Interstate 94 Westbound, take the 5th Street exit.
From Hiawatha/55, use the 3rd Street exit.
From Interstate 94 Eastbound, follow the signs [more info to follow]

BY LIGHT RAIL

Light rail train service runs along the Hiawatha Corridor, which runs from the Mall of America to downtown Minneapolis (the ends of the line are MOA and Target Field). Most people who use this service park at the Fort Snelling park-and-ride lot. The Mall of America does not have an official park and ride area, but I know some people still park there before catching the train.

Ball Park Chaser Tip--After the game, always walk the distance to the next subway stop in order to avoid the huge crowd waiting otherwise it may take 30-60 minutes to even board the train. Whereas taking the 7-10 minutes to walk will put you to the front of the line when boarding the train. Before the game make sure you don't get caught out at the "Mall Of America" within the hour of game time as the crowds are bigger for the subway because of the free parking there. Also pre-pay for your transportation fare to avoid line-ups. You can buy day passes on the light rail for $6-$8.

WHERE TO STAY?

All options below are less than 1 mile from of Target Field.

Unlimited Budget

<u>The Grand Hotel</u> Minneapolis
<u>The Westin</u> Minneapolis
<u>Residence Inn by Marriott</u> Minneapolis at the Depot

Moderate Budget

<u>The Marquette Hotel</u>
<u>The Hotel Minneapolis</u>
<u>The Depot</u> Minneapolis
<u>Hilton Garden Inn</u> Minneapolis Downtown

Chaser Budget Traveler

<u>Best Western</u>-The Normandy Inn & Suites
<u>Crowne Plaza Downtown</u>

WHERE TO PARK?

Located in the historic warehouse district of downtown Minneapolis, Target Field is being acclaimed as the most transit-friendly ballpark in America. Since there isn't a centralized parking lot around the ballpark, we recommend taking either the: Hiawatha Light Rail, Bus, Northstar Commuter Rail or Game-Day Express Bus. The Hiawatha Line has a Target Field terminal and offers 19 stations between the Mall of America and downtown Minneapolis. Numerous bus routes will connect with the trains at Hiawatha Line stations. Ballpark Chasers recommend purchasing the "Event 6-hour Pass" for a cheap round-trip to and from the ballgame.
The Northstar Commuter Rail Line provides rides from Big Lake to the Target Field station with stops in Elk River, Anoka, Coon Rapids and Fridley. The Northstar only delivers service to a select number of Twins games, so <u>make sure</u> your game is one of them.

When driving into downtown Minneapolis and Target Field, look for street parking, meter parking, garages and paid lots. Depending on the direction you are coming from, you will want to find the <u>easiest route</u> to Target Field. Street parking will always be the cheapest option (sometimes free, if you are lucky)! Just make sure you follow the <u>meter signs</u>. The easiest and yet most expensive options are the <u>dozens</u> of paid lots and garages surrounding Target Field. As with all event parking the closer to the ballpark, the more expensive the lot. Adjacent to Target Field is the AMB/Hawthorne garage which holds almost 7,000 parking spaces. Ballpark Chasers suggest finding a parking spot in a lot or garage further away from Target Field to avoid the post-game traffic.

WHERE TO EAT?

Hubert's Bar & Grille, a local Minneapolis favorite for the past 26 years, just opened a new location by Target Field. Modeled after their first restaurant which is filled with sports memorabilia, large screen televisions and great bar food, Hubert's is a must stop before a Twins game. Another close option is Kieran's Irish Pub, just 2 blocks from Target Field. Ballpark Chasers come for their famous fish and chips and corned beef Reuben's, but stay for their live music and drink menu. If you prefer a younger and livelier crowd, we recommend Sneaky Pete's, located 3 blocks from Target Field. Sneaky Pete's is open 365 days of the year and serves a full meal until 1am. With 55 high definition televisions showing every game live, what is not to love about this place (did we mention the beautiful servers)! This is the spot to be in downtown Minneapolis after a sporting event as Sneaky Pete's dance floor is open every night until 2am.

Christening a new ballpark brings tons of new and exciting concession stands and ballpark treats! Twins fans welcome this much needed upgrade as the old Metrodome had some of the worst food in all of baseball. Minnesotans will be excited to hear that local favorites such as: Murray's Steakhouse, The Loon Cafe, J.D. Hoyt's and Kramarczuk's Sausage are going to be offering their specialties around Target Field. Other new and noteworthy items you have to sample are walleye on a stick and pork-chop on a stick. Have you ever had a burger with the cheese melted inside the patty? Neither have we but Jucy Lucy burgers figured it out and made it taste really good at the same time. Look for these in select concessions around the ballpark. As for hot-dogs, the Twins went back to their original routes of Metropolitan Stadium for the same recipe of "Original Twins Dog". As for the Metrodome favorite "Dome Dog", they have done away with it and replaced it with a quarter-pound "Twins Big Dog". Two other styles to sample are the "Dugout Dog" and "Dinger Dog".

Ballpark Chasers Tip: with the exception of opening day, every Monday home game at Target Field is Dollar-A-Dog Day. The original Twins Dog are sold for the unheard of price of $1 (limit 2 at a time).

INTANGIBLES:

Being a brand new ballpark and outdoors for the first time since 1982 has returned Minnesota to back to weather induced temperatures. The ballpark has an incredible view in any of the concourse scenery to see the whole field of play. The fans have risen to the challenge with selling out every baseball game which is a far cry from the last decade when the Twins were talked about in contraction. It is definitely 'Twins Territory' at Target Field!

WHERE TO BUY TICKETS?

Over the past 8 seasons, the Twins have ranked in the bottom 1/3 of Major League Baseball attendance. However, with the combination of another race for a playoff spot and this season's new stadium, Target Field ought to be a tougher ticket to come by during the 2010 season. With any ballpark's inaugural season, it is always a good idea to purchase your tickets in advance, in case of a sell-out. Otherwise, bring a load of cash as scalpers will be ever present in the streets surrounding the ballpark.

WHEN TO GO?

On average, the Twin Cities are the coldest metropolitan cities in the nation. Because the Twins no longer play in the comforts of a dome, weather should certainly play a factor when planning your baseball trip. The last thing you want is a rain or snow out! For this reason, Ballpark Chasers highly recommends planning your trip to Minnesota in June, July or August.

WHAT ELSE TO SEE?

Despite the lack of top rated attractions in the Minneapolis/St. Paul area, there are a few baseball museums worthy of a visit. The Minnesota Amateur Baseball Hall of Fame, located on the second floor of the St. Cloud Civic Center, is a must see for those hard-core baseball fans. The museum specializes in Minnesota's amateur, minor league, college, high school, and legion baseball history. The MHOF showcases memorabilia dating back to 1857, including such items as uniforms, photos, bats, balls, programs and so much more. The Hall of Fame is open to the public and currently offers free admission! Call the St. Cloud Civic Center Office at 320-255-7272 for hours of operation.

Another free museum in the area is the Original Baseball Hall of Fame Museum of Minnesota. Founded by Ray Crump, a Washington Senators batboy and the first ever equipment manager of the Minnesota Twins, Ray showcases his collectibles from years past. This self-guided museum is a must for any Twins fan, but will still captivate any baseball purist. Located across the street from Gate A of the old Metrodome, stop by before the game and see Kirby's shrine and the world's largest Twins bobble head! Allow about 30 minutes to walk through at your leisure.

The Mall of America is our final recommendation and is a short 15 minute drive from Target Field. This 4 story mall is one of the largest in the world and houses over 500 stores! To put it in perspective, seven Yankee stadiums could fit inside of this building! I know; we didn't believe it either!

BALLPARK CHASERS VACATION?

Unfortunately, Target Field is all alone in the northern, central part of the United States. Ballpark Chasers recommends a weekend trip to Target Field to see a few games as well as the local museums. However, if you are itching for a long road trip, it is possible to combine Target Field along with Miller Park or Kauffman Stadium. A trip to Miller Park is 333 miles or 5.5 hours away while Kauffman Stadium is 440 miles or roughly 6.5 hours from Target Field.

15. <u>THE BALLPARK IN ARLINGTON</u>

<u>ARLINGTON, TEXAS</u>
<u>HOME OF THE TEXAS RANGERS</u>

<u>TRANSPORTATION:</u>

DFW—(DALLAS/FORT WORTH) is 13 miles and 30 minutes away from the park. 'DFW' is one of the cleanest and nicely run airports in the country. 85% of the flights are operated by 'American Airlines.' Unfortunately, travelling anywhere in the State of Texas is very costly.

DAL—(DALLAS/LOVE FIELD) is 23 miles and 32 minutes to Rangers ballpark. DAL is mostly known for being a hub for 'Southwest Airlines' and cheaper commuter flight airlines in Continental Express and Delta Connection.
You may save some money for the flight but you will pay it back in car rentals as rentals are very expensive anywhere in Texas unless it is the weekend.

You can pay $70-100 for a weekday rental and the weekend is extremely low at $20-$30. It is much more pleasant to drive rather than be put through the high Texas temperatures while waiting for public transit or cabs. The good news is there are no tolls. You must take a tram in order to arrive at the transportation center at 'DFW'.

<u>WHERE TO STAY?</u>

<u>Unlimited budget</u>- there is no 5 star hotels near Rangers Ballpark that we recommend.

<u>Moderate budget</u>- All the following lodging is within 1 mile of Rangers Ballpark

<u>Wingate by Wyndham</u> Arlington (ask about the Texas Sports Package)
<u>Candlewood Suites</u> Arlington
<u>Sheraton</u> Arlington Hotel
<u>Courtyard by Marriott</u> Arlington Ballpark
<u>Hyatt Place</u> Arlington

<u>Chaser budget traveler</u>-The following lodging is within 1 mile of Rangers Ballpark.

<u>Sleep Inn</u> Main Gate Six Flags
<u>Holiday Inn Express</u> Arlington Six Flags

<u>Ballpark Chasers Tip</u>: all hotels listed above are part of the Arlington Trolley line. Check with the front desk staff on how to catch a complimentary trolley to the Rangers game.

WHERE TO PARK?

If you stay at a hotel other than those suggested above and are forced to drive to the park, the Texas Rangers offer general parking on the North and East sides of the ballpark for $12. Valet parking runs $30 and if you drive a Lexus to the ballpark, valet parking is free!

WHERE TO EAT?

Bobby V's Sports Gallery Café is our top pick for local restaurants in the Arlington city limits. Although it is roughly a 20 minute drive from Rangers Ballpark, Bobby Valentine's sports bar is covered with sports memorabilia and televisions and is definitely worth the trip.

The Arlington Steak House has been serving since 1931 and is Ballpark Chasers favorite locally owned restaurant in Arlington, Texas. Just 5 miles from Rangers Ballpark, this steak house is famous for making meals from scratch and refusing to use microwaves. Oh yeah, the chicken fried steak is to die for – don't miss out!

Inside Rangers Ballpark, Rawlings All American Grille is the best place to grab a pre-game meal and mingle with the local Ranger fans. Located behind Right-Field, Rawlings provides a great view of the entire field. Come for the food, but don't leave without trying the "Margariter Liter". As far as the concession stands, Rangers Ballpark has a number of delicious options for all appetites. Ballpark Chasers favorites include: Turkey Legs (section 16 & 34), Hickory Smoked Sausage, BBQ sandwich (section 16 & 34) and the 1/2 hot dog (Section 17). Whatever you decide, make sure you leave room for a warm cinnamon roll found only outside of section 10.

INTANGIBLES:

Make sure you check out the bullpens view from center field. By far, the view of watching the players warm up pitching exceeds any other vantage point in the majors and is great for pictures. Also in the immediate vicinity there is a little slush house that has picnic tables and full air conditioning to cool down. Very ideal for kids.

WHERE TO BUY TICKETS?

Despite a World Series run, the Texas Rangers ranked in the middle of Major League attendance during the 2010 season. For this reason, box office tickets are readily available prior to the first pitch and can easily be purchased on game day or through your favorite online ticket broker.

Ballpark Chasers Alert: selling tickets outside of Rangers Ballpark is illegal and undercover police officers are there to make sure of it. Therefore, don't count on easily finding scalpers as you would for most other Major League Baseball stadiums.

WHEN TO GO?

The summer months in Arlington are hotter than hot! Temperatures average in the 90s during June, July and August! If you prefer milder temperatures, Ballpark Chasers suggest planning your trip to Rangers Ballpark in April or early May.

WHAT ELSE TO SEE?

When visiting Rangers Park in Arlington, make sure to leave time to visit Legends of the Game Museum located on the stadium grounds. This interactive museum is filled with more than just Major League Baseball memorabilia. Exhibits include Negro Leagues, Texas Leagues, Women Baseball Leagues, Texas Rangers baseball and fun activities such as catching a Nolan Ryan fastball! Tickets are just $12 and are a perfect way to spend a few hours before the game.

Another fun option is right next to Rangers Ballpark. Six Flags over Texas Amusement Park is a must for those who enjoy roller coasters. Six Flags is home of "The Texas Giant", which happens to be the tallest wooden roller coaster in the world, measuring 14 stories high with speeds up to 62 mph!

BALLPARK CHASERS VACATION?

Rangers Ballpark is part of Ballpark Chasers "Texas Dos" Vacation which includes seeing the Astros at Minute Maid Park. We suggest searching for flights to both cities to determine which airfare is the cheapest. Expect a 4 hour drive (256 miles) between ballparks, with heavy traffic in both directions.

16. DODGER STADIUM

LOS ANGELES, CALIFORNIA
HOME OF THE LOS ANGELES DODGERS

TRANSPORTATION:

Los Angeles Int'l Airport-(LAX) is 20 miles away from Dodger Stadium and can take from 30-60 minutes to arrive there depending on LA traffic.

Your only real choice (for night games) is to drive a car in Los Angeles and brave the traffic—that is if you wish to watch the full game. Read below on how to take transit to the games (you can do this for matinee games). For car rentals at LAX you have to catch a shuttle bus from any of the waiting areas outside that say-"Courtesy Shuttle For Car Rental.' Rental cars in Los Angeles can range from $50-100 for a weekday depending on the season. Weekends are a little cheaper. California State is right up there with 'NY' State for leaders in car costs. All of the rental car places are a good 10 minute shuttle ride from LAX—that is where your preferred card programs of can save you time and effort once you arrive at: AVIS/THRIFTY/NATIONAL/HERTZ/NATIONAL. Both Northbound and Southbound highways will take you to the 110 highway east or west—you want exit 24B for Dodger Stadium.

IF YOU FLY IN FROM JOHN WAYNE AIRPOR-(SNA)—Take Highway 5 till the merge towards N-110 PASADENA FWY. Your prices for car rentals and flights will be 15-25% cheaper for 'SNA' (John Wayne Airport) but the accessibility of driving to Dodger Stadium is still better coming from LAX. 'SNA' is suited nicely for the Angels, not the Dodgers.

PUBLIC TRANSIT FROM DISNEYLAND-'MATINEE GAMES'

From South Harbor Blvd you board the 460 Metro-Express Bus towards downtown Los Angeles. It is a 2 hour ride that features 70 stops, but is not a bad way to see lots of the city. From there you take the 45 Lincoln Heights-you board this bus from 6TH and Broadway. It will take you to BROADWAY/ BISHOPS/ where you walk up the hill 20 minutes—same deal on the way back take the 45 San Pedro-Rosecrans to 5th and Broadway then take the 460 'DISNEYLAND EXPRESS BUS.'
Website for Los Angeles transit at www.metro.net

WHERE TO STAY?
The following lodging is within 2 miles of Dodger Stadium

Unlimited budget

The Westin Bonaventure Hotel & Suites/Los Angeles
Omni Los Angeles Hotel
The Standard Hotels Downtown Los Angeles

Moderate budget

Ramada Inn Limited Downtown Los Angeles
Best Western Dragon Gate Inn
Comfort Inn West Sunset Blvd

Chaser budget traveler

The Mayfair Hotel
Super 8 Los Angeles Downtown
Clarion Hotel Downtown Los Angeles

DCB RECOMMENDED HOTELS:

I would recommend staying in 'Orange County' to save money---there are 2 hotels near 'Disneyland.'

Candy Cane Inn--For just over $100 a night you are 3 miles from Disneyland/ 2 miles from Angels Stadium and 18 miles from Dodger Stadium. You receive an amazing hot continental breakfast and a free shuttle ride to and from Disneyland.

Motel 6-Orange County On W Chapman Ave/I-5
This one is for $50-65 per night and you have a 24 hr-Denny's conveniently located in the same parking lot---you are walking distance to Angels Stadium and buses to Disneyland/Knotts Berry Farm.

Ballpark Chaser Traveler Tip: For $50 Roundtrip per person you can book the 'Disneyland Shuttle Bus from LAX to any of the hotels near Disneyland including the Candy Cane Inn

DCB —'BALLPARK CHASER SPECIAL'

LOS ANGELES HI HOSTEL—FULLERTON- www.hihostels.com
$22.00 per night for this deal—yes like the others it is bunk beds at a golf course-but is quiet and where else can you get that deal? I stayed there after a matinee day and slept all day until an early morning flight out of either airports SNA or LAX. This will only works as a singular traveler and have a car-it is 10 miles from Angels Stadium and is 28 miles up Hwy-5 north to Dodger Stadium. These hostels are perfect to shower, sleep and catch up on laundry while you are on the road!

WHERE TO PARK?

The Los Angeles Dodgers make it easy for their guests by offering a large, centralized parking lot in front of the stadium. The lot is broken up into two sections: "preferred" and "general" parking. The Preferred Parking lot is for season ticket holders; the General Parking lot is for all others. Expect to pay $15 for any spot in the general parking lot.

Ballpark Chasers Tip: if you are attending a Dodger's playoff game, or any other that is heavily attended, come early as the general parking lot will sell out!

WHERE TO EAT?

Due to the location of Dodger Stadium, Ballpark Chasers find that it is not convenient to walk to restaurants before or after a game. However, if you have transportation, we suggest a trip to "the birth place of the French Dip Sandwich". Philippe the Original has been serving sandwiches since 1908 and is a So Cal favorite. Don't leave without getting a French Dip, but watch out for the hot mustard!

Another local favorite is Tommy's Original Hamburger. This "world famous" hamburger shack has been flipping burgers in LA since 1946! Don't leave here without a burger and chili cheese fries. Another fun Los Angeles landmark and quick spot is Pink's Hot Dogs. Pink's has been serving hot dogs to Hollywood stars since 1939. Needless to say, Ballpark Chasers recommend the dogs!
Once inside Dodger Stadium, look for the nearest Dodger Dog stand to grab Major League Baseball's most famous ballpark food. Other great concession stands include: Carl's Jr. for a big and juicy cheeseburger, Saag's Gourmet Sausage, California Pizza Kitchen and Camacho's for their cheesy nachos.

Ballpark Chasers Tip: if you could do without another hot dog and hamburger, look for sections 33 and 104 for a break in traditional artery-clogging stadium food. Healthy Plate concessions serve everything from vegetable wraps to fruit salads to veggie and turkey dogs.

INTANGIBLES:

Maybe the best backdrop of mountains in the Majors-the crowd is also the liveliest at its peak in the majors. Designed beautifully in that you never feel crowded—most rows are 10-12 seats longs with aisles in between. It is quite the hike to your seats the higher you go, so do take that into consideration. This ballpark is way better in person then it looks on TV. Of course when you are there you will be amazed at how late the crowd arrives and soon they are to exit. Next time you see Kirk Gibson's homerun clip watch all of the taillights in the parking lot leaving even thought at the time the Dodgers were down only one run in the ninth.

Note: Take a radio with you to the game so you can listen to legendary broadcaster Vin Scully describe the game in his incredible solo act way. You can hear it at certain points in the building but if the crowd becomes too loud you will miss out.

WHERE TO BUY TICKETS?

The Los Angeles Dodgers ranked #3 in Major League Baseball attendance in 2010. Therefore, we recommend buying your tickets in advance. If you are stuck trying to get tickets last minute, make sure to look for scalpers outside of the Dodgers parking area. Selling tickets within the ballpark parking lot is illegal.

Ballpark Chasers Tip: Can you eat a lot? If food was free, would you eat during all 9 innings? If so, Ballpark Chasers recommends the "Right-Field All You Can Eat Pavilion." This exclusive section is home of unlimited dodger dogs, popcorn, nachos, peanuts, soda and water, with the purchase of your ticket. If you would prefer to upgrade the quality of your food and location of your seat, check out the Dugout Club. Located directly behind home plate, these seats start at a whopping $500 but serve top quality 5-star lobster, steak, shrimp and prime rib.

WHEN TO GO?

You can pretty much count on Los Angeles to have great weather during the entire baseball season. On the other hand, the smog will make you thankful you are only visiting! We recommend May through July as the best months to travel to Los Angeles and the So Cal area.

WHAT ELSE TO SEE?

Where do we begin! Few cities offer as much to do and see as Los Angeles. Start with Hollywood's Walk of Fame on Hollywood Boulevard and conclude with a flick at the famous Chinese Theater. If your ballpark trip is a family affair, make the kids happy spending the day at Universal Studios, Knott's Berry Farm, Six Flags, Disneyland or Magic Mountain. For a complementary event, check out the Griffith Observatory. This museum has free parking and free admission. The Observatory sits over 1,100 feet above sea level atop Hollywood Hills with gorgeous views of the city and the famous Hollywood sign.

If you desire an even closer look at the Hollywood sign, try horseback riding up to it! Sunset Ranch offers 1 or 2 hour rides and even a 4 hour evening trip that concludes with a Mexican dinner after the sun has set!

The perfect way to spend an afternoon before catching a dodger's game is Paul Ziffren Sports Resource Center. Created in 1985, The Ziffren Center is home of the world's largest sports library, including: game programs, 100 year old sports publications, books, films, media guides, photographs and game used equipment. The Ziffren Center is the best kept secret in the Los Angeles area for any sports or history buff.

BALLPARK CHASERS VACATION?

If your baseball trip to Dodger stadium involves traveling a great distance, why not extend your vacation by visiting one or more of the stadiums below.

1.) <u>Angel Stadium</u>- 30 miles/30 minutes
2.) <u>Petco Park</u>- 125 miles/2 hours
3.) <u>Oakland Coliseum</u>- 365 miles/5.5 hours
4.) <u>Chase Field</u> – 375 miles/5.5 hours
5.) <u>AT&T Park</u>- 380 miles/6 hours

DOUBLEHEADER ATTEMPTS:

Two attempts can be made with the Angels across the freeway and also with the San Diego Padres just 100 miles down the road. With the LA Dodgers it is easier with those Padres' matinees at 12:35 to have LA as the second leg of the doubleheader attempt.

17. MINUTE MAID PARK

HOUSTON, TEXAS
HOME OF THE HOUSTON ASTROS

TRANSPORTATION:

George Bush/Intercontinental-(IAH) is 20 miles and about a 30 minute drive away from the park. 'IAH' features 700 flights that leave from 'Continental Airlines' daily. It is one of the most expensive cities to fly in and out of. You can be sure to rack up the air miles by travelling here!

Car rentals are very expensive anywhere in TX unless it is the weekend. You can pay $70-100 for a weekday rental and the weekend is extremely low at $20-$30. It is much more pleasant to drive rather than be put through the high Texas temperatures while waiting for public transit or cabs. The good news is there are no tolls and the gas is not bad to purchase.

WHERE TO STAY?

Unlimited budget- all 3 are within walking distance to Minute Maid Park

Inn at the Ballpark - Luxury Hotel
Magnolia Hotel- Houston (free cookies and milk each night on the second floor)!
Four Seasons Hotel- Houston

Moderate budget – all 3 options are within walking distance to Minute Maid Park

Residence Inn by Marriott- Downtown Convention Center
Holiday Inn Express- Downtown Convention Center
Hyatt Regency – Houston

Chaser budget traveler- the following lodging is within 5 miles of Minute 'Maid Park.

Holiday Inn Select Hotels – Greenway Plaza
Courtyard by Marriott Houston- West University
Comfort Inn- Downtown Houston

WHERE TO PARK?

Minute Maid Park is a downtown stadium that offers street, metered, garage and paid lot parking. There are over 25,000 parking spaces within a ½ square block radius of Minute Maid Park. To make it easy and stress free, look for one of the three main garages: Convention Center (corner of Polk

Street and Avenida de las Americas), Toyota Center and the Harris County Courthouse building (corner of Austin and Congress).

Ballpark Chasers Tip: if you are staying at a hotel that is not within walking distance, ask the front desk staff if you are close to Houston's light-rail system. This quick ride will drop you off just 6 blocks from the stadium!

WHERE TO EAT?

Let your trip to Minute Maid Park start across the street at <u>Home Plate Bar and Grill</u>. The menu is full of amazing burgers, sandwiches, salads, dogs and wings. The Home Plate offers much needed air conditioning during an Astros day game or a nice outdoor patio for those cooler Texas evenings. Other restaurants just a few feet from Minute Maid Park are Picazo's and Landry's Seafood House. Both options are recommended before or after an Astros game.

Inside Minute Maid Park, the Astros offer a plethora of food options that rank as one of the top in the country! Ballpark Chasers suggest starting with the best: Rosa's Taqueria fajitas. They can be found in carts throughout the concourses. Other fun options include Sliders (mini hamburgers), sausage sandwiches and a superstar dog with chili cheese (warning- these are messy)! If you prefer sit-down dining, try the newly opened FiveSeven Grille in center field. In tribute to Astros' greats Jeff Bagwell and Craig Biggio, the FiveSeven Grille packs a mean plate by offering "Texas size portions". This is a great choice to grab a meal before the game. Otherwise, the FiveSeven Grille offers to-go dining in order to eat at your seat while watching the game!

INTANGIBLES:

Minute Maid Park is an awesome facility but like most indoor stadiums make sure you bring your flash as pictures are harder to take. Houston is one of the better cities at honoring the U.S troops. The train in the left field bleachers is unlike anything in baseball. Only Seattle can also claim to have train sounds emanating from the ballpark!

WHERE TO BUY TICKETS?

Although the Astros have a good fan base and new stadium, Minute Maid Park is not ranked within the top 10 of Major League attendance. Unless you are attending a game against a big-market team, it is not a problem to count on box office tickets to be available before the game. Also, scalpers are noticeably present along the streets of Houston and love to bargain during the last 30 minutes of the first pitch.

WHEN TO GO?

The summer months in Texas are a scorcher! Temperatures average in the upper 80s and low 90s during June, July, August and September. For this reason alone, Ballpark Chasers suggest a trip to Minute Maid Park in the early part of the season. April and May are your best bets for an enjoyable sunny day. As far as rain, not to worry as Minute Maid Park has a retractable roof that can close within 10 minutes.

WHAT ELSE TO DO?

A fun, relaxing and free option located just blocks from Minute Maid Park is Discovery Green. This newly opened park is full of entertainment for all ages. Everything from recreational games, to playgrounds, concerts, natural gardens, and art displays can be found all throughout this 12 acre park. Don't leave without trying the Lake House French fries served in a compostable cup! A trip to Texas just isn't complete without a stop at the Houston Space Center. Located 30 minutes from Minute Maid Park, Houston's Space Center is a great way to spend an afternoon before catching a night game. Regular attractions include: theater presentations, space simulations, NASA tour, kid's activities, galleries and memorabilia.

Ballpark Chasers Hidden Gems: Finger Furniture store at 4001 Gulf Freeway. I know! What could possibly be inside a furniture store that a Ballpark Chaser needs to see? Well, the Houston Sports Museum of course! Still confused? The location is the exact spot of old Buff Stadium, home of the Houston Buffaloes. Inside the furniture store holds the exact location where home plate once laid as well as a bunch of other amazing local sports memorabilia. Just a heads-up, there is no sign outside the Finger Furniture store, nor a website that you can Google to find more information. Trust us, it's there! For those Astros fans, or any true fan of baseball, make the 45 minute trip south to Alvin, Texas, home of the Nolan Ryan Foundation and Museum. Once here, look for the exhibit to feel what it's like to catch a Nolan Ryan fastball.

BALLPARK CHASERS VACATION?

Minute Maid Park is part of Ballpark Chasers "Texas Dos Trip" which includes seeing the Rangers at Rangers Ballpark in Arlington. We suggest searching for flights to both cities to determine which airfare is the cheapest. Expect a 4 hour drive (256 miles) between ballparks, with heavy traffic in both cities.

18. THE GREAT AMERICAN BALL PARK

CINCINNATI, OHIO
HOME OF THE CINCINNATI REDS

TRANSPORTATION:

Northern Kentucky International Airport-(CVG) is 13.7 miles and 20 minutes to Great American Ball Park. The airport serves over 600 flights daily for 'Delta Airlines'. Unfortunately, this small airport charges a lot of money for flights so you are better off flying out of Dayton (1 hour away) or Indianapolis which is 2 hours and is one of the cheapest airports to fly in and out of. The greatest feature about flying out of Cincinnati is flying out west— you gain one to three hours with going from Eastern Time to Central/Mountain or Pacific Standard. Cincinnati is a few hundred miles from the 1st time zone change (you can catch flights to Chicago or Milwaukee that are 15-40 minutes in real time once the time change is factored in).

The airport in Dayton offers cheap flights from Air Tran Airways if you can search for them at www. airtran.com.

Car rentals in Cincinnati are reasonable at $40-$60 per weekday (you may also find one-way rental drop offs that are cheap from this airport). For those people that are travelling within Chicago, Milwaukee, St. Louis, Cleveland or Detroit there are supersaver deals from 'Greyhound Bus Lines' that range from $35-$60. Please check fares at www.greyhound.com for more details.

WHERE TO STAY?

All lodgings below are within 1 mile of Great American Ball Park.

Unlimited Budget

The Westin- Cincinnati
Marriott- Cincinnati Rivercenter

Moderate Budget

Comfort Suites- Newport
Hampton Inn- Cincinnati Riverfront

Chaser budget traveler

Travelodge- Newport Riverfront

WHERE TO PARK?

The Cincinnati area offers plenty of on-site parking lots and garage options on the East and West sides of the stadium. Expect to pay between $10-12 for close parking and $5-$10 for vendor parking further out.

Ballpark Chasers Tip: The 255 Fifth Parking Garage is an easy walk to the stadium and only $7. Otherwise, park on the Kentucky side of the river for a nice walk over the Southgate Bridge!

WHERE TO EAT?

It's a must for Reds fans to visit the Machine Room Grille to see old Redleg photos and memorabilia. Located in the left field of Great American Ball Park, the Machine Room opens 3 hours before each home game, just in time for batting practice.

Don't forget the Cincinnati Coney dogs! Look for sections 116, 130 or 518 for the Skyline Cheese Coney station. Another must eatery is Montgomery Inn in section 124. The locals rave about this stuff and the Ballpark Chasers crew has to concur!

Ballpark Chasers Tip: the Reds and Great American Ball Park are doing their part to help out the fan during the 2010 season. Look for $1 concession items along the first base side (Fan Zone and View Level). Popcorn, peanuts, hot dogs, soda, ice cream and taffy are all $1. Even the beer is discounted to $5!

If you want to dine outside the park, make an effort to stop at Arnold's Bar & Grill-(Located at 210 East 8th St.) Arnolds has been serving since 1861 and will make you feel right at home. If you want a quick bite close to the park, check out the Game Day Café or In Between Tavern. Both are located within 2 blocks of Great American Ball Park and are where the local fans like to hang out before and after a Reds victory!

When parking or coming from the Kentucky side, check out a local favorite called Hofbraushaus Newport (don't worry if you can't pronounce it). This German style restaurant is truly one of the only authentic Hofbraushaus' in North America. You have your choice of dining in their Bier Hall which offers live Bavarian music or a quiet dining room to avoid the crowd. Check out their monthly beer selection to help choose your best month to visit.

INTANGIBLES:

Nothing says Cincinnati Reds like Pete Rose, right? Here is the horrible fact of life of what the Pete Rose saga has meant; his name and number are nowhere to be found inside 'Great American Ball Park' almost as if #14 never played for the club. On the other hand, across the street in the Cincinnati Hall of Fame, Pete Rose is everywhere. Of particular items the baseball team has 4192 baseballs incased in glass leading up in 5 stories in the building. It is an amazing display. There are great honors paid to all of the great Reds' teams including statue's of the 'Big Red Machine.'

WHERE TO BUY TICKETS?

No need to pre-order your tickets as the box office will have plenty of seats on game day as the Reds continue to fight their way back to a playoff caliber team. If possible, plan on catching one of the Friday night fireworks' shows. It's a top-notch presentation that caps off a great night at the old ballpark!

Ballpark Chasers Tip: if you're looking for an inexpensive ticket, get a low row in section 521. This section has a great view of the entire field, looking out onto the Ohio River and is a perfect seat for the firework shows!

WHEN TO GO?

From May through September, expect temperatures in the 80s with humidity. On average, July tends to be the hottest month, while May is the wettest month. Nothing to worry about as a late afternoon shower will cool off a night at GABP! Ballpark Chasers suggest making your trip to the Cincinnati area in the month of June.

WHAT ELSE TO SEE?

Whether you are a fan or the Reds or not, they are the oldest Major League ball club and have a lot of history. Therefore, we recommend coming early to the park to walk through the Cincinnati Reds Hall of Fame. Located on the grounds of Great American Ball Park, it is just $10 for a game day pass and takes roughly 30 minutes to go through and experience the rich past of the Redlegs.

Also close to the stadium is the National Underground Railroad Freedom Center. This Museum is one of the best in the United States. A $12 ticket will enlighten you on the secret network of escape routes that slaves used leading up to the civil war and our country's fight to end slavery.

Don't leave Cincinnati without taking a stroll through Fountain Square. Just blocks from Great American Ball Park, this entertainment hub is home to great shops, dining, landscaping and people watching!

BALLPARK CHASERS VACATION?

Cincinnati is in the heart of the Midwest and can easily be combined with travels to other ballparks. The closest stadium is Progressive Field in Cleveland (roughly a 4 hour drive). The toughest part is deciding how many to see! We suggest one of the following sceneries:

1.) Great American Ball Park, Wrigley Field, US Cellular, Miller Park
2.) Great American Ball Park, Progressive Field, Comerica Park, PNC Park

19. US CELLULAR FIELD

CHICAGO, ILLINOIS
HOME OF THE CHICAGO WHITE SOX

TRANSPORTATION:

Refer to The Chicago Cubs Chaser Guide for O'Hare Airport. Midway Airport, (MDW) is much closer at 9 miles and 16 minutes. Midway Airport is actually a lot like New York's 'LGA' in that they dropped an airport in the middle of a suburban area. However, if your preferred airline is Air Tran, Delta or Midwest, then these are the main trips for Chicago at MDW. So if you fly into MDW, you are about a twenty minute drive to the park on the 55 hwy-S. The 90-94 HWY gets you there to the 35th ST turnoff---you should give yourself plenty of time due to heavy traffic. The subway is still the best way from downtown as you can take the Red Line-Dan Ryan Exp-95 (it is only 15 minutes from downtown and a $2.50 charge). Unless the game is sold out, it is decent in returning downtown via the subway-Red Line Howard.

WHERE TO STAY?

Unfortunately, there is no lodging within walking distance of U. S. Cellular Field. All of our recommendations are within 3.5 miles of the stadium and tend to be more expensive than other cities. Look to stay outside of the city limits if you want to save money.

Unlimited budget

Hyatt Regency McCormick Place
Chicago Essex Inn
Hilton Chicago

Moderate budget

Club Quarters Chicago
Best Western Grant Hotel
Holiday Inn & Suites Downtown Chicago

Chaser budget traveler

Club Quarters Wacker at Michigan
Howard Johnson Downtown Chicago
Travelodge Hotel Downtown Chicago
Ballpark Chasers Tip: be careful when reserving a motel in downtown Chicago. There are numerous

"bargain motels" around the city that will leave you wanting to sleep in your car, rather than in your motel bed.

For the extreme ballpark chasers specials for Chicago please refer to the write-up in the Chicago Cubs Chaser guide.

WHERE TO PARK?

Ballpark Chasers recommend taking public transportation to anything in the Chicago area. The CTA Red Line makes stops directly outside the stadium and is a much cheaper and stress-free option, as the parking lots tend to be a nightmare after the game.
If you feel that you need to drive to the park, U.S. Cellular Field offers several cash lots around the stadium. Game day parking is $23 for cars and can be accessed using Lots F, G and L.

Ballpark Chasers Tip: be extremely careful when trying to park in a non-designated paid lot. Street parking is rare and if it seems too good to be true, it probably is. Most street parking around U.S. Cellular Field is residential-only and requires a parking permit. Trust us, we learned the hard way.

WHERE TO EAT?

Ballpark Chasers rave about Chicago's south side Schaller's Pump. This local jewel has been in operation since 1881 and is Chicago's oldest restaurant. Schaller's is the place to go before a White Sox game if you want hang out with the local fans and relax with a good plate of comfort food. Prime rib, corned beef, and butt-steak - it's all so good!

For an authentic Chicago pizza parlor, look no further than Freddy's Pizza. Located about a mile from U.S. Cellular Field, Freddy's serves up some tasty pizza pie and will leave you wanting to walk to the stadium to ease your full stomach. Other than a great slice of pizza, they also make an amazing and quite gigantic beef sandwich. Although not our favorite item on the menu, their double sausage is popular among the locals. If you're a Ballpark Chasers budget traveler, check out Kevin's Hamburger Heaven. Even though it's not the cleanliest restaurant and doesn't have the nicest ambiance, they do make a mean greasy burger and shake. Ballpark Chasers also rave about 35th Street Red Hot. Use this as a quick stop for a good hot dog and a great side of freshly cut French fries. If you are running late, take it to go and bring it in with you to the game. U.S. Cellular allows outside food and drinks.
New for the 2010 season, U.S. Cellular Field is offering half-pound turkey burgers and "build your own burrito's" (chicken or beef) for $8. For a sit-down meal, try the Miller Lite Bullpen Sports Bar. With a valid adult ID and an additional $15, fans can sit just beyond the Right-Field fence for a great field view and a chance at a home run ball. For those fans of wine please look for the cart around the ballpark selling a selection of red and white wine, ranging from $7.50 to $9.50 per glass.

Ballpark Chasers Tip: arrive at the ballpark early and be rewarded with '2 for the price of 1' hot dogs during the first hour after the gates open (note: only All-Star concessions have this special promotion).

INTANGIBLES:

There are countless music acts outside the ballpark before the game. Also, there are many monuments and statue's that chronicle one of the most storied franchises in 'MLB.' The fireworks shooting out of the pillars on the scoreboard are fantastic. The back end tickets for most of us Ballpark Chasers is not so great, if you buy an upper deck ticket you are staying at that level only. Be prepared to take a few elevators and then walk down the concourse ramp of five stories. The fans are amongst the liveliest.

WHERE TO BUY TICKETS?

White Sox tickets are readily available on game days. With that being said, a "Windy City Showdown" will sell out. The arrival of the Yankees and Red Sox will also bring a packed house. If you need last minute tickets, scalpers will be found outside U.S. Cellular grounds, as selling tickets on-site is strictly prohibited.

WHEN TO GO?

The Chicago area is known for its extreme climates and seasons. During the baseball season you can expect temperatures gradually increasing through the summer months with the peak coming in July and August. Thunderstorms are quite common in the summer. June typically gets the most rainfall, so don't forget to pack a light jacket.

WHAT ELSE TO SEE?

The windy city offers so much to do and see that the toughest part is deciding. From the world renowned Art Institute of Chicago to the Magnificent Mile, tourists can easy spend an entire week here. One stop not to miss is Millennium Park, located roughly 5.5 miles from U.S. Cellular Field. The newly opened 24 acre park is home of amazing and unique art, music and architecture. Don't leave without checking out the Crown Fountain, a 50 ft. tower that projects facial images with an opening that shoots water out of the image's mouth! Another attraction at Millennium Park is the Cloud Gate sculpture. Imagine a gigantic 66 ft. long upside-down jelly bean that looks like mercury and has a mirror-like finish which reflects the viewer's image back in weird shapes. Sounds pretty cool, huh?

Another quick, fun and inexpensive destination in the Chicago area is the Sears Tower, North America's tallest building (110 stories tall). On a clear day, the view from the sky deck allows you to see over 40-50 miles out, including Michigan, Indiana and Wisconsin! Try and time it so you can catch a sunset by arriving at the sky deck about 30 minutes before the sun sets.

BALLPARK CHASERS VACATION?

U.S. Cellular Field is part of Ballpark Chasers Midwest Extravaganza! Plan your trip to allow visits to the north side of Chicago for a game at <u>Wrigley Field</u> and then off to Milwaukee to see the Brewers at <u>Miller Park</u>. Only 10 miles separate Wrigley from U.S. Cellular which makes it possible to take in a rare day/night double header. <u>Miller Park</u> can be reached by car in just under 2 hours from Chicago.

20. PETCO PARK

SAN DIEGO, CALIFORNIA
HOME OF THE SAN DIEGO PADRES

TRANSPORTATION:

San Diego International Airport-(SAN) is 3.8 miles away which is a 15 minute drive to Petco Park. Rarely does 'SAN' have cheaper fares then 'LAX' OR 'SNA' in L.A-but you might find a Delta Airlines or Air Tran deal if you are flying from the Midwest. You really do not need a car in San Diego if you are staying downtown. It is only a $15 cab ride anywhere. If you end up going with a rental for sightseeing, you can expect to pay between $65-90 during the week and is not much cheaper on the weekends.

WHERE TO STAY?

The following lodging is within 1 mile of Petco Park.

Unlimited budget

Omni Hotel (Connected to Petco Park - just take the Sky Bridge)
San Diego Marriott Gaslamp Quarter
Hotel Solamar

Moderate Budget

Comfort Inn Gaslamp Quarter
Ramada Gaslamp/Convention Center

Chaser Budget Traveler

Days Inn Downtown/Convention Center
Best Western Bayside Inn

BALLPARK CHASER-'DCB SPECIAL':

Hostel at San Diego- www.hihostels.com is the most convenient of all of the hostels in the USA. You are literally a block from Petco Park for $28 per night. There is a Subway Restaurant nearby and you are a few blocks from the 'Gaslamp Quarter District'. I highly recommend this for Ballpark Chasers who also enjoys the 'nightlife'.

WHERE TO PARK?

The Padres offer plenty of street, metered, paid lots and garage parking.
Ballpark Chasers Tip: purchase your parking space online to allow more time to enjoy Petco Park.

PARKING LOTS	ADDRESS	DIRECTIONS	FEES
Padres Parkade	440 11th Ave.	Enter on 10th Ave. between Island and J St.	$20
Tailgate Park	12th Ave & 14th St.	Enter on 13th Ave and K St.	$20
8th and Harbor Garage	801 E. Harbor Dr.	Enter on 8th Ave. and Harbor Drive	$10
D1/D2 Lot	1 Park Blvd.	Enter on 11th Ave. across from MTS Structure	$20
Horton Pacific Garage	1069 1st Ave.	Enter on 1st Ave. between F and E St.	$8
11th & C Lot	1095 10th Ave.	Enter on 10th Ave. between C St. and Broadway	$8

WHERE TO EAT?

If you have a rental car, check out Trophy's Sports Grille about 5 miles north of Petco Park. Trophy's is a Ballpark Chasers top-rated restaurant. Trophy's is filled with tons of sports memorabilia and large screen televisions. Make sure to get the Ballpark Chaser Meal: a cup of Trophy's white chili, sliders and a beverage of your choice. If you need something closer to the stadium, other fun sit-down options include Henry's Pub, Moose McGillycuddy's Pub and Café, and the Yard House. If you want a quicker option, try Gaslamp Pizza for awesome pie by the slice.

Once inside Petco Park, head to the Mercado. Located on the main concourse (by section 108), the

Mercado is a food lover's smorgasbord! From seafood, to Mexican food, to barbecue, to Italian food, the Mercado has it all along with gorgeous views of Coronado Island and the San Diego Bay. If you are seeking a full service restaurant, check out the Padres Hall of Fame Bar and Grill located on the 5th floor of the Western Metal Supply Co. Building. Ballpark Chasers suggest eating here before the game as the balcony field-view is reserved for group ticket holders.

INTANGIBLES:

Petco Park probably has the best ice-cream parlor in the majors—located in the concourse along the 1st base side nearing the foul pole. Also, the ballpark is the most 'pet' friendly parks in the Majors as fans are able to bring their dogs to the park past the bleachers at any time. I suppose with the name of the ballpark they kind of have to be!

WHERE TO BUY TICKETS?

Ballpark Chasers very seldom have difficulty purchasing tickets at the Padres box office before a home game. With that being said, big market teams such as Boston, New York and Chicago will bring out more local fans so we recommend purchasing ahead of time if seeing these teams.

One of the most unique seats in all of baseball lies in left field of Petco Park. The 98 year-old Western Metal Supply building offers rooftop seats for only $49 and includes a pre-game buffet and snacks during the 3rd inning.

WHEN TO GO?

We cannot say enough about the weather in San Diego and all of California. Enjoy the sun all season long but don't forget your sunscreen! Ballpark Chasers recommend late May through July, or whenever you're able to take a break from your day-to-day routine.

WHAT ELSE TO SEE?

Just 2 miles north of Petco Park is an undiscovered gem for the San Diego sports fan or anyone who has an appreciation for sports in general. The Hall of Champions Sports Museum is the nation's largest multi-sports museum specializing in the rich history of San Diego athletics. From locals such as Ted Williams to Tony Gwynn, the Hall of Champions has plenty for the sports enthusiast!

End the day by heading to the water and spending time at the San Diego Harbor. This is a beautiful area to walk, shop, people-watch and enjoy amazing seafood! Also, find a harbor cruise for a better look at the San Diego Bay and a chance to see some dolphins. Speaking of dolphins, if you haven't had the opportunity to visit a Sea World, now is your chance. Only 15 minutes away from Petco Park, Sea World is a great way to spend time with the family of marine mammals. Day passes currently run $61 so plan on spending an entire day here. Public transport is available with light rail going to and from 'Petco Park' right into Historic 'Old Town' to connect with the local buses to Sea World Another great sightseeing day is to visit 'Old Town's Village' and eat dinner at the "JollyBoy's Restaurant'. Afterwards, check out the gift shops that feature 'Mexicana' clothing shops with great styles of leather—particularly with wallets, belts and boots.

BALLPARK CHASERS VACATION?

The California area is perfect for seeing more than one stadium. Ballpark Chasers recommends combining your trip to Petco Park along with 1 or more of the 5 stadiums below.

1.) Angel Stadium- 94 miles/1.5 hours
2.) Dodger Stadium – 124 miles/2 hours
3.) Chase Field- 355 miles/5.5 hours
4.) Oakland Coliseum- 487 miles/7.5 hours
5.) AT&T Park-503 miles/8 hours

Both Los Angeles teams are available for doubleheader opportunities for those Petco matinee day games that start at 12:35 PM. The Angels having 12:55 PM weekend matinee games makes this double doable as Angels Stadium is 20-30 minutes closer then Dodgers Stadium.

21. NATIONALS PARK

WASHINGTON, D.C.
HOME OF THE WASHINGTON NATIONALS

TRANSPORTATION:

The 'RONALD REAGAN AIRPORT'-(DCA) is 6 miles from the park and is an unpredictable length of drive based on crazy D.C traffic. DCA offers hourly flights to and from New York City and Boston along with being a hub for US Airways and Delta. The prices are cheap if you can get them in advance. The car rental facilities in DCA are a quick shuttle ride away. It is quite pricey for weekdays at $60-75 per day but weekends are more affordable at $40-$55. There is not a big need for a car in Washington but if you can brave the traffic you can see much more of the city by taking a casual drive. If you are coming from Baltimore, take the 95 HWY S until you merge to S-295.

WHERE TO STAY?

All options below are within 3 miles of Nationals Park.

Unlimited Budget

Mandarin Oriental Hotel
The Hotel George
Washington Court Hotel

Moderate Budget

Courtyard by Marriott – Capital Hill/Navy Yard
Residence Inn – Washington DC/Capitol
Holiday Inn – Washington Capitol
Courtyard by Marriott – Washington Convention Center

Chaser Budget Traveler

You will need to leave downtown to find anything under $100 per night like:
Harrington Hotel

'DCB' RECOMMENDED HOTEL:

While it is an expensive city, I have one rare nugget for you if you are willing to drive 50 miles south to Fredericksburg, Virginia in order to save some money. Here lies a 'Best Western' (Central Plaza),' that has hotel rates of just $50-60 per night which is unbelievable in that area of the country. Better suited for off hours driving like passing through to drive South after a night game in D.C. on your way to Georgia or Florida.

WHERE TO PARK?

If you don't mind the walk, parking at Nationals Park can be as low as $5. However, anything close to the stadium will run between $30-40. If you are driving to Nationals Park, we recommend pre-purchasing your parking ticket online.

During the 2008 season, 53% of visitors to Nationals Park came via the metro! If you are staying at a hotel not within walking distance of the stadium, Ballpark Chasers suggest taking the Metro. Hop on the Green Line to Navy Yard station, which is just one block from Nationals Park. If you need a cab after the game, head out the Center Field gates and make a left. The taxicab stand will remain open for 30 minutes after the final out.

Ballpark Chasers Tip: free parking is located at RFK stadium! Really? Yes, and they will even shuttle you to the game! Find Lot 8 at RFK stadium and hop aboard the "Nats Express" for a complimentary round trip shuttle to the Nationals game.

WHERE TO EAT?

Surprisingly, Nationals Park does not have a great selection of restaurants and sport bars around the stadium. Therefore, we recommend grabbing a ride on the Circulator bus that connects Union Station, Eastern Market, Barracks Row (8th St.), the Navy Yard Metro station and Nationals Park. For only $1, you can ride on Circulator running every 10 minutes at the Union Station– Navy Yard Metro. There are dozens of restaurants along this route for you to choose from, but our recommendations are on Barracks Row and Pennsylvania Ave. Ballpark Chasers favorites include: The Pour House, The Ugly Mug, Lola's Barracks Bar & Grille, Matchbox, Las Placitas, Café 8 and Banana Café & Piano Bar. With the exception of The Pour House, all other restaurants and sports bars listed above can be found along 8th Ave.

The concession stands inside Nationals Park are one of the best in baseball! Our favorites include: the Triple Play Grille, the Taste of the Majors, Hard Times Café and Red Hot & Blue. The Nationals serve everything from Cuban sandwiches, shrimp burgers, crab sandwiches, meatball subs and "quasi-dillas" (chicken quesadillas). Ballpark Chasers favorite vendor has to be Ben's Chili Bowl for their chili dogs, chili burgers, turkey dogs and signature chili. For those Chasers watching their waistline, Nationals Park offers a Healthy Plate stand that features vegetable platters with hummus, fresh fruit and gourmet fresh salads. For those who don't care about calorie count, stop for dessert at Gifford's Ice Cream and Candy Shop along the first-base side for awesome milkshakes, sundaes and hand-dipped cones. And finally, on the warm and humid DC afternoons, head to the center field plaza for a serving of Krazee Ice, the New Orleans style shaved ice that comes in 31 delicious flavors.

WHEN TO GO?

The D.C. area tends to be warm, sunny and humid during the summer months. Expect upper 80s and low 90s during July and August with frequent afternoon thunderstorms. Ballpark Chasers recommend visiting Nationals Park during the last week of May or any part of June for comfortable warm weather and less chance of rain showers.

WHAT ELSE TO SEE?

One could easily spend an entire week in Washington D.C. and not experience everything. Planning ahead is essential when traveling to Nationals Park and DC in order to see all of the attractions on your wish list. If you are making Nationals Park a quick baseball trip, without much time to see the historical sites, we recommend taking the City Segway Tour. The 3 hour tour will give you an excellent and fun way to see the White House, US Capital, Ford's Theatre, Washington Monument, Supreme Court, National Archives, Smithsonian Air & Space Museum, National Galleries of Art, Smithsonian Natural History, Smithsonian American History Museum, FBI Headquarters and more. If you haven't had the opportunity to ride a Segway, this is a perfect chance to take a cheap ride without forking over $5000 to purchase one. Because of the limited number of Segway's per group, reservations are required. If you have several days to devote to local sites, Ballpark Chasers recommends seeing all of the above in greater length along with the Lincoln Memorial, Washington National Cathedral, US Holocaust Memorial Museum, Vietnam Veterans Memorial, Library of Congress, National Gallery of Art and the National Mall.

INTANGIBLES:

The ball club has done a good job marketing the team since moving to Nationals Park but has a problem with transient governments coming and going depending on the parties who are leading the current regime of the nation. The Curly W's signage everywhere in the park is a good touch and the announcers have fun with it. Seriously, there is nothing funnier to witness in baseball quite like the President's Race.

BALLPARK CHASERS VACATION?

Nationals Park is part of the "East Coast Swing" Ballpark Chasers vacation. This trip includes seeing the Phillies at Citizens Bank Park and the Orioles in Oriole Park at Camden Yards. We suggest finding the cheapest flight to Washington DC, Baltimore or Philadelphia and getting a rental car to drive in between. Expect up to a 1 hour drive from DC to Baltimore, 2 hours from Baltimore to Philadelphia, and a 3 hour drive between Philadelphia and DC. Keep in mind that these times reflect little traffic but that will never happen during the weekdays. The "East Coast Swing" can easily be done in three days but plan for 5 to have time at local attractions and museums. If there is a scheduling oddity then you can see a doubleheader with the Baltimore Orioles or if there is a Sunday Night game in Philly it could be combined with the Nats as part of a day-night doubleheader by car on the weekend.

WHERE TO BUY TICKETS?

The Nationals are in the middle of the pack in terms of Major League Baseball attendance. It isn't necessary to pre-purchase tickets to a Nationals game unless the opposition is a big market team. If needing tickets when arriving at the stadium, scalpers are easy to find around the metro stop. If you are looking to sell your extras, make sure to be at least 100 ft. from Nationals Park grounds. It is illegal to sell tickets at any price this close to the ballpark.

Ballpark Chasers Tip: the most fun seats in Nationals Park are in section 100 (the center field reserved and center field lounge). These red painted seats, located just beyond center field, are the only ones in the ballpark (the rest are blue). In addition to the great panoramic view, the center field lounge also gives direct access to the Red Porch Restaurant along with a $20 food, beverage and/or merchandise credit!

22. TURNER FIELD

ATLANTA, GEORGIA
HOME OF THE ATLANTA BRAVES

TRANSPORTATION:

'WILLIAM B HARTSFIELD AIRPORT'-(ATL) is 9 miles and about a 20 minute drive from the airport. When you are arrive at 'ATL' you will need to give yourself plenty of time to make it to the game as the 'Car Rental Facilities' are all a few miles from the airport. You will need to catch your car rental's specific shuttle in order to rent a car.

'ATL' is the busiest passenger traffic airport in the world amongst being the biggest for space as well. The airport is the main hub for Air-Train Airways and Delta Airlines. You can purchase many cheap flights with these airlines and it serves well for quick flights to Baltimore, Tampa Bay, Miami, New York and Boston. Car rentals will cost you anywhere from $45-60 for a weekday and about half that price for weekdays. Since the public transport is not that quick in this city you are better off renting a car. Cabs will also incur you big fees should you try to use this method of transport.

WHERE TO STAY?

 All options below are within 2 miles of Turner Field

Unlimited Budget

The Ellis Hotel on Peachtree
The Ritz Carlton – Atlanta
Omni Hotel at CNN Center

Moderate Budget

Atlanta Marriott – Downtown
Hampton Inn & Suites – Atlanta
Holiday Inn Select – Atlanta Conference Center

Chaser Budget Traveler

Country Inn & Suites – Atlanta Downtown (across the street from Turner Field)
Comfort Inn at Turner Field

WHERE TO PARK?

The Braves offer several parking lots surrounding Turner Field. Paid lots range from $8-$20, depending on the distance to the stadium and the day of the week (weekends are more expensive). There are also several independent lots that will provide parking for under $10. If you arrive at least 2 hours before the first pitch, check out the south side of the stadium for a chance at street parking.

Ballpark Chasers Tip: Don't get fooled into pre-purchasing your parking tickets through Ticketmaster. After Ticketmaster's "convenience" and "delivery" charges, there is no savings.

WHERE TO EAT?

Because of the location of Turner Field and the surrounding highways, there is only one worth-while option to eat and walk to the stadium. Bullpen Restaurant is located at the southwest gate of Turner Field, offering "Atlanta's best BBQ and wings". Ballpark Chasers enjoy their "Kickin Combos". Restaurants further from the park that require a cab ride include: Fat Matt's Rib Shack, Six Feet Under and The Varsity. All three options are within 3 miles of Turner Field. Fat Matt's serves a mean plate of ribs, beans and some of the best mac and cheese we have sampled in all of North America! Six Feet Under is the greenest restaurant in the Atlanta area. From running off of wind energy to eliminating plastic water and soda bottles, Six Feet Under is doing their part in the sustainability movement. Oh, they also serve the best seafood along with a beautiful selection of spirits. Finally, The Varsity is the country's biggest drive-in restaurant, serving in the Atlanta area since 1928! Traditional drive-in food can be found at the Varsity. Our favorites include the hot dogs, hamburgers, chicken burgers, salads and shakes.

Once inside Turner Field, the food is just as good! Ballpark Chasers are in heaven with all of the options to choose from. The Chop-House is the Braves center field multi-level restaurant and bar. As for concession stands, our favorites include Skip & Pete's BBQ, La Taqueria and the Taste of Majors. If you can only do one, Skip & Pete's is a must!

INTANGIBLES:

Turner field has the famous 'tomahawk chop' that is a tradition unlike any other tradition in the majors. Be prepared to do the chant 'oh-oh-oh-oh-ohhhh….oh-oh-ohhhhh! Kids especially love this as it is a fun participation. Turner also has several days where kids can run the bases after the game.

WHERE TO BUY TICKETS?

The Braves were in the middle of the pack of Major League Baseball attendance over the course of the 2010 season. Consequently, tickets are generally available and easy to come by at the stadium box office before the game. Also, scalpers can be found on Hank Aaron Drive and Ralph David Abernathy

Boulevard, from Pryor Street to the stadium. Unless you are seeing a near sellout or playoff game, always offer 60% of the face value and then negotiate from there.

Ballpark Chasers Tip: 2-1/2 hours before game time, skyline seats go on sale for $1! The only place to purchase is at the ticket office window located next to the museum entrance in Monument Grove. This is a great option if you are more interested in the ballpark than the game.

WHEN TO GO?

You can count on a hot and humid vacation to "Hotlanta" during the summer months. To get a little relief, Ballpark Chasers recommends traveling to Turner Field in late April or any part of May. On average, July tends to bring the most rainfall as well as the hottest temperatures and is therefore best avoided. Because there are no other Major League parks around the Georgia area, we suggest staying for a weekend series in order to ensure seeing a game and not a rainout. There is nothing worse than traveling across the country for a cancelled game.

WHAT ELSE TO SEE?

Open year-round at Turner Field is the Braves Museum and Hall of Fame. The Museum showcases the Braves rich history of professional baseball, dating back to the days of the Milwaukee and Boston Braves. The Braves Museum provides over 600 different artifacts and photos to view, including the 1995 World Series Trophy and Hank Aaron's 715th home run bat and ball! The Museum and Hall of Fame opens 2.5 hours prior to the first pitch and closes at the middle of the seventh inning. Admission is just $2 on game days and $5 on non game days.

For those fans of sports museums, check out the Georgia Sports Hall of Fame in Macon, Georgia. About a 1.5 hour drive from downtown Atlanta, the GSHF is the largest state sports hall of fame in the country! Traditional and interactive exhibits will provide hours of entertainment.

Another museum not to miss is the Ty Cobb Museum in Royston, Georgia (about a 2 hour drive from Turner Field). Although Cobb was not the most model citizen, he is arguably one of the greatest ballplayers of all time. The museum houses a theatre, artifacts, memorabilia and photographs of the great "Georgia Peach". The Museum is open year-round, Monday through Saturday and has a $5 admission fee for adults over the age of 18.

A trip to Atlanta is not complete without visiting the Martin Luther King Jr. Historical Site. This national historical landmark includes a visitor center and museum, the famous Ebenezer Church, a Gandhi Promenade, the King Center and Dr. King's birth home and gravesite. Leave at least a half-day to comfortably see the entire MLK historical site.

23. <u>CHASE FIELD</u>

<u>PHOENIX, ARIZONA</u>
<u>HOME OF THE ARIZONA DIAMONDBACKS</u>

<u>TRANSPORTATION:</u>

'SKY HARBOR INTERNATIONAL AIRPORT'-(PHX) is 5 miles and a 15 minute drive away from 'Chase Field'. It is actually quicker to take a cab to the ballpark then it is to take the 4 mile shuttle bus to the 'Car Transportation Center' to rent a car. Car rentals will cost you $45-60 for a weekday and about half of that for the weekend. The good news is that tax in Arizona is a lot less than in most states.

The airport is a strong hub for American Airlines and Southwest Airlines. Unless you are flying in from the surrounding states or early in the morning, be prepared to pay hefty fees for your airline fares. Note here is Phoenix never changes its time for 'Daylight Savings Time' in the summer. However, if you are flying from the 'East' you can enjoy Phoenix being on PST time in the summer.

<u>WHERE TO STAY?</u>

The following lodging is within walking distance to Chase Field

<u>**Unlimited budget**</u>- there is currently no 5-star hotels within a close proximity of Chase Field.

<u>**Moderate budget**</u>

<u>Holiday Inn Hotel & Suites</u>
<u>Wyndham</u> - Phoenix Downtown

<u>**Chaser budget traveler**</u>

<u>SpringHill Suites</u> - Phoenix Downtown
<u>Hotel San Carlos-</u> ask about the ghost story!
<u>Super 8 Motel Phoenix</u>

<u>WHERE TO PARK?</u>

When entering downtown Phoenix, look for electronic message boards on the highway and streets to direct you to the best route to avoid traffic. Street, paid lots and garage parking is available around Chase Field and Copper Square. Parking can range from $5 to $25 on a typical day. Look east of the stadium for the least inexpensive lots (between Washington and the railroad tracks).

Ballpark Chasers Tip: with so many hotels near Chase Field, avoid driving and parking by choosing a hotel within walking distance to the stadium. Otherwise, we have reports of free parking southwest of the stadium, on Grant St. between 2nd & 3rd (only about a 10 minute walk from here).

WHERE TO EAT?

Pizza Bianco is the Mecca of pizzerias. People travel across the country to try their pie! Just two blocks north of Chase Field makes Pizza Bianco extremely difficult to get seating before and after a Diamondback game. We highly suggest coming several hours before game time in order to get through the line (seriously)! If you don't have the patience or the time—head over to one of the most unique atmospheres in all of baseball located across the street from Chase Field (Westside). Sliders American Grill is the place to be before and after a Diamondbacks game! Come for a great meal and stay for the people watching.

If looking to dine with a ballpark view, check out Friday's Front Row Sports Grill, located just behind the left field grandstand. Friday's is a great spot and open year-round but if eating during the game, we suggest calling ahead. Other fun options within the park include Cactus Corn flavored popcorn, Fatburgers and Peter Piper Pizza. Don't forget the Ballpark Chasers Meal: a Gordon Biersch burger, fries and a Gordon Biersch beer (located in section 121 & 314).

INTANGIBLES:

Chase Field has a hot tub sauna in Center Field that is quite unique to most ballparks. Although Chase Field has a retractable roof, inside the ballpark is quite muggy when temperatures reach over 100 F degrees outside (particularly when the Field is at capacity).

WHERE TO BUY TICKETS?

Ballpark Chasers around the Phoenix area tell us that box office tickets and scalpers are easy to come by over the past several seasons.

Ballpark Chasers Fun Fact: The famous RideNow Powersports Pool, located in center field, is actually a suite and can only be purchased as a group package. This one of a kind package seats up to 35 people and will only set you back a cool $6000-$7000!

WHEN TO GO?

The last time we checked, Phoenix was in the middle of the desert! Therefore, desert equals HOT weather! Throughout downtown, local businesses have misters spraying water outside for their customers. Average temperatures are over 100 degrees in the months of June, July, August and September. We highly suggest planning a trip in the months of April or May. Keep in mind, Chase Field does have a retractable roof and air conditioning inside the ballpark for a more enjoyable experience.

WHAT ELSE TO SEE?

Within walking distance of the stadium lies Heritage Park. This is home of the <u>Arizona Science center and IMAX Theater</u>. Also close by is <u>Copper Square</u>- more great restaurants and an AMC Theatre to catch a flick. If you are feeling a little tired (or just too hot to walk), hop on a Rickshaw!

To work off some of those greasy ballpark foods, take advantage of wonderful hiking trails surrounding the Phoenix area. Some of the top rated include: Camelback Mountain, South Mountain Park, Summit Trail and Echo Canyon Trail. Another great way to get a view of the desert is through the <u>Arizona Bound Jeep Tours</u>! Also top rated attractions from locals and tourists are the Phoenix Zoo and the Botanical Gardens.

BALLPARK CHASERS VACATION?

If you are traveling a great distance to come to Arizona, we highly recommend turning Chase Field into the West Coast 4 Ballpark Chaser vacation. This includes traveling to <u>Petco Park</u> in San Diego, <u>Angels Stadium in Anaheim</u> and <u>Dodger Stadium</u> in Los Angeles. The longest stretch of a drive is from San Diego to Phoenix, which takes roughly 5 hours (356 miles). Find the cheapest plane ticket to any of these four destinations and get a rental car with good gas mileage!

24. PROGRESSIVE FIELD

CLEVELAND, OHIO
HOME OF THE CLEVELAND INDIANS

TRANSPORTATION:

CLEVELAND/HOPKINS AIRPORT-(CLE) is about 15 miles and a 20 minute drive away by car. Alternatively, if you are staying downtown you can take the light rail train all the way into to the 'Tower City Hall' station which only takes about 35 minutes. There is a station in the bottom deck of the airport that is adjacent to the 'Arrivals' level. If a car rental is in your plans then you have chosen one of the cheapest airports for rental cars. Renting a car in Cleveland or nearby airport 'CAK' (45 miles away) for a week or more can run only $18-25 per day. Otherwise, it is $30-40 to rent a car for a normal weekday rate with it being $20-25 on the weekend. Subsequent insurance is also very cheap to make it a nice place to rent a vehicle. In Cleveland you only pay $8-10 for full auto coverage where most of the nation pays-$16-$27 per day just for full auto coverage. Other cheap cities for full auto insurance are: Milwaukee, Rochester, Chicago and St. Louis on weekends and of course Phoenix! If you are planning a 4 or 5 city trip Cleveland or Akron are good cities to fly into in order to return at the end of the trip. Cleveland is a strong hub for Continental Airlines and their smaller aircraft carrier of ExpressJet. 'CAK' Airport is a large hub for Air Tran Airways which feature several cheap flights anywhere domestically. We recommend including both of these airports in searches in order to find the cheapest fare.

WHERE TO STAY?

All options below are within 1 mile of Progressive Field

Unlimited Budget

The Ritz-Carlton Cleveland
Hyatt Regency Cleveland at the Arcade

Moderate Budget

Cleveland Marriott Downtown at Key Center
Holiday Inn Express Cleveland Downtown
Hilton Garden Inn Cleveland Downtown
Radisson Hotel Cleveland Gateway
Residence Inn Cleveland Downtown

Chaser Budget Traveler

As of now, there are no recommended Chaser Budget motels in the downtown Cleveland area. We highly suggest spending a few extra dollars and getting a great moderate budget hotel by Progressive Field.

WHERE TO PARK?

The downtown Cleveland area offers a vast amount of paid lots, garages, street and metered parking. Parking prices can range from $5 to $25 depending on the day of the week, location of the parking spot, and the opposing team. This is one stadium to circle the park a few times to find the best deal.

Ballpark Chasers Tip: Leaving the ballpark after an Indians game can be a nightmare. Ballpark Chasers recommends avoiding the lots within 2 blocks of Progressive Field to prevent getting stuck in bottlenecked traffic. You may also park at the 'Rock N Roll Hall Of Fame Lot' for a $10 flat rate special if you are watching a matinee and wish to see both the park and this attraction in the same day. It is only a mile up the road to walk to the ballpark from the 'RRHOF'.

WHERE TO EAT?

The selection of restaurants and sports bars outside of Progressive Field ranks in the top 5 of Major League Baseball cities. With such a wide assortment, Ballpark Chasers of all ages find the hardest part just choosing which one to try. The closest to the park (within walking distance) include Panini's Bar and Grille, Winking Lizard Tavern, Flannery's Pub, Fat Fish Blue and The Clevelander Bar and Grille. Our intentions were to rate them and give you a recommendation, but they are all so good. Try hitting up one before and after the game and let us know your favorite! A little further out is the Great Lakes Brewing Company, one of the "greenest" breweries in North America. No worries about finding a cab as Great Lakes shuttles their patrons to and from Indians games in their "eco-friendly Fatty-Wagon"! A round-trip ride on their vegetable oil-powered shuttle is only $1. Don't leave without getting the Ballpark Chasers meal: the sausage sampler, Brewhouse Burger and a Dortmunder Gold Lager.

Once inside Progressive Field, the action is in center field. The Market Pavilion offers numerous concession choices ranging from I-shaped soft pretzels served with Bertman's mustard, super nachos, wings and slider burgers from "Cleats". For those budget chasers, try a value meal for $5. The value meal consists of a hot dog, bag of peanuts and fountain drink. If for some reason you want to go to the ballpark and eat healthy, look for the "Go Foods" near Gate A (Section 162). Go foods offers menu items with no trans-fat, less than 4 grams per serving of saturated fats and sugars and 100% whole grains. Back to the fun stuff – for dessert, it is required to try Strickland's homemade ice cream! They serve up vanilla on a daily basis as well as 2 specialty flavors that rotate throughout the season. It's by far one of the best ice cream stands in baseball.

INTANGIBLES:

Much like Detroit, there are several in house participation venues to pitch, throw and catch inside the stadium. The Indians has several remarkable wall murals which show the history of the ball club. You can't watch any game as a fan without remembering or hearing reference to the movie 'Major League' which featured the ball club in its movie. Look for the drum player in right field bleachers just like in the movie.

WHERE TO BUY TICKETS?

On an average night at Progressive Field during the 2010 season, the stands were only 40% full. With that being said, Indians games rarely sell out unless the Red Sox or Yankees are in town. Tickets can be easily purchased before the game at the Indians box office or from the local scalpers working the streets.

Ballpark Chasers Tip: Have you ever wanted to stand on the field and watch batting practice? Well, the Indians give you that opportunity. Purchase a "Batting Practice XTRA" ticket and stand at the warning track directly behind home plate for Indians pre-game batting practice. Although the ticket does not include a seat for the game, it does come with a t-shirt and disposable camera.

WHEN TO GO?

Summers in Cleveland are usually hot and humid, with occasional rain showers. Mid to upper 80 degrees and even temperatures into the 90s are common from mid June through August. On average, July is the warmest and rainiest month in Cleveland. Ballpark Chasers find the best months to travel to Progressive Field are June, August and early September.

WHAT ELSE TO SEE?

If you only have time for one attraction in Cleveland, make sure it is the Rock and Roll Hall of Fame and Museum. Celebrating rock musicians, bands, songwriters, producers and legends, the Rock and Roll Hall of Fame does a tremendous job preserving the greats. Some of our favorite artifacts found inside the museum are: John Lennon's jacket, Madonna's bustier, Jimi Hendrix hand written lyrics to "Purple Haze", Muddy Watters electric guitar and Jim Morison's Cub Scout shirt! But if Rock N' Roll isn't your thing, you can always visit Cleveland's Polka Hall of Fame!

Enjoy the outdoors by taking a day trip to Lake Erie. Whether you want to swim, fish, parasail, canoe, scuba dive, Jet Ski, shop or simply lay on the beach, Lake Erie has it all! Expect a 2 hour round-trip drive from Cleveland to Lake Erie.

Did you know that Northeast Ohio has over 300 golf courses? Our favorite courses are part of Cleveland Metropark, which consists of 7 courses in the Cleveland surrounding area. Depending on your level of play and your expectations for a round of golf, there is a great course waiting for you. Check out their handy golf quiz to determine your best match. Not to worry as you can easily rent a set of clubs at any course.

BALLPARK CHASERS VACATION?

Progressive Field is part of "The Rust Belt" Ballpark Chasers vacation. This trip includes seeing the Pirates at <u>PNC Park</u> and the Tigers at <u>Comerica Park</u>. Those Ballpark Chasers looking for a longer vacation also include Cincinnati to see the Reds play at <u>Great American Ball Park</u>. On average, the drive from Progressive Field to PNC Park takes 2 ½ hours. With Cleveland Thursday matinee games in the summer you could do a Cleveland-Pittsburgh day-night double header comfortably because of the 12:10 pm starts at Progressive Field. The longest leg of the trip is from PNC Park to Comerica, roughly a 5 hour drive. If you need to return to Cleveland, plan on a 3 hour drive from Detroit. To prevent the last leg of the trip, try booking 2 one-way tickets. This way you can fly into Detroit and out of Pittsburgh, or vice versa. If you want to squeeze in Cincinnati, plan for a 4 hour drive from Progressive Field.

25. ANGELS STADIUM

ANAHEIM, CALIFORNIA
HOME OF THE LOS ANGELES ANGELS OF ANAHEIM

TRANSPORTATION:

We covered from LAX- in the Los Angeles Dodgers guide. We covered the hotels and transportation mostly except this is a good area to talk about John Wayne Airport-(SNA). Again with both of these airports mostly all carriers are available and you can get good rates. Of course you must remember that most of the overnight flights are out of LAX. From 'SNA' it is a quick jaunt up hwy 55-north to the park of about 12 miles and 20-30 minutes depending on traffic. The good news is the car rental facility is right across the street from SNA. Note to Chasers here***** 'SNA' is the worst airports for security line-ups in America and have an average wait of nearly 45 minutes—once you are through security you get an unusual take off experience—as the airlines have to shut off the airplane engines once you reach 1000 feet in the air until they pass the outskirts of Orange County and Santa Ana. The car rental facility is miles away from a gas station. Hit a station a few miles before getting off hwy 55-preferably in Santa Ana when it is time to return your car.

There are some cheap non-stop 'Alaska Airlines' flights within the Pac Coast. TIP***Always click the icon at www.kayak.com in 'the nearby airports column below said city,' this can give you cheaper flights at close by airports. Car rentals are a lot cheaper (15-25%) out of 'SNA' as compared to 'LAX'.

WHERE TO STAY?

The following lodging is within 1.5 miles of Angel Stadium.

Unlimited budget

Residence Inn Anaheim
Ayres Inn of Anaheim

Moderate budget

Holiday Inn Anaheim Resort
Doubletree Hotel Anaheim
Hilton Suites Anaheim/Orange

Chaser budget traveler

Comfort Inn of Anaheim

<u>Super 8 Motel</u> Anaheim/Near Disneyland

WHERE TO PARK?

Angel Stadium is one of a handful of parks around Major League Baseball that offers a centralized lot for all fans. The parking lot opens 2 ½ hours before the first pitch and is located on 2000 Gene Autry Way. You can access the lot via Douglass Road, State College Boulevard, and Orangewood Avenue. Expect to pay $8 for game day parking.

Ballpark Chasers Tip: make note of where you parked in the Angels lot. It is very easy in this full parking lot to misplace your vehicle after the game. Oh, and don't rely on your car alarm to save you as everyone else is trying the same thing!

Extreme Ballpark Chaser Tip-We found a free parking place just off of W Chapman and hwy 5 past the Ramada Inn. Turn onto Rampart Street North—keep driving a mile or so up road until you reach S Town Plaza Center Pl Street. Turn right after that and the parking spaces on the right are free if you can find a spot and you only have to walk up to the light and cross over the street of E Orangewood Street. Of course if you stay at the Motel 6 you only have to walk 2-3 miles up Rampart Street anyway as it is across from the 'Ramada Inn.'

INTANGIBLES—'DCB SAYS':

The staff used to be in 'Crcaker Jack Uniforms' when I first visited the Angels Stadium but have since retreated a little from that. I like the waterfall in center and of course there are great pictures to be had near the big 'A' outside the ballpark.

WHERE TO EAT?

The Catch is hands down the place to go before an Angel's game. Located across the street from Angel stadium, The Catch is known for their steaks and seafood. Other fun sit-down options near Angel Stadium are JT Schmid's Restaurant and Brewery, National Sports Grill and Throwbacks Sports Bar and Grill.

If you want a quicker option, try <u>In-N-Out Burger</u>. For those not on the west coast, this will be a treat. Believe it or not, they actually have fresh beef (not frozen patties), fresh potatoes peeled in front of you and they use real ice cream for their shakes! Needless to say, you will not find a microwave, freezer or heat-lamp at In-N-Out Burger!

Inside the park, Angel Stadium offers one restaurant open to all ticket holders. Homeplate Club is buffet style ($25 for adults and $10 for children) with a great view of the main entrance and the large, red signature Angel hats! They open 1 ½ hours prior to the first pitch so come early for a good seat. Other good eats within the ballpark are California Pizza Kitchen, The Beach Pit BBQ and Ruby's.

WHERE TO BUY TICKETS?

Because the Angels are currently one of the top teams in Major League Baseball, we recommend to plan and purchase your tickets in advance. Scalping tickets is more challenging at Angel Stadium since scalpers are required to stay outside of the main parking lot. If you need last minute tickets, look for the guys holding the signs "I Need Tickets" between Gene Autry Way and State College Blvd.

WHEN TO GO?

Ahh, beautiful California! Enjoy baseball all season long with wonderful temperatures and very little chance of rain. Ballpark Chasers recommend late May through July or whenever your hometown is still experiencing spring temperatures.

WHAT ELSE TO SEE?

Within minutes of Angel Stadium, Disneyland is a perfect way to spend a day or two in Anaheim. Despite the notion that Disneyland is only a place for children, we recommend it for all ages. To really appreciate Orange County, make a trip to Newport Beach. Only 20 minutes from Angel Stadium, Newport Beach is a gorgeous area to work on that tan and get some rest and relaxation.

DOUBLEHEADER OPTIONS:

LA Dodgers and San Diego Padres. Saturday and Thursday matinee games sometimes start at 12:55 which lends to viable doubleheaders when these two other teams are playing as there are lots of opportunities for this combination.

BALLPARK CHASERS VACATION?

The California area is perfect for seeing more than one stadium. Ballpark Chasers recommend combining your trip to Angel Stadium along with one or more of the five stadiums below.
1.) Dodger Stadium – 31 miles/39 minutes
2.) Petco Park- 94 miles/1.5 hours
3.) Chase Field- 356 miles/5.2 hours
4.) AT&T Park-409 miles/6.2 hours
5.) Oakland Coliseum- 394 miles/6 hours

26. ROGERS CENTER

TORONTO, ONTARIO CANADA
HOME OF THE TORONTO BLUE JAYS

THIS 1ST PART IS AN ALL 'DCB' CHASER GUIDE

TRANSPORTATION:

From 'LESTER B.PEARSON INT'L AIRPORT'-(YYZ) is about a 30 minute drive through the rigors of downtown traffic. We suggest going to a day game in Toronto for easier road trips. There is a downtown shuttle that you can purchase at the airport for $28 roundtrip. The shuttle takes you right to Union Station which is a mere mile from the ballpark. Also, if you are coming from Cleveland, Pittsburgh or Detroit and have more games to attend back in the states, a round-trip Greyhound bus trip is always around a hundred dollars. This puts you so close into downtown and can save on parking and gas. Ballpark Chasers does not recommend flying into Toronto if you are combining other ball games into your trip as it is very expensive to fly in and out of. You are better off flying out of Buffalo, Detroit or Cleveland and to use ground transportation into Canada.

Car rentals in the city go for about $50 a day. If you are lucky enough to be there on the weekend, you can steal a $20-25 rental sometimes at www.bcaa.com under the car section. The car rental facility is right outside the airport so it is very accessible. Again, Budget and Thrifty rentals are your best options with the preferred programs to eliminate waiting in line at the airport.

One last option is to take Sedan Service to and from the game. It is very cheap at $50 per trip. You can use this service to the airport after a day game last year and was at the airport 25 minutes after being picked up. While you will spend more money in Canada usually for things this is one instance you will not! This is a good alternative for Americans so they don't get a $300 speeding ticket on the streets in Ontario.

As for driving on the 401 hwy, give yourself ample time as Toronto is one of the biggest cities in North America.

FOOD

While it does not get enough credit, outside of the 'Rogers Center' are some of the best street vendor hotdogs you will find. These guys make a living from selling their food down the street at 'Union Station' all day before coming out to the park. You can buy dogs and drinks for a dollar. If that doesn't suit you, there is the 'Hard Rock Cafe' bar at 'Windows Restaurant, (just inside the entrance of Rogers Centre). There you can eat awesome pub food while you watch batting practice. I highly recommend the rib sandwich with Au Jus sauce. This is a great way to spend the time before a ballgame.

Back in 1989 when the park was the 1st of its kind, they had much more selection of food—now with dwindling crowds you are much better off eating at the aforementioned places before or after the games.

TICKETS

Extreme Ballpark Chaser tip: If you know anyone that lives in Canada ask them to cash some of them in for redeemable ticket voucher's (from Gate 9 only in person) that are great deals for great tickets. www.airmiles.ca is the website you can get your Canadian friends to lend you their Canadian address(Your US Safeway club card number will work) and then sign up here with their address again for a hundred free bonus miles---in which you can redeem for 2 ticket vouchers in the 500 section (a $25 value). It is a first come first serve basis so you can redeem these vouchers for the prime games like NY and BOS. If you are Canadian you are probably already familiar with air miles so just collect enough. This year it is 125 air miles for $50 outfield tickets and 180 air miles for $70 field level baselines tickets.

Earn Air miles for free with normal internet searches with the Air miles Toolbar. You can earn 360 air miles for the year by doing 300 searches a month that qualify you for 30 air miles a month. So between that and the Safeway deal you can earn $150 worth of Toronto Blue Vouchers for not really doing anything at all. More of a Canadian Ballpark Chaser tip—but if you are going to do Toronto anyway save the money!

Tickets are always up for sale at ww.ebay.ca as well for major discounts. It is always a buyer's market for Blue Jays tickets. You can always find guys outside the park selling tickets for half price as well. This is an ideal solution for Yankees and Red Sox fans that are sick of paying hundreds of dollars in their hometown to save a boatload of money to see their team.

INTANGIBLES:

Being the only Canadian team makes it hard for the hardcore ballpark chaser. It penalizes both the U.S and Canada. I would not suggest flying in and out of Toronto if you can avoid it. Canada has so many taxes on their flights that it is almost double the cost for a flight. You are better off driving from Detroit or Cleveland to fly out of those cities. The only practical flights are to New York with the American Carriers.

# BALLPARK CHASERS GUIDE
_(from ballparkchasers.com)

WHERE TO STAY?

 All of the following Ballpark Chasers recommended lodging is within walking distance of Rogers Stadium

Unlimited budget

Residence Inn Toronto Downtown (entertainment district)
Hotel le Germain Toronto
Soho Metropolitan Hotel
The Westin Harbour Castle

Moderate budget

Renaissance Hotel Toronto Downtown
The Strathcona Hotel

Chaser budget traveler

Super 8 Toronto
Travelodge Toronto Downtown

Ballpark Chasers Tip: although it isn't the nicest hotel in Toronto, the Renaissance Hotel offers a once in a lifetime chance to sleep in a Major League Baseball stadium! There are over 70 rooms with a field view, so start saving and reserve several months in advance.

WHERE TO PARK?

Rogers Centre is located in the heart of downtown Toronto and can be difficult to navigate if you are not familiar with the area. The Blue Jays underground parking is the most convenient option. Otherwise, garages, paid lots and street parking are readily available in the surrounding city blocks. Expect a price range of $10 to $30 for parking, depending on the distance to the stadium.

WHERE TO EAT?

Downtown Toronto provides numerous restaurants and sports bars. "The Great One" has his very own restaurant with a unique name, "Wayne Gretzky's Restaurant". Okay, so the name isn't that original but the décor and food make up for it. Where else can you find continuous highlight reels from the remarkable career of Wayne Gretzky and hundreds of memorabilia items throughout his playing days? Not to mention, the food is pretty good too. Don't leave without trying their famous meat

Another fun sports hangout is the Armadillo Texas Grille. You can't go wrong if you love large portions, local fans, and great margaritas! Make sure to arrive early on game days as this spot becomes the place to be for Blue Jays fans. Our last recommendation for eating outside of the ballpark is Pizza Rustica. We were quite surprised to find a local pizza joint in Toronto that could make a great pie and live up to Ballpark Chasers standards. Come check them out and decide for your self.

Inside the stadium the food takes a turn for the worse. Ballpark Chasers does not recommend any concessions at this time because they are only serving average hot dogs, hamburgers and boring stadium pizza. Your best bet is to arrive when the gates open and get a seat at the Hard Rock Café, located in Right Field. Serving on game days only, the Hard Rock is an ideal way to catch the game while enjoying a good ol' classic American meal.

WHERE TO BUY TICKETS?

The Blue Jays were died last in ballpark attendance during the 2010 season. This is good news for Ballpark Chasers traveling to Rogers Centre. Blue Jays tickets are easily available before home games through their box office, located at Gate 9 (Bremner Blvd, just east of Spadina Ave). Purchasing tickets from scalpers is another choice and you will find them very visible on all sides of the stadium. As long as the Blue Jays are not competing for a playoff spot and the seats are wide open, purchasing tickets from scalpers usually presents a better deal than through the box office. Remember, there are dozens of scalpers all competing for your business, so feel free to negotiate!

Ballpark Chasers Tip: if you just want in the game and don't care about where you sit, plan your trip to see a Tuesday game to take advantage of a $2 ticket in all 500 level and some 200 level seats!

WHEN TO GO?

Rogers Centre was the first Major League Baseball stadium to build a retractable roof. The Blue Jays will not only close the roof with rain, but also during those hot, summer afternoons. Spring and fall temperatures tend to be on the cooler side in Toronto; therefore, Ballpark Chasers recommend the months of June, July and August when traveling to Rogers Centre.

WHAT ELSE TO SEE?

Just blocks from Rogers Centre lie two of Toronto's must see attractions. The CN Tower and the Hockey Hall of Fame are a perfect way to spend the day before a Blue Jays game. To get the most out of the 1,800 ft. tall CN Tower, Ballpark Chasers recommends purchasing tickets for the "Total Tower Experience". This package includes glass floor elevator rides, sky pod and look-out observation decks, a documentary film and motion theatre ride. The Hockey Hall of Fame is a short walk from the CN Tower and is the "Mecca" for hockey fans. For just $13, one can see the Stanley Cup, slap shots at real-time goalies, test your goalkeeping skills (by taking shots from Wayne Gretzky and Mark Messier), watch hockey movies, and be a play-by-play announcer, while taking in the world's largest collection of hockey memorabilia!

If you have a rental car and are up for a two hour drive, head west to visit the <u>Canadian Baseball Hall of Fame and Museum</u> in St. Mary's, Ontario. Although it isn't as grand as Cooperstown, the CBHF is still worth the trip for any baseball fan. The museum pays tribute to over 80 Canadian baseball heroes, with tons of baseball memorabilia, artifacts and souvenirs. Coming soon to the CBHF is "The Great Canadian Dream Park", a 32 acre site that will hold a new baseball stadium, three baseball fields, walking trails, picnic grounds, and a new interactive museum and education center. With a target completion date of 2013, the new Canadian Baseball Hall of Fame looks to be the next home for baseball in Canada.

27. KAUFFMAN STADIUM

KANSAS CITY, MISSOURI
HOME OF THE KANSAS CITY ROYALS

TRANSPORTATION—'DCB SAYS':

KANSAS CITY AIRPORT- (MCI) is 26 Miles and a 35 minute drive from the airport to the yard. The 'Car Transportation Rental Center is a 3 miles shuttle bus ride. There is no further ballpark from the airport in the majors then in KC. If you are only in town for the game, for $50 you could have sedan service to Kauffman Stadium. Keep in mind, the gas station at the car rental center is not open for business from 12am-6am and there is not another gas station for 7-8 miles (so they can charge you $6.99 a gallon when the tank is not full). Our suggestion is to stay at the Best Western at 'MCI Airport' for about $70-and if you need to get around rent a car. Otherwise, if it is just to the ballgame and back you can pay a sedan driver $110 roundtrip for up to 4 people. Car rentals go for about $50-60 for the day, plus the optional $25 insurance, $15 for gas and $10 for parking at Kauffman

MCI Airport is a not really a hub for any airline but sees the most traffic from the airlines 'Frontier and Southwest Airlines.' The fares are quite expensive all around. If you are planning to combine St. Louis in your travels, it is better to fly into to and return out of STL-LAMBERT.

WHERE TO STAY?

Unlimited budget- There is no 4 or 5 star hotels close to Kauffman Stadium

Moderate budget -All 3 options are within walking distance of Kauffman Stadium

Sheraton Kansas City Sports Complex Hotel
Clarion Hotel Sports Complex
Drury Inn & Suites Kansas City Stadium

Chaser budget traveler - The following lodging is within 4 miles of Kauffman Stadium

Super 8 Independence, MO
Best Western Truman Inn

WHERE TO PARK?

Parking at "The K" has never been so easy! The Kansas City Royals are one of a handful of ball clubs that offer a centralized parking lot in front of their respective stadium. General parking is only $10 and the Royals provide an <u>easy-guide</u> that has directions to either the east or west parking lot, depending on the direction you are coming from.

WHERE TO EAT?

One of our crew's favorite restaurants in all of baseball is just 15 minutes from Kauffman Stadium. Chappell's Restaurant and Sports Museum is a must see when coming to Kansas City. Chappell's not only serves great food, but also is home of the country's largest collection of sports memorabilia (within a restaurant). Don't leave here without trying the famous half-pound burger, meeting Jim Chappell (the owner) and finding the autograph baseball from Ty Cobb and the authentic 1974 World Series Trophy!

If you haven't noticed in the other Ballpark Chasers Guides, we love "hole-in-the-wall" restaurants and the local favorites. If you feel the same way, look no further than LC's BBQ. Just 4 miles from Kauffman Stadium, LC's can practically be smelled from the seats! Well, that may be an exaggeration, but LC's is arguably the best BBQ joint in all of Kansas City. Our mouths are watering just thinking of their burnt end sandwiches and fries. A few miles further lay one of the coolest interactive restaurants in the country, The 810 Zone is the place to go to find food made from scratch, interactive televisions at each table, a radio broadcast booth and a colossal collection of high definition televisions and sports memorabilia! If that isn't enough, bring your best swing for their golf simulator game that claims to be accurate within .3 percent! We recommend <u>calling ahead</u> for a tee-time if you want to play Pebble Beach.

The 2009 season opened with a newly renovated Kauffman Stadium. Some of the new features include a restaurant in Right-Field, a Royals Hall of Fame exhibit and miniature golf in Left Field. Rivals Restaurant is now open just beyond the Right-Field bleachers and is serving up traditional sports bar cuisine. To keep you up on the game, Rivals offers a number of flat-screen televisions, including a 103 incher! Rivals Restaurant makes for a perfect stop during those cool spring nights or blistering hot and humid summer days in Kansas City. For dessert, look for Sheridan's Frozen Custard in the new "Outfield Experience". Sheridan's is the only custard stand operating in a professional sports venue!

INTANGIBLES:

Some of the best pictures can be taken inside Kauffman Stadium because of their waterfalls. It is better to see a game at night because of this aspect as well. Kauffman also features the biggest Videotron in the major leagues. Wherever you are in the park you can see this monstrous screen. Be sure to have your picture taken with the statue George Brett in right field.

WHERE TO BUY TICKETS?

The Kansas City Royals have consistently been in the bottom half of fan attendance for quite some time. The struggle of the Royals on the field translates into a struggle filling up the stands of Kauffman Stadium. Needless to say, tickets were relatively easy to come by during the 2010 season. Ballpark Chasers can pick up tickets right before the game at one of the box office locations outside of Kauffman Stadium or online using their interactive seating chart. If you can, plan a Friday night game to catch a great fireworks show following the game.

Ballpark Chasers Fun Fact: One of the most coveted and hardest to come by seats in all of baseball is the famous red seat found in Section 101, Row C, Seat 1. The Royals placed this red seat in honor of the legendary Kansas City Monarch, Buck O'Neil. Don't expect to find the seat on eBay, as the Royals front office donates this seat to a member of the Kansas City community for each home game.

WHEN TO GO?

Summers in Kansas City tend to be hot and humid! Expect temperatures in the 90's with the lowest probability of rain during the months of July and August. If you prefer less humidity and cooler temperatures, plan your trip in April, May and/or June. Just be prepared to bring your umbrella.

WHAT ELSE TO SEE?

Besides the Hall of Fame in Cooperstown, no other attraction comes close to the Negro League Baseball Museum in Kansas City. Founded in 1990, the NLBM is a non-profit organization with a privately funded mission to preserve the history of African Americans in baseball. Located in the historic district of 18th and Vine (10 minutes from Kauffman Stadium), the NLBM will provide hours of entertainment and will leave you with a greater appreciation of the Negro Leagues. Ballpark Chasers recommends making a day out of it by purchasing a combo ticket ($8) which includes a ticket to the Jazz Museum next door. After a day at the museums, head over to the Country Club Plaza for 15 blocks of restaurants, shops, concerts, entertainment and a unique atmosphere that cannot be replicated anywhere in the greater Midwest. If your trip to Kansas City is spent with the love of your life, don't leave the Country Club Plaza without a Venetian style Gondola ride.

BALLPARK CHASERS VACATION?

Ballpark Chasers rave about the "Midwest 3" baseball road trip! This includes seeing Kauffman Stadium, Busch Stadium and Coors Field. We recommend finding the cheapest airfare to either Denver or St. Louis and using a rental car to drive in between. The drive from Denver to Kansas City is roughly 9 hours, or about 610 miles; whereas the drive between St. Louis and Kansas City is about 240 miles or 4 hours.

28. **TROPICANA FIELD**

ST. PETERSBURG, FLORIDA
HOME OF THE TAMPA BAY RAYS

TRANSPORTATION:

Tampa International Airport-(TPA) is about 22 miles and a 35 minute drive from Tropicana Field. Unless you are only staying for the baseball game it is going to be necessary to rent a car when you land into Tampa. You are a quick shuttle to any of the main car rental agencies. Car rates will run you about $45-60 for a weekday and not much cheaper on the weekend with Florida being such a popular tourist destination. The airport is a strong hub for both cheap Airlines Air Tran Airways and Southwest. For these reasons alone the city is very cheap to fly in and out of. If you plan on visiting Miami after Tampa it is much better to fly to Tampa and return at the end of your trip. Flights between cities run about $70 should you choose to fly between which is an ideal option.

WHERE TO STAY?

There are no hotels within walking distance to Tropicana Field. Ballpark Chasers recommends reserving a rental car from the airport as all hotels below are within 1-3 miles of the stadium

Unlimited Budget

The Pier Hotel
Renaissance Vinoy Resort and Golf Club

Moderate Budget

America's Best Inn St. Petersburg
Courtyard by Marriott Downtown St. Petersburg
Hampton Inn & Suites St. Petersburg Downtown

Chaser Budget Traveler

Comfort Inn & Suites at Tropicana Field

Ballpark Chasers hidden gem: Hilton St. Petersburg Carillon Point (about 10 miles from Tropicana Field but worth the drive)

DCB SPECIAL:

Best Western-St. Petersburg/Clearwater is about 8 miles from the ballpark and costs only about $60 per night with a hot complimentary continental breakfast. It is only a $15-20 cab ride from the ballpark and a $35 cab ride from the airport.

WHERE TO PARK?

The Rays organization makes parking a snap, offering 9 lots around Tropicana Field. Rays parking is $20 for the premium games, while select games drop to just $10. To find pricing information for your game and reserve a spot in advance. A more affordable option is the commercial and city owned lots surrounding Tropicana Field. For select games, a free baseball Shuttle picks up passengers on Second Street mid-block between Central Avenue and 1st Avenue South (under the Bank of America Tower's pedestrian bridge) and drops passengers off near Gate 4 at Tropicana Field. The baseball shuttle operates 90 minutes before game time and until one hour after the game is over. A city-owned garage on 1st Avenue South, just east of 2nd Street South, is the designated shuttle parking facility and costs $5.

Ballpark Chasers Tip: the Rays are doing their part to encourage car-pooling by offering fans free parking when arriving at the game with 4 or more people in the same vehicle!

WHERE TO EAT?

Rays fans love to grab food and drinks at Ferg's Sports Bar and Grill before every home game. Located directly across from Tropicana Field, Ferg's boasts about their numerous awards from the local online community. Start with some scrumptious boneless chicken wings and follow it up with "The Devil Ray" burger.
If you're in the mood for some good Southern comfort cuisine, look for The Savannah Café on Central Ave, one block from Tropicana Field. Just make sure to save room for dessert as the pineapple upside-down cake is amazing.
Our final suggestion is a little further out but well worth the walk. Captain Al's Waterfront Grill & Bar is located right next to the historic St. Petersburg Pier which offers gorgeous views of Tampa Bay. Make sure to take advantage of their outdoor seating, specialty mixed drinks, live music and endless sunshine. Grab a table with a view and enjoy a Ballpark Chasers meal by ordering the crispy calamari for starters, a grouper sandwich for the main course and your choice of their many house specialty drinks.
Once inside Tropicana Field, the concession options are nothing to write home about. Ballpark Chasers only suggests the Columbia Restaurant (really just a stand) for quick Cuban style food and the Centerfield Brew House, for a sit-down restaurant. The Brew Pub opens 2 hours before game time and serves traditional bar food and drinks. Don't forget to check out the Ted Williams Museum and Hitters Hall of Fame and the 10,000 gallon tank filled with live Rays after your meal.

INTANGIBLES:

Tropicana Field might be hard to get to and it might be hard to look at but the park is very fan friendly for kids and families. There are many activities for the kids inside the building and they have the most kid friendly mascot, 'Raymond'. Tampa Bay's management has done a great job creating family specials to encourage families to the park. It is also a great way to avoid the hot temperatures outside in the summer months.

WHERE TO BUY TICKETS?

Despite the Rays being highly competitive, Tropicana Field sat nearly half empty during the 2010 home games. Even the World Series didn't fill up the stadium! Don't expect a sell-out until Tampa brings a new ballpark to Tampa. Tickets can be purchased at the main box office or from your favorite online broker. Scalping is illegal on stadium property; however, reselling tickets at or below face value can take place on the west side of the stadium, between Gates 5 and 6. Look for plenty of action in this area and great bargains starting about 2.5 hours before every home game.

WHEN TO GO?

It's Florida! Enjoy the sun and no need to worry about rainouts as Tropicana Field is one of the few remaining domes in Major League Baseball. Ballpark Chasers favorite month to travel to Tropicana Field is May due to the warm, but comfortable temperatures and less rainfall than the rest of the summer brings.

WHAT ELSE TO SEE?

The beautiful Florida sun provides numerous outdoor activities throughout the summer. Ballpark Chasers favorite is Busch Gardens, just 35 minutes from Tropicana Field. Busch Gardens is much more than just an amusement park, offering everything from an animal park, live shows, safaris, a bird garden, a water park and a children's play area. But who are we kidding; you come to Busch Gardens for their roller coasters! Sheikra is America's first "dive coaster" – 200 feet up followed by 90 degrees straight down! Gwazi is the area's largest and fastest double wooden coaster that will make you question how a bunch of wood (1.25 million board feet to be exact) can keep the coaster up! Check out the Montu for a 60 mph inverted roller coaster that reaches G-force of 3.85. To put that in perspective, Space Shuttle astronauts experience a similar force upon lift-off. The best of all has to be Kumba! The 135 ft. drop will make your stomach rise up to your throat!
Ballpark Chasers suggestion: take these coaster rides on an empty stomach!
Tampa's best kept secret is the Big Cat Rescue. This nonprofit organization rescues exotic cats from being abused and/or abandoned and provides them with a safe home. Day tours are offered Monday through Saturday (children under the age of 10 can only take the Saturday tour) and include seeing over 140 animals from over 15 different species of wild cat. This is truly one of the few opportunities to see up close cougars, tigers, bobcats, lions, leopards and lynx as many of them are now endangered

or even extent in the wild. Keep in mind that the Big Cat Rescue is not a zoo and tours are the only way to see the cats. Also, cameras are allowed but no tripods. Umbrellas are forbidden. Make sure to wear an old but comfortable pair of walking shoes.

BALLPARK CHASERS VACATION?

Tropicana Field is part of the "Sunshine Pair" Ballpark Chasers Trip, which includes seeing <u>Sun Life Stadium</u> in Miami. The drive between stadiums is roughly 253 miles, or about 4 hours. Ballpark Chasers recommends searching for airline tickets to either Tampa International Airport or Miami International Airport to find the cheapest ticket from your home city.

In order to break up the 4 hour drive, check out a game at one or more of the Florida State League ballparks. Our favorite is Charlotte Sports Park in Port Charlotte, Florida. The newly renovated stadium is home to the <u>Charlotte Stone Crabs</u>, the High-A Affiliate of the Tampa Bay Rays. Further south is Hammond Stadium in Fort Myers, Florida. The Twins Advanced Single A Affiliate, the <u>Fort Myers Miracle</u>, play here and offer a great beer garden along with fabulous turkey legs!

29. SUN LIFE STADIUM

MIAMI, FLORIDA
HOME OF THE FLORIDA MARLINS

TRANSPORTATION:

Sun Life is 18 Miles/25 minutes from FT. Lauderdale Airport-(FLA).
Sun Life is 15 Miles/25-40 minutes from Miami Int'l Airport-(MIA).

The best option is to visit www.kayak.com to find the best fare you can as both airports are similar distance away. If there is a similar price and you are driving it is better to fly into FLL. The car rental facilities are all a few miles off the airport in 'MIA' and you are in a deep residential area that can make you lost before you go anywhere—where as FLL has all of the car rental agencies on-site. Car rentals are quite expensive at $55-70 per weekday and the weekend is not much cheaper. You will want to bid at www.priceline.com in order to reduce the fare.

FLL- serves the cheaper airlines of Air Tran Airways, Southwest Airlines and Jet Blue.

MIA- serves the legacy airlines of Continental and American Airlines.

WHERE TO STAY?

All options below are within 15 miles of Sun Life Stadium

Unlimited Budget

Seminole Hard Rock Hotel & Casino
The Westin Diplomat Resort
The Caroline Ocean Beach Hotel

Moderate Budget

Hilton Garden Inn - Miramar
Shulas Hotel & Golf Club
TownePlace Suites by Marriott
Courtyard - Miami Lakes

Chaser Budget Traveler

Quality Inn and Suites - Hollywood Boulevard

<u>El Palacio Sports Hotel</u> - the closest option to Sun Life Stadium

WHERE TO PARK?

The Florida Marlins offer convenient and inexpensive parking around Sun Life Stadium. Gate 4 opens 2 ½ hours before the first pitch; all others open 2 hours prior. All parking is just $10 per vehicle for the 2010 season.

Ballpark Chasers Tip: we highly suggest renting a car after flying in to Miami International. Because of the location of the Sun Life Stadium and the lack of hotels, restaurants and entertainment surrounding, you will want to have your own vehicle.

WHERE TO EAT?

Unfortunately, there are no worthy restaurants or quick-food stops within walking distance of Sun Life Stadium. The closest option is The Mahogany Grille, an upscale restaurant located about 1 mile from the stadium. The Mahogany Grille is open Wednesdays through Sundays and is known best for serving up delicious "soul food". Order the plate of Fish and Grits and enjoy their nightly live music. A little further away is Tony's Pizza Café, arguably the best pizza pie in all of South Florida. Make sure to bring your appetite as Tony's serves big portions of everything on the menu, including true New York style pizza. Our last recommendation, Shula's Steak House, is approximately a 15 minute drive from the stadium. Don Shula opened a chain of these restaurants centered on a common theme of perfection- trying to serve the perfect steak. We think he did a great job as the steaks are definitely worth the trip! Ballpark Chasers will go for the 48 ounce porterhouse steak at an attempt to join the infamous "48-ounce Club"!

Do yourself a favor and eat before coming to the game. Sun Life Stadium has a fair amount of concession stands to choose from, but nothing worth the money. If you are stuck and need a snack, the empanadas from Maggie's Empanada Bistro are our lone recommendation.

INTANGIBLES:

The stadium does change names every year so you might want to make sure you know the directions on how to drive to and from the park depending on where you are coming from. Be sure to buy your tickets in advance as half of the tickets purchased are day of the game sales. If you are a football fan be sure to bring your camera to take pictures of all the 'DOLPHIN'S' pictures in the building. Be sure to visit in 2011 as there will be a new park unveiled in 2012!

WHERE TO BUY TICKETS?

Over the last four of five seasons, the Florida Marlins and Sun Life Stadium boast the prestigious honor of holding Major League Baseball's worst attendance. You never need to worry about purchasing a ticket in advance unless seeing the Marlins in a playoff or World Series game. Because you are experiencing a baseball game in a football stadium, there isn't much to take in. Therefore, Ballpark

Chasers enjoy a seat in the Marlins "All you can Eat Seating", located in the club level of Sun Life Stadium. Starting at $47, these club-level seats are fully air-conditioned and come with unlimited gut-busting hotdogs, nachos, popcorn, peanuts and soda.

Ballpark Chasers Tip: sign up for the Marlins "E-Saver" newsletter to receive discounted ticket offers throughout the season.

WHEN TO GO?

South Florida is no surprise a tropical climate region that offers year-round sunshine. In terms of rainfall, June through September tend to be the rainiest months for the Miami area. Ballpark Chasers suggest planning a trip to Sun Life Stadium in the beginning of the season when your home city is still struggling to break 60 degrees.

WHAT ELSE TO SEE?

A trip to Florida isn't complete without taking a trip to the beach. Although there are many to choose from, South Beach is in a league of its own. After you get your fill laying on the beach and catching some vitamin D, make time for the art deco walking tour to fully appreciate the history of South Beach. No reservations are required; however, tours depart only once per day, so make sure to plan accordingly.

Explore Miami via water by embarking on a 2 hour Ocean Force Adventure aboard a Zodiac RIB boat (the same used by the FBI and other law enforcement agencies)! This sightseeing/thrill ride travels roughly 40 miles across the ocean to witness marine life, historical landmarks, celebrity homes and gorgeous views of the Miami skyline. With only 6 passengers per boat, reservations are a must.

If you just can't get enough of the water and are feeling brave, head south until you come across Coopertown, Florida where the population is under 10! After trying some frog legs and gator tails for lunch at their local neighborhood restaurant, embark on an airboat tour through the Florida everglades. Coopertown Airboats offer a one-hour or two-hour ride that will show you the wildlife of Everglades National Park up close and personal. Make sure to bring your camera as alligators and crocodiles like to come out and play during the tour. Come see why Mickey Mantle made a point of taking a ride on one of the most unique tour operations in all of America.

BALLPARK CHASERS VACATION?

Sun Life Stadium is part of the "Sunshine Pair" Ballpark Chasers Vacation, which includes seeing Tropicana Field in Tampa, Florida. The drive between stadiums is roughly 253 miles, or about 4 hours. Ballpark Chasers recommends searching for airline tickets to either Tampa International Airport or Miami International Airport to find the cheapest ticket from your home city.

30. MCAFEE COLISEUM

OAKLAND, CALIFORNIA
HOME OF THE OAKLAND A'S

TRANSPORTATION:

'OAKLAND INTERNATIONAL AIRPORT'-(OAK) is a really small airport but is one of the hubs for Southwest Airlines-which also means no fees for 2 pieces of luggage! Ideal for flying in from the Midwest cities such as: KC-STL and COL if you are looking for a day game. Oakland's Airport is located a few miles only from the ballpark which is very convenient at least.
The car rental facilities are about a 3 mile shuttle bus away from the airport. Once you see the ballpark in the distance you have to choose parking. The car rentals are decently priced in comparison to San Francisco, still use the Priceline website to go cheaper. You should be able to get a car for $40-50 during the weekday and about $25-35 for a weekend day rental

WHERE TO STAY?

The following lodging is within 1.5 miles of the Oakland Coliseum

Unlimited budget- There is not any 4 or 5 star hotels within 2 miles of Oakland Coliseum

Moderate Budget

Holiday Inn Express Airport
Hilton Oakland Airport
Courtyard by Marriot Oakland Airport

Chaser budget traveler

Days Hotel Oakland Airport (walking distance to the stadium)
La Quinta Inn Oakland Airport Coliseum

WHERE TO PARK?

The Oakland Athletics make it trouble-free for their guests by offering a large, centralized parking lot in front of the stadium. Expect to pay $17 for any spot in the general parking lot and keep in mind parking attendants will not accept a bill larger than $20. Also note that the Coliseum lot opens 2 ½ hours prior to the first pitch for those looking to catch batting practice.

<u>*Ballpark Chasers Tip*</u>: fans get free parking on <u>most</u> Tuesday games during the 2010 season! No such luck when the Yankees and Red Sox are in town.

WHERE TO EAT?

If you only have one day in the Oakland area, it is critical to make your way to Walnut Creek, California to find <u>McCovey's Restaurant</u>. Inspired by the "Gentle Giant", Willie McCovey, this restaurant is like no other. From the outside architecture to the inside layout, McCovey's is a mini replica of AT&T Park with their walls overflowing from sports memorabilia that make it fell like a mini Cooperstown! The 30 minute drive from Oakland is well worth it for the amazing selection of comfort food. Ballpark Chasers recommend not leaving without trying the "Grand Slam Double-stacked Hamburger" and finding the signed baseball by Satchel Paige!

The most convenient and quickest option to grab a bite before or after an A's game is at Doug's BBQ. This local Oakland favorite is within walking distance to the stadium and offers great burgers (veggie as well), BBQ and chicken items. If you go with a rental car, the 15 minute drive to <u>Zachary's Pizza</u> is most certainly worth it! Come for a Chicago style pizza pie and see why Sports Illustrated rated it as one of their best places for a slice!

Ballpark Chasers Tip: Unfortunately, there aren't many good things to say about the food within Oakland Coliseum and therefore we highly recommend eating before the game. If you are desperate, check out the Kinder's BBQ for a decent sirloin hoagie sandwich.

INTANGIBLES- "DCB SAYS":

The Oakland A's have won 4 World Series and they have had some incredible players (Henderson-Jackson-Giambi-Eckersley-Catfish Hunter). The Athletics pay decent respect to these players throughout their stadium. I like the tailgating done in the parking lot before the game--boy did I get harassed for wearing a Mickey Mantle jersey during one moment outside the park. The foul grounds of the park are unique in size and it looks nice aesthetically if you sit in the third deck behind home plate.

For such a horrible stadium, the A's had one of the better decades of late. They are in desperate need of a new stadium.

WHERE TO BUY TICKETS?

Unless the A's start winning again, don't expect the fans to come out until they open Cisco Field in 2012. The box office will have tickets available unless it's a Bay Series against the San Francisco Giants. If you happen to catch a Wednesday A's game at Oakland Coliseum, check out the $2 tickets and $1 hot dogs during the 2010 season.

Ballpark Chasers' Tip: Do you dream of going to the ballpark and eating whatever you want, without opening your wallet? If so, Ballpark Chasers recommends Oakland Coliseums "All You Can Eat Seating." These exclusive sections are home to unlimited hot dogs, popcorn, nachos, peanuts, Pepsi products and even ice cream! This belly-buster is included with the purchase of a $35 ticket in sections 316, 317 and 318.

WHEN TO GO?

The weather in Oakland is very similar to the San Francisco area- mild summers that are not sweltering hot. Average temperatures are in the mid 70s during the summer with very little humidity. Ballpark Chasers recommend June through August as the best months to travel to Oakland; these are the warmest and driest.

WHAT ELSE TO SEE?

Most people think that Oakland wouldn't have much to offer other than the A's, Raiders and Golden State Warriors. Au Contraire, my fellow Ballpark Chasers! Jack London Square is Oakland's waterfront district full of vast shopping, dining and entertainment. Make sure to stop for a drink and Heinold's First and Last Chance Bar. This local pub has been in operation using gas lamps since 1883 and was built from remnants of an old wailing ship. Watch out for the uneven floor that still remains from the San Francisco earthquake of 1906!

If you have not had the opportunity to see redwood trees in person, Oakland will give you that chance. Redwood Regional Park is just a few miles outside of downtown Oakland and is home to nearly 2,000 acres of Redwoods that stand up to 150 ft. tall! Bring your trail shoes as this park has plenty of paths to choose from.

Still not impressed with Oakland's attractions? Well, San Francisco is only a 10 minute drive away!

BALLPARK CHASERS VACATION?

If your baseball trip to Oakland Coliseum involves traveling a great distance, we suggest extending your vacation by visiting one or more of the stadiums below.

1.) AT&T Park- 16 miles/30 minutes
2.) Dodger Stadium- 365 miles/5.5 hours
3.) Angel Stadium- 394 miles/6 hours
4.) Petco Park- 487 miles/7.5 hours

FEATURED BALLPARK CHASERS AND THE AUTHORS:

Roger Ratzenberger

Roger Ratzenberger Jr. is 50 years old and his hometown in Milford CT.
Website-www.Ratzenberger.net
Approximate date of first baseball park visit-July 1967
Number of parks usually visited in one year-10
Favorite Ballpark old and New-Fenway Park and PNC Park
Usually sits on field level but always goes out for long walks during the games.

ROGER'S STORY:

I have been passionate about baseball ever since, at the age of 7, I attended my first Major League Baseball game at Yankee Stadium. As a Mets fan, it's still hard for me to accept that my first Major League game was a Yankee game. It did, however, provide me an opportunity to see the great Mickey Mantle and the unconventional, long-haired Joe Pepitone in person. A year later, I saw my first New York Mets game at Shea Stadium and I have been an avid Mets fan ever since. My loyalties are pledged to the Mets, but my passion extends to all aspects of the great game of baseball and its history.

I am extremely fortunate to have a wife who is just about as enthusiastic and knowledgeable a baseball fan as I am. She's just not quite as fanatical. Cathy grew up about 15 minutes from Shea Stadium and is a Mets fan as well. She had been to more games than I had when we first met. We share the same birthday, April 26, which luckily falls during baseball season, as does our wedding anniversary of September 10. For two baseball fans, we decided that there is no better way to celebrate our special occasions than at a ballpark watching a baseball game. As such, we've celebrated many birthdays and anniversaries at Shea Stadium, Citi Field and on some specially chosen "road" trips.

When I was young I thought that it would be interesting to see a game in all of the active Major League Baseball Stadiums but I didn't consider it to be a realistic goal. By my early-30's, I had only witnessed games at Shea Stadium, Yankee Stadium, Fenway Park and Veteran's Stadium. It wasn't until 1991 that the idea of my "quest" began to take shape. That was the last year of Baltimore's Memorial Stadium and Cathy and I wanted to see a game there before the stadium was lost. It was special to us because it was one of the venues where the 1969 Miracle Mets World Championship played out. So, we took a quick trip to Baltimore and saw one of the last 20 or so games played at the stadium. It was Cal Ripken, Jr's birthday and I recall a woman running onto the field in an unsuccessful attempt to give him a kiss (I don't believe that it was Morgana, the Kissing Bandit). The stadium may only have been a mere shell of what it once was but it provided us with a glimpse into the baseball's past and another connection to our beloved 1969 Miracle Mets.

The quest gained momentum in 2000, when I again visited a stadium in its final year of existence. This time it was Three Rivers Stadium. Returning from a business trip, I met friends and colleagues, Wes Kirschner and Phil Jacques, in Pittsburgh where we attended a Reds/Pirates doubleheader. A unique part of this trip was the boat ride that we took to the game. This trip was the first in a string of several annual trips with Wes and effectively kicked off my quest in earnest.

As my sons, Bobby and Dan grew older and my frequent flyer miles piled up, the family started to join me on the long distance trips as well as the "local" ones. This not only provided me with the opportunity to add new stadiums to my list, but also it allowed me to re-visit ones that I had previously enjoyed. Sharing these experiences with my family was a fun and interesting way for us to explore different parts of the country. My favorite encore trip was a return to Wrigley Field, US Cellular Field and Miller Park with the obligatory pilgrimage to the Field of Dreams in Dyersville, Iowa.

My family and I embarked on our most ambitious trip in 2009. We rented a minivan and set out to see games in Pittsburgh, Cincinnati, Detroit and Cleveland. To ease our way into the trip, on the way to Pittsburgh we stopped in Reading, Pennsylvania to witness a doubleheader between the Reading Phillies and the Binghamton Mets at FirstEnergy Stadium. We then proceeded to enjoy games at PNC Park, Great American Ballpark, Comerica Park and Progressive Field. We even walked across state lines to the Cincinnati game from our hotel in Covington, Kentucky via the historic John A. Roebling Suspension Bridge. After a rainy, somewhat stressful trek back home, we completed the 1,800+ mile loop of 6 games at 5 stadiums in 8 days with a collection of memories to last a lifetime.

On another memorable trip, we followed our Mets to California. We saw them play at Dodger Stadium (another favorite of mine) and the Padres' Qualcomm Stadium. In between, we sandwiched in an Angels' game at Edison Field and some additional historical baseball stops. The highlight of the Dodger Stadium game was Dan's obtaining an autograph from the Mets' Turk Wendell. When Bobby was unable to get near enough to get one himself, he tossed his ball to Dan and asked his brother to get it signed. Upon seeing Dan return Turk said, "Didn't I already sign a ball for you?" Dan replied that it was for his brother and pointed him out back in the crowd. Turk then called to Bobby with a smile saying, "don't be lazy, come down here and get it yourself", which he did.

The most exciting play witnessed during my quest occurred on a quick trip to the new Citizen's Bank Park in Philadelphia with my friend Dave Wanta and our boys. Leading the Astros 7-2, the Phillies had the bases loaded with no outs. With ex-Met Todd Pratt batting I said that if the scene was ever set for a triple play, it was now with the slow-footed Pratt at the plate. David Weathers then induced Pratt to hit a ground ball to third which was fielded by Morgan Ensberg. Ensberg stepped on third and threw to Jeff Kent, who got the force out at second before throwing to Mike Lamb at first base to complete a rare around-the-horn triple play. That play woke up the Astros' offense and they ended up winning the game 12-10. It was ironic that three ex-Mets were involved in the triple play: Todd Pratt, Jeff Kent (who was a homerun short of the cycle) and David Weathers. It made us feel right at home.

Our visit to Dolphin Stadium added an unexpected souvenir to my memorabilia collection. During batting practice, as I was taking photographs as a part of my ritual walk around the inside of the park, someone on the field yelled for me to look out. I looked up just in time to turn and catch a ball hit by Stephen Drew. Proud of my accomplishment, I returned to our seats and showed the ball to Cathy and Dan. Bobby had also been taking a stroll around the stadium and when he returned, I proudly showed him my new souvenir. He smiled widely as he proceeded to pull out of his pockets, one at a time, the four balls that he had caught.

It's amazing that on all my trips, only one game was rained out. There were several close calls, such as my first visit to Comerica Park with Wes when it poured during our entire drive from Cincinnati to Detroit only to have the sun fortuitously peek out just prior to game time. Then there was the drive to Minneapolis/St. Paul with tornados following just a few miles behind us for most of the way. And the family visit to Cleveland, when a monsoon erupted just prior to the start of the game with howling winds and tornado warnings. Happily, there was just a half hour delay to the start of the game. The sole rainout occurred when Cathy and I took a weekend trip to Atlanta. Luckily we were able to take in a game the next day but we ended up spending almost the entire weekend in Turner Field which, by the way, is the friendliest stadium that we have ever visited.

We pride ourselves for never leaving a game before it's over regardless of its length. However, I reluctantly have to admit that I did leave one game early. On a business trip I was able to squeeze in my first visit to Wrigley Field. In order to catch a flight we had to leave the game in the bottom of the 8th inning. As we were leaving the stadium, we heard the crowd roar and later found out that Sammy Sosa had hit a homerun. That's why you never leave early. You never know what you might miss.

I completed my Major League Baseball Stadium quest for the first time in 2008 with a Mets/Nationals game at Washington's Nationals Park. It was the last of the 30 active Major League Baseball Stadiums on my list and my 39th overall. I "completed" it again in 2009 by attending games at the 2 new, New York Stadiums: the new Yankee Stadium and Citi Field. I realize that as old ballparks are retired and are replaced with new ones, "complete" is not a permanent state. However, there are fewer and fewer *old* ballparks and currently only 4 of the active 30 were opened prior to 1987. Heck, Dodger Stadium is the 3rd oldest but is only 48 years old, having opened in 1962. Of course, there are still a couple of general purpose stadiums in the ranks and a team or two that are relocation candidates. So, there's still opportunity for new venues.

My travels have taken me to all corners of the continental US as well as to Canada and Japan. From the big cities of New York, Los Angeles and Chicago to the small markets of Kansas City and Minneapolis/St Paul to the corn fields of Iowa. It's very cool being able to watch any Major League Baseball TV broadcast with the notion of "been there, done that" and the sense that the familiarity with the stadium brings. All of that aside, my visit to the Field of Dreams in Dyersville, Iowa with Cathy, Bobby and Dan was the preeminent stop on my quest thus far. The four of us playing catch on that field, in that setting, encapsulated the magic of the baseball experience. Time seemed to stand still and the joy of that day will remain forever etched in our memories.

Originally, the intent of my quest was to attend games at each of the active Major League Baseball Stadiums. It has been a great way to enjoy the game of baseball and its history, to experience different parts of the country (and the world) and have fun while spending quality time with my family and friends. What started out as a well-defined mission has evolved into an odyssey of somewhat mythological proportions. It is no longer bound by its initial objective but has grown to encompass visits to all sorts of baseball related sites and events. When I once again cross the last active Major League Baseball Stadium off my list, there will still be Minor League Stadiums, international and amateur parks, special events (e.g. the Midnight Sun Baseball Game in Fairbanks, Alaska) and historic sites to visit. Of course, that's not to say that I won't continue to return to my favorite Major League Baseball Stadiums and enjoy what they have to offer until the new ones arrive!

30 BALLPARKS AND A BABY

Roberto Coquis, Judy Pino and Sofia

Website-www.30ballparksandababy.com

OUR STORY:

"When you finally decide to make the pilgrimage to visit all thirty Major League Baseball Parks you certainly don't think of doing it with your newborn baby in tow! But we did. My wife Judy and I took our baby daughter, Sofia, on the road trip of a lifetime that began with a job search and a baseball game

Like most Americans in 2009, we had both lost our jobs and to make things even more interesting, we were blessed with the birth of our daughter in early February. At just 11 weeks old we took Sofia to watch our home team play at Nationals Park and proudly introduced her to the great American Pastime. While still basking in the glory of parenthood, I got a job interview opportunity in Indiana and took my family with me with the prospect of possibly moving out there if things worked out. The sports fanatic that I am I had convinced Judy that we should stop along the way and catch a game (or two). We visited Cleveland's Progressive Field and Chicago's Wrigley Field before stopping in Indiana for the job interview.

As fate would have it, the job didn't work out. Feeling a bit defeated and in search of a new perspective, we decided to visit our family in St. Louis to figure things out. Baseball really does make everything better. So, while in Missouri we visited Busch Stadium took a day trip to Kauffman Stadium and on the way back home we stopped off at PNC Park in Pittsburgh. You can imagine the conversations in the car now that Indiana was off the table. *What do we do now? Where should we be applying for jobs?* But summer was fast approaching, we had some vacation money saved up, and I kept thinking: BASEBALL!

We already had six Major League Baseball ballparks under our belt at that point and I figured-why not keep going? Of course this took some convincing. Judy thought I was crazy. Our daughter was only three months and we were both still jobless. After much consideration, we decided to make it a family-focused summer and move forward with the ballpark tour on the condition that we would make our time in each city count towards our efforts to find a job. Who knew? Perhaps our dream jobs were somewhere outside the Beltway? So we updated our resumes, packed our bags, and called friends and family that we could stay with in their baseball towns.

We dubbed our tour "30 Ballparks and a Baby" and started a website to chronicle our journey. We also created rules about our visits to the ballparks. We would always cheer for the home team, and secondly we would then leave a resume with the Human Resources Office. We would also collect items from each team to auction off at the end of our tour to raise funds for a charity that benefits girls and women in sports.

We prepared a mini-multimedia campaign that included press availability, A Facebook Fan Page and a Twitter account-@30Ballparksbaby, in addition to our website www.30ballparksandababy.com . The response was phenomenal. We got coverage from the local media in almost every city we visited. As a result, we received items, but also fans saw our story in their local news. People called us offering advice on job leads in their community, and we met with organizations that benefits girls in women in sports in order to determine who we would support.

During our tour we drove 15, 171 miles, visited 30 MLB parks in the U.S and Canada, logged 89 hours of love baseball, cheered 15 home wins and mourned 15 home losses, caught a foul ball, made it on the JumboTron, and witnessed when Derek Jeter tied Lou Gehrig's hit record for the New York Yankees. But the trip was not just about baseball. We also saw 38 states in our great country, visited three U.S National Parks, made lasting friendships in and out of the ballparks, raised over $2,500 to benefit the *The Woman's Sports Foundation-GoGirl!Go! Program* and watched our daughter grow right before our eyes. Our trip was about self-discovery, and accomplishing wonderful things as a family. In the end our pilgrimage to the ballparks was not just about baseball, but what baseball can do.

Roberto Jose Coquis and Judy Pino live in Washington D.C with their daughter Sofia. Roberto is pursuing his love of sports with a Master's Degree in Sports Industry Management

at Georgetown University and Judy now works as a media consultant.

Paul Swaney And Son

Website-www.stadiumjourney.com

PAUL SAYS:

"On September 29, 1985, I traveled to my first ballpark with my dad and younger brother. I was 9 years old, and the destination was the Old Tiger Stadium at the corner for Michigan and Trumbull.

I don't have a clear memory of the game, so my childhood trips back to Tiger Stadium, (usually once a year after that first visit) have all merged into one consolidated recollection. Dark concourses, Marty Castillo signing a program, and my brother shouting "Lou" for Lou Whitaker from the stands all may have happened that day, or years later.

For years, I told the story that my first game pitted Jack Morris against Roger Clemens in an 8-4 victory for the Tigers. Turns out I had the score right, but it was in the Red Sox favor, and the pitchers were Juan Berenguer and Rob Woodward.

I guess that is what baseball is for a child though, an idealized world where the grass is always greener. It remains that way today.

It took me a long time to realize how important those visits were. My son was born in 2007, and as I held him in my arms, I began to think about the finite nature of life. We were all small like this at one point, and someday we will all be gone. This awareness led me to think about what it is that makes me happy, and my thoughts inevitably led me to those childhood days at Tiger Stadium.

When I took my son to Wrigley Field around his first birthday in 2008, it all became clear. I was happiest when I was at the ballpark, stadium or sports arena.

I began my own website, StadiumJourney.com later that year as a way for people to share their experiences of attending live sporting events, and ensure that their visits are as enjoyable as possible.

Baseball remains my favorite sport to attend. I live near enough to Wrigley Field to walk to a game, and I have been to 25 Major League Stadiums so far. I prefer in almost all cases to sit in the front row of the upper deck behind home plate. I think that is the best viewpoint in the stadium

Meg Minard

Visiting Baseball Stadiums

MEG SAYS:

"I was asked to write about my baseball park visit experiences from a 'female' perspective. At first thought, I didn't really think there was a difference between a 'male' and a 'female' perspective. We're all baseball fans and we all enjoy visiting stadiums, right?"

Then I mulled it over and began thinking of things that might be different: age, binocular usage, travel planning, meeting other females who do the same thing I do, things I like/don't like about attending a game, meeting people.

Age

When I was younger (many years ago) and visited ballparks (minor league – Greenville, SC – Municipal Stadium) folks would ask me if I was a scout. I keep score and have a clipboard, binoculars, and usually some kind of stat sheet.

Or, more often, I would be asked if I was a wife or girlfriend of one the players.

This past summer (2010) when attending a game in Greenville, SC – Fluor Field this time - (many years later), I was asked if I was the mother of the pitcher. **Great...**

Binocular usage

I guess another difference between gals and guys visiting baseball and baseball stadiums is the use of the binoculars.

I use my binoculars to:

See who is warming up in the bullpen
Get a better look at arguments on the field
Get a better look at injuries
Check out batting stances
Check out pitcher stances and movements (love Matt Daley's stance)
Check out what the players look like. Yes, I do check out how good looking a player is.

A friend of mine once said if the World Series was based on looks and not the ability to perform, the 2007 Rockies would have won the championship that year.

And, I like the hi-socks look. It is tidier and very attractive, sexy almost. I'm not quite sure why more players don't wear their uniforms that way.

Meeting another female baseball park visitor

Probably for about 12+ years or so, here I am, a single female, making baseball stadium trips and vacations. I'm doing the planning, the checking out the schedules, determining when I can take vacation days from work, finding hotels and car routes, plane reservations… All THAT stuff. I like the planning part of the trip.

I thought I was the only female who took vacations tailored towards visiting ballparks as well as one who traveled on these types of vacations by her self.

One year, I was in Arizona, and there was a woman in front of a map in Scottsdale Stadium. "Would you take a photo of me?" Being a lover of maps, I of course did and then proceeded to get my photo taken in front of the same map by her.

We started talking and realized we were similar type women. Independent women, baseball fans, similar job functions, perfectly fine with vacationing solo, and loved baseball, and visiting baseball stadiums …..

Wow. I'm not the only one. THAT is priceless.

We (Barbara and I) have, of course, become friends.

Travel Safety
Another difference in planning a baseball park visit between male and female fans might be the concern of the safety of where a hotel might be located and if it is in a safe area of a city and how safe it might be to travel around the area and to and from the stadium.
I prefer taking public transportation to major league stadiums and travel safety is a big piece of public transportation. Do the trains/buses go through a 'bad' neighborhood? How safe is it to wait at a train station or bus stop?
I've never had to plan a visit for a man to make a 'baseball road trip' so I'm not quite sure what that gender considers safe or unsafe or if it is even a concern.
One of the reasons I like http://www.ballparkchasers.com is I can always ask beforehand.

Hotels for me… Holiday Inn Express, a Hampton Inn, La Quinta, or Best Westerns are generally in safe areas.

Things I like/don't like

Things I like about going to a game:
It gets my mind off of 'life,' 'work,' 'family,' 'etc.' for three hours or so. It's a welcomed break from day-to-day stress, pressures, and issues.

I like the local brewery and beverages.

I like strategies of the game, especially watching a National League game.

My ritual: Hitting the rest room when entering the stadium, taking photos if it is a new stadium for me, getting a beer and a bite to eat, finding my seats, checking out my neighbors, pulling out the scorecard, radio, and binoculars, honoring America with the National Anthem, writing the starting line up, checking out the players wearing hi-socks, pitch speed, pitch count, relief pitchers…… hits, home runs, fielding, stuff like that; finally…..visiting the rest room after the game. It is all a part of the game and game experience. And, I do the same things every game I attend.

Things that irritate me when going to a game:

I hate a kid getting cotton candy in my hair.

When the person sitting in front of me is going to stand up (blocking my view of the game) and start chatting with their neighbor (who was just sitting next to them) and the bases are loaded with a 3-2 count and the batter's team is down 5-2 and it's a Todd Helton, Derek Jeter, or Albert Pujols at bat. In fact, it doesn't really matter who is at bat.

Music/Manufactured Noise between pitches.

Music/Manufactured Noise level – when I have to yell at the person sitting sight next to me just to talk and when the music level is played so loud you can not hear the player change announcements.

Ahhhhhh, if those were the only things I had to worry about in life….. I'd be set.

Meeting People

I do get to meet a lot of people in my baseball stadium travels, like my friend, Barbara, mentioned above. I've met quite a few of my baseball stadium visiting friends over the internet and have, in fact, met many of them in person.

I meet people over the internet because I'm a proofreading dork when it comes to reading baseball stadium websites. When I find one I like a lot and I see a typo or some text that needs correction, I write the webmaster with the recommended changes. Not every webmaster replies with a response but some do and are very appreciate. Often times we end up emailing each other back and forth and becoming email friends. On quite a few occasions, those individuals would be traveling to a game near where I live(d) or attending a game at the same or similar time I would be at a stadium. So, we'd meet up in person.

I've not yet met a person who visits baseball stadiums as a hobby whom I have not gotten along with.

Josh Robbins-'Land Record Holder'-30

Baseball Games in 26 Days!

Website-www.thirty27.com

Commentary by Chuck Booth:

"I never knew it at the time-but when I was chasing my 1st streak attempt at the previous world record—Josh was establishing a new record. I was even in the same park in Milwaukee July.11/2008 when Josh set the record of 30/26-(unbeknownst to me of course). In the fall of 2008, and just before I was going to submit my tied world record claim-I discovered my tied record had just been beaten by 3 days. So I acquired all the motivation I needed to try and break the record again considering I no longer held the record in any form any more.

While I did set the New World Record for visiting all 30 ballparks in 24 days the next summer in 2009-Josh's record of 30 games in 26 days, (all by car) should be represented as incredible achievement as well. In fact, there should be a new category represented as such. Glad to have you as a friend Josh, and thanks for inspiring me to chase your record. "

Here is Josh's biography:

Josh is a freelance videographer-journalist and baseball historian in Chandler, Arizona. In 2010, he earned a Master's Degree in Sport Management from CSU-Long Beach. From June 16 to July 11, 2008, he watched a game in all 30 MLB stadiums in an 'all-land' record 26 days by car. His quest was featured on an episode of This Week in Baseball on August 9, 2008 http://mlb.mlb.com/video/play.jsp?content_id=3295802. You can visit his website and learn more about it at Thirty27.com.

Here is an article written about Josh that summed up his record attempt.

By Nancy Peters

There are multitudes of die-hard baseball fans in the country, even in the world, who have never been to a major league baseball game. Many fans have listened to the radio and heard that distinctive sound of wood hitting the leather ball, over the fence and out of the park. Some who have visited a major league baseball park tell the story many times in their lifetime, as a visit to the House That Ruth Built (Yankee Stadium), or to Veterans' Park, or Wrigley Field, or Fenway Park are now becoming visits of legend as the old parks make way for new, and names are interchanged as the newest sponsor buys the land.

Josh Robbins, a lifelong New York Yankees fan, moved to southern California from his upstate New York hometown. He and high school friends, Sven Jenkins, John Treadwell, and Bob Adney still talk about the games the Yankees play even though Bob and Josh live on the West Coast nowadays. But a lifelong personal goal for Josh will be fulfilled with the help of his three boyhood friends, his Dad Jonathan, and Robbins' wife, Suganya (Sue) when Robbins leaves southern California on June 16 for a 27-day automobile trip to visit all 30 major league baseball parks.

"My friend Bob will meet me in Seattle. Along the way I'll meet up with my Dad in Kansas City. Sue will meet me in Minneapolis, and John and Sven will join me in Baltimore for that leg of the trip. From Seattle to San Diego, from Arizona to Florida, from Atlanta to Boston, Chicago, Kansas City, Cincinnati, Pittsburgh, Toronto, Baltimore, Texas, Colorado, not in that particular order, are all on the itinerary," said Josh. "We hope to raise $10,000, with half paying for the trip and the other $5,000 being donated to the Jim Thorpe Little League."

The trip does have some sponsors in Toyota USA, The Mattel Corporation, Rawlings, and Homewood Suites by Hilton. But donations are being accepted for expenses not paid by the sponsorships secured. In-kind donations for auctioning at the year-end picnic for Jim Thorpe Little League are also being accepted. And the website, thirty27.com, has information on making donations by mail or PayPal.

"When we first started telling friends and relatives about our trip we got great feedback," shared Josh. "People were willing to 'bet' that we would or wouldn't make the world record and that got me thinking about how we could launch something that would also give back to a community group and, of course, Little League was an obvious recipient."

District 37, Jim Thorpe Little League received a gross of baseballs from Rawlings. Toyota USA and Homewood Suites will sponsor the road trip and accommodations in several major league cities. Airfare between several of the cities and living expenses, for things such as beer and hot dogs, peanuts and soda at all the parks (editorial note: writer's creative license used here) will be taken care of by donations.

At a recent Hawthorne City Council meeting, Josh Robbins presented his project and received enthusiastic support from Mayor Larry Guidi and the City Council. "Little League is a fond memory for many young people in this room tonight," said Guidi, "and I hope that some of you will go back to those memories and support this project which will benefit Little League in Hawthorne."

"Young people should be allowed to experience the excitement of playing baseball and participate in one of America's favorite pastimes. We developed our passion for baseball as Little Leaguers," recalled Josh. "We wanted to fan that passion we have by visiting the parks, but our 50% sharing of donations with Little League is now a very important component of the project."

Josh is a video production assistant for several local cable stations in the South Bay, Hawthorne, Lawndale, and Torrance included. He will be filming a video log and journal of the trip for the 27 days to produce a documentary of the World Record-breaking project and to showcase at film festivals around the country. Josh Robbins will leave on June 16 for the first game, Florida Marlins at Seattle Mariners, and visit the last ball park in Milwaukee when the Brewers play the Cincinnati Reds on July 12, the day after his birthday. With the help of the community to complete his achievement of the World Record of 30 ball parks in 27 days, Josh will give back to his community and to Jim Thorpe Little League. By the 7th inning stretch of the 27-day trip, somewhere between the LA Dodgers at Houston or Philadelphia at Atlanta, Josh and his trip mates may be longing for a comfortable couch and a radio. But with a World Record to make it into the books of Major League Baseball history, they will keep rounding the bases of the superhighways until July 12 at 7:05 p.m. when the Umpire yells, "Play Ball!" and the last out is pitched.

Dutch Van Duzee

DUTCH SAYS:

"MY BASEBALL STADIUM TRIPS-I have been to several ballparks over the years. Each time that I visit a new park-I always take notes. The picture above is taken right outside of Target Field last year. Here are write-ups of the last 4 parks that have opened in the majors. This has brought my overall count to 40 Major League Parks."

37ᵗʰ PARK OVERALL

7/11-13/08   Washington DC-Nationals Park

I joined many other Astros fans for the weekend series in the inaugural season of Nationals Park. Great stadium but it was built in a part of town (near Navy Yard on banks of the Anacostia) with not much activity although plans for future development in the immediate area were evident. I stayed at the Courtyard just a few blocks from the stadium and near the Metro station. It reminded me of Citizens Bank Park in Philly with much activity beyond the outfield concourse (Red Loft and Red Porch bars, and Walk Up bar behind the big scoreboard). Good view of the Capital can be seen from the upper sections beyond LF wall. Astros dropped the opener but won the next 2 to take the series.

38TH PARK OVERALL

6/17/09-New York, NY-New Yankee Stadium

My third 2009 baseball trip was to NYC to visit the inaugural seasons of new Yankee Stadium in the Bronx and Citi Field in Queens. I had planned 2 games at each stadium; due to rains on last year's trip to NYC, I missed one of two planned games at the old Yankee stadium. This year, rain posed a challenge again as I missed the second game of the trip, a Thursday matinee which was delayed 5 ½ hours before they ended up playing the game later that night. I wasn't all that impressed with new Yankee stadium...has the look of the old stadium, but of course with club level suites. Field level seating (the number of seats) seemed smaller than most stadiums, and I was sitting 30 rows up, on the last possible row, under the overhang from the next deck, which I don't like. I did like the Hard Rock Cafe at the stadium. I wanted to go on a tour of the stadium to see Monument Park, and some of the other areas you wouldn't normally be able to see but the tours were sold out. The old stadium still remains next to it. The Nationals beat the Yankees in the interleague match up on Wed night.

39TH PARK OVERALL

<u>6/19-20/09</u>   New York, NY-Citi Field

The Mets were playing the Rays in interleague games on Fri night and Sat afternoon. When I arrived in Queens on the 7 train, I didn't realize Shea had been demolished already. No sign of Shea as it was completely paved over as the new parking lot for Citi Field. Hands down, I thought the Mets built a better ballpark than the Yankees. The entrance – Jackie Robinson rotunda is impressive as escalators take you up into the park. Citi has a lot of neat features beyond the outfield...mini ball field for the kids, a dunk tank, expanded food and microbrew selections, etc. And of course the Big Apple in CF was brought over from Shea. The seating configuration was better at Citi (compared to Yankee stadium) at Citi...more field level seating and the seats in the upper promenade, particularly the promenade box (sect 400s) seem a lot closer to the field than the upper sections at most other parks. The Mets won Fri night, but the Rays came back to win Sat in a game that was nearly rained out. The skies cleared just in time to get the 4 o'clock game in.

40TH PARK OVERALL

<u>6/11-13/10</u>   Minneapolis, MN-Target Field

After 28 yrs in the Metrodome, outdoor baseball returned to MN this year with the opening of Target Field. I attended the weekend interleague series vs. the Braves, which was a rematch of the great '91 World Series. The ballpark, which rests right next to the Target Center in downtown, is a huge upgrade from the dome and one of my new favorites. With a seating capacity of around 40,000, the stadium seemed more compact, with seating (on all levels) seemingly closer to the field than most other parks, and it was full of fans for all 3 games. I was impressed with the crowd; rivals the Cardinal Nation. The park featured several nice statues of past players and a large Gold Glove; however, all of these were just outside of the park – it would have been nice to have some of these features inside the park along the concourses. The highlight of the games was Liriano's 7K's in a row, one shy of tying the AL record.

I can't wait for more parks to open In Florida and for the Oakland A's in the coming years-you can rest assure I will add those to my other 40 ballparks I have already seen. In addition to each park's first visit-I also take notes on any single game I attend as that is my tradition!

Bob Devries

Website: http://30ballparks-in-1season.com/

BOB SAYS:

"On September 10, 2008, my wife, Shawn Marie DeVries (shown in this picture above), passed away from Arrhythmogenic Right Ventricle Ventricle Dysplasia (ARVD). She was only 35.

In 2009, as part of my recovery from Shawn's passing I toured the country and attended a baseball game in all 30 MLB ballparks. I was fortunate to come into contact with Laura from the SADS Foundation (www.StopSADS.org) because of my travels. I have learned that there are so many others out there like me searching for answers to how we could have prevented the passing of our loved ones.

In 2010, I decided to tour the country again attended a game at all 30 MLB ballparks only this time the trips were not about me, but about raising awareness of SADS conditions.

This has been a long, strange but thoroughly amazing journey this summer. It all started on Easter Sunday at Fenway Park for the opener of the baseball season where I saw the Yankees play the Red Sox. I was single and living in Boston at the time and now I am now living in Columbus, OH and have a wonderful girlfriend. Everything that has happened in the middle has been a blur.

What I do remember from the blur are all the wonderful people I have met along the way. All the lives we have touched and I do say we. This journey this summer has been a team effort. You may not realize it but you have made a difference as well. From the kind messages of support to helping spread the word about SADS – we all have made a difference. When we are done tallying the donations we will be well over $22,000 – who would have thought!!

If you are so inclined to donate to various charities and Foundations, please take a moment to consider the SADS Foundation. They are a small group that does wonders in saving lives and assisting with people like me who have lost a loved one and if you don't think your donation matters think again. At lunch the other day with Laura her Blackberry kept beeping and she told me that she gets an email every time a donation is made to the SADS Foundation. The VP of Marketing gets an email with every donation!!! Very cool knowing your donation will not go unnoticed."

Kenneth A. Lee (co-author)

Website: www.seeall30.com

KENNETH SAYS:

"My name is Kenneth Lee and I am a ballpark addict….

They say that admitting you have a problem is the first step on your way to recovery. Well, I have been an addict for years and I don't see my "problem" going away any time soon. Just last night as we watched "I Survived A Japanese Game Show," I commented to my wife, "It would be fun to go to Tokyo, we could catch a game at the Tokyo Dome!"

My addiction started innocently. It was 1977. After a few months of listening to Seattle Mariners games on radio, as they were only on television once or twice a year during those first several years, my Dad asked my brother and I if we would want to go to a game. OF COURSE WE DID! Our first game was the Mariners vs. the Yankees at the Kingdome. As we walked up and into the dome I saw the field for the first time, and I was hooked! I know people talk about their first ever game being at Wrigley or Yankee Stadium, Fenway or Tiger Stadium… mine was at the Kingdome, and I loved it! The grass may have been fake, and the sun certainly didn't shine on the field and you couldn't feel the wind blow, but it was a beautiful sight for a 4 year old, and one that will stay with me forever.

Over the next 10 years we went to several Mariners games. My parents would take us up for weekend games where we would see the Saturday night game and double back for the Sunday afternoon game. We only lived an hour from Seattle, but we would stay in a hotel just south of Seattle on those weekends. I still remember those weekends like they were yesterday. Even after my father passed away in 1986, Mom made sure we still went to games and had our weekends without fail.

In 1987 as we were visiting family in Northeast Oklahoma a group of us decided to go to Kansas City to catch a Royals game. It's an over 3 hour drive from Picher, OK to Royal Stadium and I couldn't hide my excitement. Until that day I had never thought I would to see a game anywhere but the Kingdome. The experience was incredible! It was hotter than blue blazes, but we had a great time. We sat in the front row, down the 3rd baseline directly by the foul pole. Bo Jackson was playing left for the Royals then and I got a great picture of him waving in our direction. All I recall of the game is that the Royals beat the Twins and Dan Gladden hit a home run for Minnesota, but I can remember the beauty of the ballpark vividly.

Even though I had my first taste of another ballpark in 1987 it was 10 years before I did it again. In June of 1997 I was in Dallas, TX with a friend attending a concert for a country singer we worked for. We decided that the day before the concert we would go to Arlington and catch a game. We sat up in the rafters and although I developed a fear of escalators after taking a ride on the one up to the upper deck, (the "Escalator to Heaven" as I call it), I still loved The Ballpark in Arlington. The design was very different than any of the few others I had been to at this point. The way they used the history of Texas in its design was so cool. I loved the green steel and red brick! It was that very night, June 14, 1997, that I decided I wanted to see all the Major League ballparks!

In 2000 I went to visit some friends in California. They took me to see my Mariners play the A's at the Coliseum. While the ballpark is a real dump, (this coming from someone that loved the Kingdome,) I loved being there to see the park, taste the local foods, and see how different fans react to the game. The M's won. They spanked the A's big time! It was this trip that made my dream of seeing all of the ballparks seems reachable…eventually.

In July 2000, I took my mom to Austin to see family. We ended up going our separate ways. She went north to Oklahoma for our family reunion and I went to Nashville for Fan Fair. We were to eventually meet up in Alabama a couple weeks later. After Fan Fair I ended up back in Texas and decided to make the drive to Houston to see Enron Field. I had seen countless games at the Kingdome with its roof, and at Safeco Field which had opened the previous year, but I never felt like I was watching baseball indoors. Enron, however, with the roof closed, felt like we were watching a game in a warehouse. I really enjoyed my walk around the park, seeing how they used the old train station in its design and all, but that roof really spoiled it for me. It wasn't until the end of the 7th inning when they finally opened the roof, you felt the rush of hot air coming in from the beautiful Houston night. At that moment, the game changed completely. All of a sudden we were watching a game the way it was supposed to be watched at night, under the stars. After eventually meeting up with mom and the rest of my family in Alabama, I found myself with a few days on my hands and decided to go to Atlanta, see Stone Mountain and stop by Turner Field. As per my luck, the Braves were out of town that day and wouldn't be at home any day that I could catch them. I still made the best of it. I took the time to see the park from the outside and was sure to visit the remains of Fulton County Stadium. I had watched a lot of Braves games when I lived in Oklahoma because the Braves via TBS was all the baseball we got on television back then. I was so bummed I didn't get to see a game at Turner Field. This just fed my fire. I vowed to make it back one day!

On my drive back to Austin I was able to take in a game at The Ballpark in Arlington. It was the Mariners vs. Rangers on July 3, 2000. The Ballpark is a great place to watch games. If it wasn't for the incredible heat of July, I would have loved to have stayed for a few more games. This was my second game at The Ballpark. It was strange to me to be back, but I loved it this time just as much.

In May of 2002, I was planning a trip to the Chicago area to see a friend for a few days, I realized that while she was busy the first couple days, I could catch some games. I flew into Chicago and made the drive up to Milwaukee to see the Braves vs. Brewers game at Miller Park. It was awesome! The land of brats & kraut didn't disappoint! I was enthralled with the way their roof opened, having just had Safeco and its retractable roof for not quite 3 seasons yet. The sight lines are great. No matter where

I walked I had a great view of the action. I stayed in town that night and caught the afternoon game the next day before driving to the South Side of Chicago to catch the White Sox vs. Mariners game at Comiskey Field.

May 2, 2002, was the first day I had ever gone to two games in two parks in two states! What a thrill that was! One American League and one National League game even! To top it off, in the nightcap, I got to see history made as Mike Cameron hit four HR's. He tied 12 others for this feat, was only the fourth from the AL to do it and only the fifth in history to do it in four consecutive at bats. In his last 2 ab's, he was plunked on the backside and hit a drive that had the right fielder literally against the wall reaching up to make the catch!). In addition to his 4 HR's, Cammy and Brett Boone went back-to-back with HR's twice in the same inning. This was the first time in MLB history that a pair of teammates had ever done so. That feat still hasn't been beat or even matched.

One of the greatest parts of going to different ballparks, for me, is meeting the people who go to those games. The couple that sat next to me at this game just happened to realize the White Sox were playing that night as they got to town on their drive to Iowa for a wedding. They decided to stop early and catch the game. What a game they got to see. I had been warned by my friend about wearing my Mariner's gear on the South Side, but I had no problem. Actually had a great time kidding around with the White Sox fans and an usher that kept dropping by to comment on the game.

July 2002 found me back in Oklahoma with family. After our family reunion I was hitting the road on my first ever "Baseball Road Trip!" My addiction was getting the best of me. After careful planning, I mapped out a route that would take me to games in Cincinnati (Cinergy Field), Cleveland (Jacobs Field), Detroit (Comerica Park) and a weekend of Cubs vs. Cardinals in St. Louis at Busch Stadium. This made 5 games in 4 ballparks in a week. This is what life is all about, yeah? It was incredible! But this just fed the appetite for my addiction and left me wanting more.

Later in 2002, a friend of mine, Bob Mason, and I planned a trip that we had wanted to do for a few years, and went to see "The Field of Dreams". While we were planning this trip Bob told me to plan it all and put in as much as we can do in the few days that we had. I naturally added a White Sox vs. Angels game at Comiskey Park and my 3rd game at Miller Park (Brewers vs. Expos). I usually go to games on my own, so this was a treat to get to share other ballparks with a friend of mine and to show him what I liked and disliked about them. I took him by Wrigley to see it, even though the Cubs were out of town. We had a great time on our baseball weekend and I couldn't wait to do more.

In early 2003 my mom asked me to take her to see family in Oklahoma, I decided that I would drop her off and plan a trip that was bigger and better than I did the previous year. I spent days working on a schedule and getting everything planned out so that when we hit the road on July 9th, I would be ready. I even planned a stop at Coors Field in Denver on our drive to Oklahoma. Before we could leave I had one last thing to do, I asked my brother, Judd, and his wife, June, if I could take my 16 year old nephew, Sean, with me. They agreed. I made sure to let them know it wasn't just about the ballparks. While we were in town for games, we would do other historical things. On July 15th we left on a trip that would have us seeing: The Negro Leagues Museum, Kauffman Stadium (no game), the Field of Dreams, Wrigley Field (no game), US Cellular Field (no game), Louisville Slugger Museum (did the tour), Great American Ballpark (Astros v Reds), PNC Park (Brewers vs. Pirates), Yankee Stadium (Monument Park, Old Timers' Day game and Indians vs. Yankees, with my favorite Yankee David "Boomer" Wells pitching), Fenway Park (Blue Jays vs. Red Sox – 1st row Green Monster seats), Baseball Hall Of Fame (only 3 hours worth), Veterans Stadium (Mets vs. Phillies), Oriole Park @ Camden Yards (Rangers vs. Orioles), Turner Field (Marlins vs. Braves) and Old Busch Stadium (Pirates vs. Cardinals). 8 games in 8 different parks! It was amazing! My first trips to Fenway Park and Yankee Stadium, I cried like a baby! Along the way we took in the Gettysburg battlefield, and toured New York City and Washington DC. We also got to see both the new and old Durham Athletic Parks as well as Shoeless Joe Jackson's grave. That trip was so amazing! I was so glad to get to share it with my nephew because I know he will never forget it! We got to do and see so much. It was awesome!

While on the 2003 trip, in Philly at The Vet, I realized that I was going to marry my girlfriend. I even told Sean and he just laughed. The day after I got back, I proposed to her and we planned a July 17, 2004 wedding. As we were thinking about our honeymoon Yvonne, (who is not a sports fan, but goes to games with me occasionally) says, "We should go to California. We can split the trip between me showing you things I love and you can take me to the ballparks you haven't seen yet." I knew I loved this woman and she just proved to me again why I did! For our honeymoon, along with Disneyland, Universal Studios, Sea World, San Diego Wild Animal Park and Sedona, we caught games at SBC Park (Padres vs. Giants), Dodger Stadium (Padres Vs Dodgers), Bank One Ballpark (Rockies vs. Diamondbacks), Petco Park (Giants vs. Padres – got my 1st ever batting practice home run ball at this game!) and Angel Stadium (Mariners vs. Angels). We even saw the Peoria Sports Complex, where the Mariners and Padres hold Spring Training. I am so addicted that even my future wife knew what I would want to do. I would have never dreamed that we would do that on our honeymoon, but we both loved every moment of it!

In 2005, my wife asked me if I would take her on an East Coast trip so she could finally go to New York. I was game because to me that meant more ballparks and she agreed! This trip found us at games at Oriole Park @ Camden Yards (D'Rays vs. Orioles), Citizens Bank Park (Marlins vs. Phillies), RFK Stadium (Mets vs. Nationals), Shea Stadium (on 05/05/05, Phillies vs. Mets), Fenway Park (roof box 1st baseline seats, Mariners vs. Red Sox) and Yankee Stadium (a tour 1 day and Mariners vs. Yankees the next). The games at Citizens Bank Park and RFK Stadium were the same day, an afternoon and night game. I just love doing that!

In November 2005 as we went to Florida to see Yvonne's nana for her 80th birthday, I took a day to go see 10 different spring training ballparks: Knology Park (Blue Jays), Bright House Networks Field (Phillies), Progress Energy Park (D'Rays), Legends Field (Yankees), McKechnie Field (Pirates), Ed Smith Stadium (Reds), Joker Marchant Stadium (Tigers), Chain Of Lakes Park (Indians), Osceola Stadium (Astros) and Champion Stadium (Braves) along with Tropicana Field. Later in that same run I got to take in the huge Dolphin Stadium. It just looked wrong to me as there was a football field where a baseball field should have been. I would have to go back and catch a real game one day.

For our trip in 2006 my wife really wanted to take her mom to see New York in December with it all decorated for Christmas. While I would have enjoyed that a lot, going in December meant no baseball. She informed me she really wanted it to be a "Girls Trip" so I could go on a ballpark trip on my own if I wanted in exchange… WOOHOO! I planned a run that had me seeing the rest of the parks I needed to see to complete my tour of all 30 current MLB Ballparks. I caught 2 games at the Metrodome (Indians vs. Twins), Miller Park for my 4th game there (Astros vs. Brewers), 3 games at Wrigley Field (2 Cardinals vs. Cubs, and 1 Phillies vs. Cubs night game), Comerica Park (White Sox vs. Tigers), Rogers Centre (A's vs. Blue Jays), PNC Park (Astros vs. Pirates), 2 games at New Busch Stadium (Cubs vs. Cardinals), and The Ballpark in Arlington (Orioles vs. Rangers.) I picked up my brother in Oklahoma and took him with me to this game, we both got batting practice home run balls at this game, in our seats, didn't even have to try, they came right to us!) and Coors Field (Mets vs. Rockies). One August 25th when I got to St. Louis, I had seen all 30 MLB Ballparks.

Even though Nationals Park opened on March 30, 2008 and I had another ballpark to see, I decided to wait until for the two new ones in New York to open the next year and do them all on the same run. Besides, this year, my wife wanted me to take her to see her Dad in Knoxville, TN for our trip. I planned it, with stops at the Metrodome (White Sox vs. Twins – where Tony Oliva left us his tickets for the game), two games at Wrigley Field (a night game and a day game vs. the Brewers) and the Rogers Centre (White Sox vs. Blue Jays). I am so addicted that I made sure to show my wife US Cellular (no game), Comerica Park (no game), PNC Park (no game), Great American Ballpark (no game) and we toured the Louisville Slugger Museum.

It was just two days before we left for our trip in 2008 that the company I work for, Jackson Hewitt Tax Service, held our 'end of the tax season' dinner and awards banquet. It was then I found out that they were sending me to Orlando in August to the Jackson Hewitt Corporate Management Summit. My addiction is so strong that all I could think was "Baseball in August in Florida! Wooohooo!!" Needless to say, our plans had us seeing games at Tropicana Field (Blue Jays vs. Rays) and Dolphin Stadium (Mets vs. Marlins) as well as seeing the other seven spring training ballparks I need to see to complete the Florida parks.

In 2009, I got to hit the road with my friend Bob Mason again. Ever since we attended 8th grade at Tumwater Middle School in Tumwater, WA, we have both had a fascination for the Civil War. We decided back then that one day we would go to Gettysburg and walk around the battlefield. In 2009 we got that chance. On that trip we were also able see Oriole Park @ Camden Yards (Mets vs. Orioles), Citizen's Bank Park (Blue Jays vs. Phillies), Yankee Stadium (Nationals vs. Yankees), Fenway Park (Marlins vs. Red Sox, where we were joined by my nephew Sean and his girlfriend Nicole), Citi Field (Rays vs. Mets) and Nationals Park (Blue Jays vs. Nationals). We had planned a doubleheader for the Yankee Stadium & Fenway Park games. The problem was that with it raining in New York as hard as it was (it was bad enough to make two guys from Washington State say "Damn, that's a lot of rain!") we were unable to see the game at Yankee Stadium. Luckily they did open the gates on time. We were able to go in, walk around and pay the extremely high concession prices before we hit the road for Boston. After hitting Citi Field and getting to the game at Nationals Park later in that trip, I had once again completed the tour of all 30 MLB Ballparks.

In late fall 2009, my nephew Sean called me to let me know he had popped the question to his girlfriend Nicole. They were getting married on July 23, 2010 in Mystic, CT and asked if my wife and I could come. I told him we wouldn't miss it for the world. At that point I got really excited, not only for their wedding, but for the possibility of more games. When the MLB schedules came out I worked up an itinerary that would allow me to see a few games while back there. Then it hit me, I needed to catch a game at the brand new Target Field in Minneapolis as well. I figured out a way to make it happen, however, to do it as planned I needed to leave town on July 17th, which is my wedding anniversary. After debating it for a while, I asked my wife if I could and she agreed. The plan was for me to fly to Milwaukee overnight, get a car in the morning and drive to Minneapolis for a game that afternoon. I would stay in town that night, catch the game the next evening, before making the drive overnight back to Milwaukee for a 6am flight to Baltimore. From there I would see Nationals Park (taking in a tour as well as a game a few days later), Oriole Park @ Camden Yards (two Rays vs. Orioles games), Fenway Park (just a tour), Yankee Stadium (Royals vs. Yankees) and Citi Field (Cardinals vs. Mets).

While the entire trip was great especially getting to Fenway yet again, the day that stands out to me the most is July 18th. That is the day I got to Target Field for the White Sox vs. Twins game. It's a special day to me because it is the day that I once again became "Whole". I was back in the "All 30" club once again... at least until the next one is built.

My name is Kenneth Lee and I am a ballpark addict..."

Come visit me at www.seeall30.com for full reports of my trips as well as my reviews of every Major League stadium I have ever been to.

To my lovely wife Yvonne: Thank you for everything! 143!!!!

Craig B. Landgren (co-author of book)
Also founder of www.ballparkchasers.com

Craig's Author Profile:

Craig is the founder of ballparkchasers.com, a baseball social network. Craig launched Ballpark Chasers with the vision of connecting baseball fans around the world, especially those with the life goal of visiting all Major League ballparks. Since going live, Ballpark Chasers has Doubled each year in total members and quickly become the Internet's largest collection of amateur ballpark photos. It was Craig's belief that there were others, much like him self, that shared the lifelong dream of visiting all 30 major league ballparks. Craig also found a void online that not only provided a service for those looking to gain help planning their ballpark vacations but also a way to scrapbook and record their trip upon returning home. Craig currently resides in the Seattle area with his wife and newborn daughter.

Chuck Douglas Booth-(Author)
World Record Holder 30/24

Website-www.fastestthirtyballgames.com (Opening in Spring of 2011)

Personal note to Jim Maclaren's in memory of his honor:

I considered "Jim" a real hero for inspiring others just by living to the best of his own so I was happy I got to raise awareness for the "Head North Foundation" again along the way. I will always remember Jim for helping me turn my life around. This World record Achievement will be cherished because I had worked 308 days in a row since I landed home in Canada after the 2008 streak attempts. I delivered over 100,000 newspapers -- and did 5,000 pizza deliveries —to save the $10,000 Canadian to put myself in that position once to take another swing at the record.

Many times I wanted to give up with the physical torque of battling the weather elements and walking/running five miles a day. Several different times it looked like I would not be able to continue the regimen I had set out to do to accomplish this mission. I always thought of Jim not giving up and I found inspiration to go after it another day.

Whether or not I broke the record or not I enjoyed and relished each game in the 2009 chase, each ballpark and nuance of all that is a baseball fan. I did not see delays from travel, weather or extra innings as a negative thing, but as part of the journey.

Now that I am done, and wrote a book about the entire experiences I hope that I will hear from you all as part of a research team to what drives all of us.

Some say that-us 'ballpark chasers' are crazy to put ourselves through these kind of things just to watch baseball, but they don't understand that this is more then just a game, it is a fabric of our being.

"While I broke the World Record in 2009—the far more memorable trip was 2008 because of my family. My 3 brothers, and my dad and I, journeyed on a 4 day 4 stadium trip together. It had been the first time we had all travelled together in 13 years. What historic parks were lined up for the streak, in consecutive days we saw Fenway Park in Boston, Old Yankee Stadium in New York, Busch Stadium in St. Louis and while I travelled onto Minnesota—in order to carry on my trip-my brothers were able to see a game at Wrigley Field. The pictures and memories will last a lifetime.

Old Yankee Stadium had proved to be the meeting place for our family when visiting my brother Trent-because he lives in New Jersey. I first visited Old Yankee Stadium with my brother Trent in 2006.

Amongst many memories was the interview I did with 'Fox Sports Central' with my dad 'Tom Booth'-right on the field level of Busch Stadium. Baseball has always been the one generational calling that has galvanized our family. For one brief road trip these guys saw what I got to do for 36 days in a row in 2008—and for 24 days in 2009.

Douglas 'Chuck' Booth currently resides in White Rock B.C Canada about two hours north of Seattle. He is now looking for full time employment with MLB.

Email: booth7629@gmail.com

PICTURES WITH

MY FAMILY FOR THE 2008 STREAK/TRIPS TO OLD YANKEE
STADIUM 2006&2007

PICTURES WITH THE SALTERS-AND ALSO THE RAIN DELAY
GAME ON JULY.23/2009

1. My dad Tom, Brother Trent and Popa Lewis. 2. Iconic pic from Busch Stadium Stands.
3.My dad and I being interviewed in STL.

1.My brother Clint 2. Great picture at Fenway Park /07/30/2008
3. My media pic by Peace Arch News.

Bottom Picture-Booth boys at ESPN NY. Top Left-Booth Boys in Chicago near Wrigleyville.
Top Right-Brothers Clint and Ken at Busch Stadium.

My brother Trent and I at Yankee Stadium in '06

Just before Game#30-24 (Left) New Yankee Stadium Rain Delay July.23/09 (Right)

Celebrating with the Salter' Boys After game#30-24 days
August.14/2009

Chuck with the Salter's@PNC-/2008

OFFICIAL WORLD RECORD TRIP DATES/GAMES 2009
ALL 30 ACTIVE MLB PARKS IN 24 DAYS
1^{ST TO} LAST PITCH OF GAME

CHUCK BOOTH'S WORLD RECORD

Game
#

1. July.22 PNC Park-Pittsburgh-Day #1
2. July.23 Rogers Center-Toronto-Day#2
3. July.23 New Yankee Stadium-New York- Day#2
4. July.24 Wrigley Field-Chicago-Day#3
5. July.24 Miller Park-Milwaukee-Day#3
6. July.25 Coors Field-Denver-Day#4
7. July.26 Minute Maid Park-Houston-Day#5
8. July.27 The Ball Park In Arlington-Arlington-Day#6
9. July.28 Oriole Park at Camden Yards-Baltimore-Day#7
10. July.29 Busch Stadium-St. Louis-Day#8
11. July.30 The Great American Ball Park-Cincinnati-Day#9
12. July.30 Us Cellular Field-Chicago-Day#9
13. July.31 McAfee Coliseum-Oakland-Day#10
14. Aug.01 AT&T Park-San Francisco-Day#11
15. Aug.02 Sun Life Stadium-Miami-Day#12
16. Aug.03 Tropicana Field-St. Petersburg-Day#13
17. Aug.04 Nationals Park-Washington D.C -Day#14
18. Aug.05 Citi Field-Flushing Meadows-Day#15
19. Aug.05 Citizens Bank Ball Park-Day#15
20. Aug.06 Progressive Field-Cleveland Day#16
21. Aug.06 Kauffman Stadium-Kansas City Day#16
22. Aug.07 Petco Park-San Diego-Day#17
23. Aug.08 Angels Stadium-Anaheim-Day#18
24. Aug.08 Dodgers Stadium-Los Angeles Day#18
25. Aug.09 Safeco Field-Seattle-Day#19
26. Aug.10 Chase Field-Phoenix-Day#20
27. Aug.11 Metrodome-Minneapolis-Day#21
28. Aug.12 Turner Field-Atlanta-Day#22
29. Aug.13 Fenway Park-Boston-Day#23
30. Aug.14 Comerica Park-Detroit-Day#24

Summary Of Record Chase Expenses

Totals in (Us Dollars)

ITEM	2008	2009

Plane Fares	$5141	$3049
Tickets for Games	$1229	$1048
Average per game-TKT	41 games- $30	34 games- $35
Food	$1050	$885
Lodging	$1100	$650
Car Rentals	$1115	$587
Sedan Services	$790	$380
Cab Fare	$320	$493
Cell Phone Billing	$495	$1509
All forms Public Transport	$127	$136
Amtrak Trains	$323	$144
Greyhound Bus	$165	$125
Clothes (including laundry)	$215	$185
Souvenirs	$121	$110
Camera expenses-film	$687	$112
Guinness Submission expenses	$43	$247
Charitable donation-business cards	$159	$126
Health Insurances	$80	$80
Tips-hotel and shuttle bus	$215	$210
Parking all around	$676	$451
Tolls Paid-Fines included	$544	$111
Credit Card Fees/Bank charge Fees	$375	$279
Internet	$245	$71
Mailing fees	$71	$44
Work Surcharge for vacation	$390	$247
	_____	
Total Money Spent	$15676	$11279
Canadian Currency Estimate	$17000	$11400

30 WEBSITES HOT SHEET FOR ROAD BASEBALL ROAD TRIP

1. www.kayak.com
2. www.priceline.com
3. www.expedia.com
4. www.stubhub.com
5. www.ballparkchasers.com
6. www.mlb.com
7. www.googlemaps.com
8. www.johnnyroadtrip.com
9. www.thirty27.com
10. www.seeall30.com
11. www.stadiumjourney.com
12. www.BallparkEGuides.com
13. www.bestwestern.com
14. www.motel6.com
15. www.amtrak.com
16. www.greyhound.com
17. www.limoquote.com
18. www.espn.com
19. www.airtran.com
20. www.continental.com
21. www.thrifty.com
22. www.nationalcar.com
23. www.southwest.com
24. www.hilton.com
25. www.en.wikipedia.org/wiki/List of Major League Baseball mascots
    —(FOR MOM'S ESPECIALLY TO KNOW)
26. www.fastest30ballgames.com
27. www.tsa.gov
28. www.theweathernetwork.com
29. www.mapquest.com
30. www.xmradio.com

These are the airport codes to list for each city-or can be combined with a neighboring city if fares are cheaper.

1. **Arizona-PHX**
2. **Atlanta-ATL**
3. **Baltimore-BWI or Dulles-(IAD)/Washington (DCA)**
4. **Boston-BOS/Manchester, NH-MHT/Providence(PVD)**
5. **Chicago-(CHC) MDW or ORD(, Milwaukee(MKE)**
6. **Chicago-(CHC) or MDW, Milwaukee(MKE)**
7. **Cincinnati-CVG/Dayton-(DAY)/Columbus(CMH)**
8. **Cleveland-CLE/Akron(CAK)**
9. **Colorado-DEN**
10. **Detroit-DTW/Flint-(FNT)/Toledo-(TOL)**
11. **Florida-FLL or MIA**
12. **Houston-IAH or HOU for Hobby.**
13. **Kansas City-MCI**
14. **Los Angeles-(LAA) or SNA/Burbank-(BUR)/Ontario-(ONT)/Long Beach-(LGB)/ San Diego (SAN)**
15. **Los Angeles (LAD) same as #14**
16. **Milwaukee-MKE/Chicago-ORD/MDW**
17. **Minnesota-MSP/Rochester, MN-(RST)**
18. **New York-NYM-LGA/JFK/EWR/Westchester County-(HPN)/Long Island-(ISP).**
19. **New York-NYY-Same as #18.**
20. **Oakland-OAK/San Francisco-(SFO)/San Jose-(SJC)**
21. **Philadelphia-PHL/NJ City-(EWR)/Atlantic City-(ACY)**
22. **Pittsburgh-PIT**
23. **San Diego-SAN/SNA/LGB/BUR/LAX/ONT**
24. **San Francisco-SFO/OAK/SJC**
25. **Seattle-SEA/Bellingham-(BLI)/Portland-(PDX)**
26. **St. Louis-STL**
27. **Tampa Bay-TPA/Clearwater-(PIE)**
28. **Texas-DFW or DAL**
29. **Toronto-YYZ**
30. **Washington-DCA/IAD/BWI**

Make sure to click the nearest city icon at <u>www.kayak.com</u>.

The following names are all people who had a part in helping me break the world record and I wanted to thank them personally. `

BRYAN MCCRON JIM MACLAREN

TRENT BOOTH	KRISTY BOOTH	CRAIG LANDGREN
KEN BOOTH	HELEN BOOTH	CATHIE ELLIS
RANDAL SCHOBER	CLINT BOOTH	HOLLY SANDERS
DAN RUSSELL	KENNETH A. LEE	TIMOTHY CATES
STU WALTERS	KENJI STEWART	STEVE LEES
RICK QUINTON	ROB BLAIR	JUSTIN DION
BROOK WARD	CASEY STERN	DAN DION
ALEXANDRA BAHOU	ANITA VERMA	VINOD VERMA
NICK GREENIZAN	NITIN VERMA	NAKUL VERMA
TOM BOOTH	NARIAN VERMA	ELAINE CAMP
NANCY BOOTH	ALEX CAMP	JUDY BUSHELL
ESTELLE BOOTH	JAN COMBE-KRAFT	DOUG KRAFT
CONNOR MCCRON	BOB ELLIOT	

SEDAN DRIVERS/TAXI DRIVERS WHO GOT ME THERE ON TIME-YOU GUYS ROCKED!!!

NATIONAL CAR RENTAL-ATLANTA AND MEMPHIS ESPECIALLY

AIR TRAN AIRWAYS

TORONTO BLUE JAYS

BEST WESTERN-CLEARWATER FLORIDA

BOSTON REDSOX

CKNW 980 SPORTS STAFF---MY HOME RADIO STATION

HEADNORTH FOUNDATION

PEACE ARCH NEWS&SURREY NOW

DETROIT FREE PRESS

A SPECIAL THANKS TO THE SALTER'S DETROIT-(JOE, DIANNE, ANTHONY, ROBERT AND JACOB)FOR SHOWING ME THE WAY IN DETROIT—IM GLAD I MET YOU GUYS IN 2008-AND THAT LAST GAME IS STILL THE BEST GAME OF THE ENTIRE TRIP! I AM ALSO GLAD THAT YOU WERE THERE TO BREAK THE RECORD WITH ME!

CHECK OUT THESE OTHER NOVELS BY DOUG BOOTH A.K.A. HUGH HAWKINS

LEAPING DEATH

THE ROOKIE BOOKIE

AVAILABLE AT- www.authorhouse.com